AP

A Critical Examination of the
Advanced Placement Program

AP

A Critical Examination of the Advanced Placement Program

PHILIP M. SADLER
GERHARD SONNERT
ROBERT H. TAI
KRISTIN KLOPFENSTEIN

Editors

HARVARD EDUCATION PRESS
CAMBRIDGE, MASSACHUSETTS

*To the high school teachers who
make advanced placement work*

Library of Congress Control Number: 2009942748

Paperback ISBN 978-1-934742-55-6
Library Edition ISBN 978-1-934742-56-3

Published by Harvard Education Press,
an imprint of the Harvard Education Publishing Group

Harvard Education Press
8 Story Street
Cambridge, MA 02138

Cover Design: Schwadesign, Inc.

The typefaces used in this book are ITC Stone Serif for text and
ITC Stone Sans for display.

Contents

PART ONE

An Introduction and Overview

CHAPTER 1

Advanced Placement in a Changing Educational Landscape

Philip M. Sadler

Viewed as an incontrovertible indicator of educational excellence by educators and politicians alike, the Advanced Placement (AP) Program[1] of the College Entrance Examination Board provides "motivated high school students with the opportunity to take college-level courses in a high school setting" (NRC, 2001, p. 246). As a testament to the popularity and support it enjoys, AP's annual growth rate of 9.3 percent during the last two decades far exceeds the 1 percent yearly increase in the number of students graduating high school (Hussar & Bailey, 2009, table 24; College Board, 2009a). Advanced Placement courses have become the juggernaut of American high school education, expanding their reach well beyond their origins in elite private schools. Public high schools in well-off suburbs have vastly increased their course offerings, while less affluent rural and urban schools now offer advanced courses where none existed previously. Twenty-five percent of graduating high school seniors in the United States have taken at least one AP exam (College Board, 2008, appendix C). The number of AP offerings has become a well-publicized proxy for high school quality (e.g., the Newsweek June 8, 2009, listing of America's top public high schools). Students see AP courses on their transcript as the ticket to ensuring entry into the college of their choice. State legislatures require AP offerings in high schools and mandate their value as college credit in state institutions of higher learning. AP now has a role in national politics. In 2006 President George W. Bush called for a near doubling of the number of AP teachers in mathematics and science by training an additional "70,000 high school teachers to lead advanced-placement courses in math and science" (Bush, 2006). U.S. Department of Education grants subsidize the expansion of AP offerings, which can include underwriting the cost of exams.

Yet, while many view AP as an unmitigated triumph, others question if the program has been oversold. In light of its rapid expansion, many worry that the College Board has lowered its standards for passing AP exams to keep students, parents, and schools supportive. Colleges and universities are increasingly reluctant about awarding credit for the AP coursework of incoming students. Many academic departments have boosted their requirement to higher AP exam scores in awarding college credit. Others have argued for the abolition of AP credit entirely. High school students complain of the dizzying pace of AP courses, and many never return to the subject again in college. Home-grown advanced high school courses and electives are eliminated in favor of increasing AP offerings, which many say is simply more "test-prep" for yet another standardized exam (Labrecque, 2006). Criticism that AP courses cover too much material, too superficially, and too quickly have surfaced from blue-ribbon panels studying advanced high school coursework, like that of the National Research Council (2002). In the effort to close the gap between students in privileged and struggling communities, AP has expanded to urban and rural schools, where AP exam scores can be dismal. Economists warn that Advanced Placement is but one lever for change; that it can be a very costly one to implement, often with meager returns; and that it reallocates scarce resources from other worthwhile and more effective programs.

Thus, Advanced Placement has its vocal boosters and detractors, its advocates and opponents. The vigorous debate about AP somewhat overshadows the consideration of alternative forms of advanced coursework, but we should keep in mind that AP courses represent but one of several different opportunities for high school students to take advanced coursework.

The International Baccalaureate (IB) originated in Geneva, Switzerland, as a way for internationally mobile students to prepare for university entry through a rigorous curriculum and standardized examinations. Unlike AP, IB is organized around a school-level curriculum that includes all academic subject areas. This includes a lengthy application process for schools, a trial period, and an on-site visit from an IB delegation. There are 668 schools in the United States offering an IB high school diploma program. Exams are scored on a 1 to 7 scale, and colleges vary in their policy of awarding credit for scores of 4 to 7. Examinations are offered in six groups (language, second language, experimental sciences, the arts, mathematics and computer science, individuals and society) and consist primarily of essay questions. Unlike the AP Program, teachers are monitored and receive feedback in addition to student test scores.

Dual credit and concurrent enrollment programs refer to ways in which high school students can take courses offered by colleges. Dual credit programs offer both high school and college credit, so high schools must explicitly adopt policies to implement this option. Concurrent enrollment students receive college credit only; this option does not require approval from a high school, but the college must be willing to accept high school students who have not yet earned their high school diploma. Both programs allow students to earn college credit that is more readily transferable when students matriculate into college. Proponents of dual credit and concurrent enrollment programs argue that they offer students an authentic college experience because the courses are taught by college faculty and populated with college students. Detractors express concern about the absence of a standardized end-of-course exam or other form of quality control given that the course grade is the only measure of student success. Home-grown advanced courses are offered by high schools in subjects where teachers have a strong interest and special expertise. Rather confusingly, they are often called honors courses, although this name does not distinguish between first-year courses often required for entry into AP courses and second-year courses that are more closely aligned with college-level curricula. These courses can be much more laboratory oriented when offered in the sciences than are other advanced courses, and they provide students an opportunity to carry out project work in an area of their interest. Many wealthy public suburban and elite private schools have turned from AP offerings to such courses, claiming that they are more similar to college. Credit can be awarded by colleges for such courses, although those that require department exams for course credit make that option available. Many students prepare for the AP exams in these non-AP courses and take them successfully.

Despite the numerous routes and opportunities for accelerated learning while in high school, the AP Program dominates the public perception of advanced coursework. Seemingly everyone with a stake in education has an opinion about the AP Program: students, parents, teachers, guidance counselors, administrators, professors, college admissions officers, policy makers, and journalists. Although there is no shortage of strong views about the merits of AP, there is a shortage of evidence about the efficacy, cost, and value of these programs. The College Board's (2009b) Web site does provide links to research on AP, but the thirty-three listed documents all appear to be internally produced research reports or glowing accounts of the AP Program from outside entities. However, additional research, much of it critical, exists that has been conducted by researchers without strong ties to the College Board. This research is spread across many academic journals, but, as a whole, it gives a far more balanced perspective of the AP Program using a variety of approaches to probe when and where AP courses work best and where they may fall short.

The idea behind this book is to bring together in a single concise volume the findings of many of the most thoughtful and rigorous researchers who have studied the impact of the AP Program. Together our contributors make use of a variety of quantitative and qualitative approaches, ranging from historical to economic, to examine this popular program from multiple angles. The authors and other interested colleagues gathered on May 11–12, 2007, at Harvard University for a conference entitled "Synthesis of Research on Advanced High School Coursework in Science and Mathematics."[2] Each contributor presented his or her latest work and had an opportunity to discuss it with other participants and a general audience in attendance. Thereafter participants drafted chapters for a broad audience that represent a wide range of perspectives and, taken together, present a comprehensive picture of the history, impact, and possible future trends of the AP Program. The result is a set of well-reasoned and nuanced findings concerning the proper implementation of the program, how AP should be viewed by colleges and universities, and the role of advanced high school coursework in education reform.

Those who will find the information in this volume valuable include educators and policy makers who are interested in educational improvement at the high school level and in the effective transition between high school and college. In addition, this book is of interest for officials involved in the college admission process, since AP enrollment is increasingly used as a tool for differentiating applicants. College faculty may also find useful information in this book because they are called on to set standards for giving course credit to entering students, and many are involved in professional development activities that support efforts to increase rigor in high school courses. Furthermore, college faculty train new teachers and administrators who will be involved in the implementation of advanced coursework at the high school level. Last but not least, parents who advocate for increasing academic quality in their children's schools will find answers to their questions about the difference AP courses can make in students' college success.

Two of the key themes that appear repeatedly and are treated by many of the authors in this book are the issues of causality and social equity. Determining the causal effects associated with the AP Program is difficult because participation is voluntary and participants are self-selected. In this way, choosing to take an AP course can be thought of as a filter that draws in a group of motivated, high-achieving students who have a strong chance of later doing well in college, whether or not they have taken an AP course. If this self-selection effect is ignored, one might easily overestimate the impact of AP course-taking on high school students. Dougherty, Mellor, and Jian (2006) said it best when they offered the following insight: "Much of those [AP] students' later success in college may be due not to the AP classes themselves, but to the personal characteristics that led them to participate in the classes in the first place—better academic preparation, stronger motivation, better family advantages, and so on. These selection effects will affect any comparison of AP and non-AP students" (p. 3).

For this reason, it is problematic to simply compare the performance of groups of AP and non-AP students and attribute any differences found to the impact of AP. With the near impossibility of conducting experimental studies in which students can be randomly assigned to educational interventions or to a control group, social scientists have developed statistical methods to account for differences in student background. The researchers in this volume are adept at such techniques, paying careful attention to other performance-related variables that would offer alternative explanations for differences between the performance of AP and non-AP students. Such methods help isolate the effects of AP experience from other confounding factors, making their findings far more defensible than much of the previous work on AP. Although such work cannot definitively prove causality, it can offer strong evidence for or against the effect of educational programs. Only a relatively small group of academics involved in AP research has conducted studies that carefully control for student backgrounds and explore relevant alternative hypotheses. Many members of that group are contributors to this book. Just as all oceangoing vessels must undergo careful "compass compensation" to remove the confounding effect of the ship's steel structure on its compass, studies of educational programs will have no guarantee of accuracy without attention to background variables.

The body of evidence presented in this volume comes from educational researchers and economists as well as from those with subject and teaching expertise at the college and precollege level. Longitudinal data sets have been collected that follow students from early interest in science (or not) through their high school experiences and into college majors and later career choices. Retrospective cohort studies, pioneered by epidemiologists, relate success in college coursework to background factors and the students' different course-taking experiences in high school. General linear models, hierarchical when appropriate, are built to explain the variance in students' college grades or interest. Econometric models are constructed to perform a cost-benefit analysis of AP programs, weighing a variety of factors and alternatives to offering advanced courses in high school. Case studies and surveys are used to examine the range of implementation of AP courses and how available resources and teacher qualifications impact the quality of student experiences.

The reader may notice that the sciences enjoy more attention in this book than other subjects. This is primarily because there are more resources available for studying the pipeline to STEM (science, technology, engineering, and mathematics) careers than in other domains. Funding from the National Science Foundation and national data sets that include science and mathematics achievement tests and attitude items (e.g., National Education Longitudinal Study of 1988) aid interested researchers in conducting rigorous studies.

The disparity in educational attainment between students of high and low economic status and among different racial and ethnic groups is a national concern. Social equity is also a stated concern of the College Board, as well as of many of the contributors to this volume. Closing the achievement gap by equalizing educational opportunity can allow students to fulfill their potential, thereby loosening the bonds of intergenerational poverty and increasing productivity. Providing access to advanced coursework to as many high school students as possible is seen by many as a way to make this happen. However, one must keep in mind that inequities in educational opportunity are cumulative. Disadvantages in the educational experience from early grades on (e.g., lack of teaching resources, fewer well-prepared teachers, less parental involvement) cannot be ameliorated by simply making advanced courses available in high school (Lee & Burkham, 2002). While well-prepared students may benefit from college-level classes, others may be lost in such classes or alienated by the subject or may slow down other students' progress.

Although many schools implement an AP program as the academic track for universally high-achieving students, AP courses can be used to provide opportunities for students who are only strong in a subset of subject areas. Although most schools require strong performance in a prerequisite course to enter AP, usually these are courses that are open to all students and are commonly taken as a part of a normal, college preparatory curriculum (e.g., biology as a prerequisite for AP Biology). Thus, a student need not be selected at an early age to make AP participation a possibility; with the proper support, any capable and motivated student can succeed.[3] By being able to take a single AP course (or many), more students can be accommodated more fluidly than by tracking or through gifted and talented programs that tend to accelerate learning in all subjects.

ORGANIZATION OF THE BOOK

This book's fourteen chapters are divided into four parts. Part I offers readers this introduction to and overview of the book as well as a look at the origins and evolution of the AP Program. Part II takes a closer look inside AP, examining the differences between AP and other courses, the variation of AP teacher characteristics and practices, and the validation of AP exam scores. Part III focuses on correlates of AP participation by reporting on several in-depth studies of representative groups that gauge the impact of AP coursework on later student performance and continuance in subject areas. Part IV applies findings to policy issues, tracing the economic issues involved in AP programs and the role of student preparedness in the success of the program. It includes a final, summary chapter that makes recommendations for the various groups of stakeholders who interact with the Advanced Placement Program.

In chapter 2 Timothy Lacy gives a concise overview of the growth and the transformation of the AP Program, from its inception as a small elite program for the best and brightest students to its current status as a standard feature throughout American high school education. The chapter explores how the institution that governs the AP Program, the College Board, has expanded and changed over time and traces the strategies, policies, and leadership of this large, nonprofit corporation.

Chapter 3 examines the varied preparation of students enrolling in introductory college science courses in biology, chemistry, and physics as well as the differences between AP and other high school courses. Advanced placement courses exist alongside regular and honors courses in a typical high school and are promoted as being far more rigorous than other courses and as covering a subject area more rapidly. Philip M. Sadler compares different levels of high school offerings, examining differences in student ability and background, teacher attributes, and structural differences that involve allocation of resources in the sciences from the assignment of the most able teachers to the purchase of specialized laboratory equipment.

In chapter 4 Pamela Paek, Henry Braun, Eva Ponte, Catherine Trapani, and Donald Powers take a closer look inside the AP course and ask, Which teacher characteristics and practices in AP Biology courses might influence their students' performance on the AP Biology exam? In a national survey study, to which nearly 1,200 teachers responded, they identified differences between less and more successful teachers of AP Biology courses. Key among the differences, the authors found teachers' professional development to be a consistently significant predictor of students' performance on the AP exam. School and class context were also found to be significant, with smaller class sizes and daily class meetings (rather than block scheduling) emerging as predictors of students' success on the AP exam.

Chapter 5 discusses the process followed by the College Board to establish the empirical validity of their exams. Maureen Ewing, Kristen Huff, and Pamela Kaliski outline the College Board's program to measure the relative achievement of AP and non-AP students in college, AP exam scores as indicators of appropriate placement level, and perceptions of the AP Program by former AP students in college. They conclude that key to the awarding of college credit for passing AP exams is their structure and the process used to grade them.

Robert H. Tai, Christine Qi Liu, John T. Almarode, and Xitao Fan explore in chapter 6 the association between Advanced Placement Program participation (i.e., students who took an AP science or mathematics exam in high school) and the likelihood that these same students graduate with baccalaureates in science-related degree concentrations in physical sciences and engineering and the life sciences. The study uses data collected from the National Educational Longitudinal Study of 1988 and spans 1988 to 2000. It analyzes a sample of nearly four thousand students, and the results indicate a strong positive association between AP

Program participation and greater likelihood of earning baccalaureate degrees in the two science-related degree categories.

Chapter 7 examines the connection between students' AP experiences and their later performance in introductory college science courses. Advanced Placement courses in biology, chemistry, and physics are offered in an increasing number of U.S. high schools, ostensibly enabling students to engage in introductory-level college coursework. Many AP students take the year-end AP exams and score well enough to bypass introductory college courses. However, either by choice or by college policy, some AP students end up taking introductory level courses despite their prior AP enrollment. Philip M. Sadler and Gerhard Sonnert use this artifact to compare the performance of students who have taken AP coursework to that of their classmates in introductory college science courses in fifty-five randomly selected colleges. By controlling for students' backgrounds and prior coursework in science, they can characterize the degree to which AP coursework predicts better introductory college course grades. The authors conclude that taking and passing the AP exam had a positive effect on students' performance in college introductory science courses in all three disciplines.

In chapter 8 William R. Duffy II investigates whether significant differences in college student persistence and performance outcomes exist among students who have taken Advanced Placement, those who have enrolled in college courses for dual credit (in high school and college), and those who have not availed themselves of such offerings. This study examines a four-year public university in west Tennessee and uses data drawn from the university student database over a six-year period, from fall 2000 through fall 2006, with a sample size of 786 individuals. Regression analysis offers inferential results that indicate no significant differences existed in student college persistence and performance outcomes among AP students, dual credit students, and those who did not participate in either program. Also, the only pre-entry attribute that showed a consistently significant relationship with college persistence and performance outcome measures was the achievement composite variable based on composite ACT score, high school GPA, and high school rank. The analysis concludes that AP and dual credit students persist and perform only as well in college as their peers, although the chapter author indicates that more studies should be conducted across multiple institutions before generalizing these findings.

Kristin Klopfenstein and M. Kathleen Thomas use in chapter 9 an economic perspective to examine the hidden costs of implementing and maintaining a quality AP program. They discuss the policies that have spurred AP growth, the ambiguous results of research studying the benefits of AP, and the unexamined costs of AP expansion and make suggestions for policy given our current understanding of the costs and benefits, especially for alternatives to the AP system that might have a better cost-benefit ratio. The authors discuss some unintended consequences of the expansion of the AP Program to traditionally underrepresented student populations, and they warn against state-mandated course offerings and the use of AP coursework as a selection criterion in the college admissions process. They question AP "helicopter drops"—that is, implementing AP as an educational reform in low-achieving schools for diminishing the achievement gap—in the absence of substantial institutional supports such as those provided by programs like AVID (Advancement via Individual Determination).

In chapter 10 Kristin Klopfenstein examines whether AP subsidies are economically justified based on estimates of the impact of AP experience on time to college degree. Public subsidies of the AP Program are increasingly available at the local, state, and federal levels for AP teacher training, exam fee subsidies for low income students, and performance incentives for teachers and students who do well on AP exams. Subsidies of the AP Program may be economically justified if AP-taking saves taxpayers money by shortening the average time to college graduation at public colleges and universities. However, there is no estimate of the extent to which AP-taking influences time to graduation or of the potential cost savings if it does so. This chapter estimates whether, on average, students who earn passing grades (three or higher) on AP exams while enrolled at Texas public high schools graduate more quickly, ceteris paribus, from Texas public universities than students who do not pass AP exams. The analysis is followed by a discussion of the magnitude of an effect necessary to offset current levels of government funding in support of the AP Program. This research finds that AP experience, either in terms of courses taken or exams passed, does not shorten the time it takes to earn a degree. In contrast to the finding of no effect for AP experience, the models consistently predict that dual credit experience does shorten time to degree. Together, these results indicate that public dollars should be diverted from subsidizing the AP Program to facilitating the development of dual credit programs.

Chapter 11 argues for the importance of solid academic preparation in the early years of schooling (especially preK–8) to prepare students for AP courses and for college. Chrys Dougherty and Lynn Mellor assert that simply expanding AP programs to low-income and minority constituencies does not work when the quality of early education is left unaddressed. Although school population AP exam passing rates can be identified as a useful indicator of a high school's academic program, population AP exam passing rates have remained low for low-income and minority students, even after implementation of Advanced Placement incentive programs designed to boost those rates. Dougherty and Mellor also take aim at the proliferation of "college preparatory" courses. According to their research, the standards of these courses might be a misleading indicator of student readiness for success on AP exams and in college. Just like an unscrupulous merchant might mislabel orange drink as orange juice, some of those college preparatory courses might not deserve their label—as indicated by the majority of low-income and minority students in Texas needing remediation in college even after completing the basic college prep curriculum.

William Lichten takes a critical look at AP expansion on the basis of a case study of the Philadelphia area in chapter 12. He argues that wishful thinking dominated policy making when AP courses were put in inadequately prepared schools as a part of a concerted surge in AP offerings citywide. He contends that AP expansion has led to serious failure in inner-city schools and discusses the causes for this failure involving both schools and students. In his view, the policy makers' decision to implement the surge apparently ignored the College Board's own research findings that predicted lack of success among students in inner-city schools on the basis of low student PSAT scores. The unfortunate history of the surge prompts Lichten to suggest the following improvements to the AP Program: AP scores should be reported openly at the school and district levels; the College Board qualification scale should be updated, because a passing grade is no longer a 3 but a 4; students who enroll in AP courses should demonstrate a readiness to do the work; and only students with demonstrated ability should be allowed into the program.

In chapter 13 Philip M. Sadler uses an empirical method to devise an appropriate bonus for AP course grades in high school grade point averages. College admissions officers must select an incoming class from the transcripts, test scores, and recommendations of applicants. Advanced Placement coursework is increasingly a part of this decision, as it is both incorporated into an applicant's high school class rank and GPA. Evidence from college science courses supports the incorporation of letter grade bonuses into the calculation of high school GPAs: one-half for honors courses, one for AP courses, and two for students who earn a 3 or higher on an AP exam. This method helps offset the effect of grade inflation and more accurately reflects the potential for student success at the college level.

In the concluding chapter, Philip M. Sadler summarizes the results of the research presented and draws lessons for the various stakeholders in the Advanced Placement Program.

ACKNOWLEDGMENTS

Although this book has been put together by four editors who provided an overall framework and worked with contributors to synthesize a cohesive volume, many more individuals contributed with their comments and advice. We would like to acknowledge the people who helped make this book possible, particularly Janice M. Earle, Finbarr C. Sloane, and Larry E. Suter of the National Science Foundation. This research has resulted from the tireless efforts of many on our research team: Michael Filisky, Hal Coyle, Cynthia Crockett, Bruce Ward, Judith Peritz, Annette Trenga, Freeman Deutsch, Nancy Cook, Zahra Hazari, Jaimie Miller, Marc Schwartz, Matthew H. Schneps, Nancy Finkelstein, Alex Griswold, Tobias McElheny, Yael Bowman, and Alexia Prichard. We also appreciate advice and interest from several colleagues in the field: Barbara Dodd of the University of Texas at Austin; Michael Neuschatz of the American Institute of Physics; Trevor Packer of the College Board; Saul Geiser of the University of California at Berkeley; Paul Hickman of Northeastern University; William Fitzsimmons, Marlyn McGrath Lewis, Georgene Herschbach, and Rory Browne of Harvard University; and Charles Alcock and Irwin Shapiro of the Harvard-Smithsonian Center for Astrophysics. The team at the Harvard Education Press, particularly the enthusiasm and talents of our editor Carolyn Chauncey, helped both to motivate the writing of this book and to shape it into a readable and comprehensive volume.

NOTES

1. Readers should note that Advanced Placement, Advanced Placement Program, and AP are registered trademarks of the College Board, which was neither involved in the production of this book nor endorses the views expressed in it.

2. This conference and the writing of this book were supported in part by the National Science Foundation and its Research and Evaluation on Education in Science and Engineering program (NSF REESE #0635090). Any opinions, findings, and conclusions or recommendations expressed in this material are those of the author(s) and do not necessarily reflect the views of the National Science Foundation.

3. Programs like Advancement via Individual Determination (AVID) provide traditionally underserved students with the support they need to succeed in advanced coursework like AP. AP provides the high standards to which AVID students aspire, and the union of AP and AVID can weaken the transmission of intergenerational poverty that is often exacerbated by early tracking in schools.

REFERENCES

America's top public high schools. (2009, June 8). *Newsweek*. http://www .newsweek.com/id/201160

Bush, George W. (2006, January 31). State of the Union address. *The New York Times*. http://www.nytimes.com/2006/01/31/politics/text-bush.html?scp =1&sq=%20Bush%202006%20State%20of%20the%2Union%20address& st=cse

College Board. (2008). The 4th AP report to the nation. New York: College Board. (2009a). Annual AP Program participation 1956–2009.http:// professionals.collegeboard.com/profdownload/annual-participation-09.pdf College Board. (2009b). AP data, reports, and research. http://professionals .collegeboard.com/data-reports-research/cb

Dougherty, C., Mellor, L., & Jian, S. (2006). The relationship between Advanced Placement and college graduation. Austin, TX: National Center for Educational Accountability.

Hussar, W. J., & Bailey, T. M. (2009). Projections of education statistics to 2018 (NCES 2009-062). Washington, DC: National Center for Education Statistics, Institute of Education Sciences.

Labrecque, R. (2006, September 21). Unfair advancement [Op-ed]. *The New York Times*.

Lee, V. E., & Burkham, D. T. (2002). Inequality at the starting gate: Social background differences in achievement as children begin school. Washington, DC: Economic Policy Institute.

National Research Council [NRC]. (2001). Knowing what students know: The science and design of educational assessment. Committee on the Foundations of Assessment. J. Pelligrino, N. Chudowsky, & R. Glaser (Eds.).

Board on Testing and Assessment, Center for Education. Division of Behavioral and Social Sciences and Education. Washington, DC: National Academies Press.

National Research Council. (2002). Learning and understanding: Improving advanced study of mathematics and science in US high schools. Committee on Programs for Advanced Study of Mathematics and Science in American High Schools. J. P. Gollub, M. W. Bertenthal, J. B. Labov, & P. C. Curtis Jr. (Eds.). Center for Education. Division of Behavioral and Social Sciences and Education. Washington, DC: National Academies Press.

CHAPTER 2

Examining AP

Access, Rigor, and Revenue in the History of the Advanced Placement Program

Tim Lacy

The College Board embodies a contradiction to its contemporary critics. On the one hand, it holds forth as a multifaceted, nonprofit, nongovernmental organization engaging in nationwide education standardization activities. Its subsidiary, the Advanced Placement (AP) Program, fills a void left by the traditional reluctance to regulate education by the U.S. federal government. The object of concern for AP in particular, and indeed the College Board in general, is the transitional period from high school to higher education. Founded in 1900 as a small nonprofit association of elite colleges, the College Entrance Examination Board, in its own words, seeks both to "help high school students make a successful transition to higher education" and to "simplify the application process for students and for those colleges' admission offices" (Lagemann, 1983, p. 99; College Board, "History"). From its beginning until the 1950s, its mission expanded to include the creation and maintenance of the Scholastic Aptitude Test (SAT) in the 1920s, and the assumption of the AP Program in the 1950s (College Board, "Fact Sheet").

On the other hand, the College Board has become a huge economic concern and is perceived by its critics as a big business. By 2009 it had evolved into multi-million-dollar organization with every appearance of a corporation. While its five-thousand-plus members each pay a relatively small $325 annual fee, in 2008 the organization generated SAT revenues estimated at roughly $58 million, with another $230 million from Advanced Placement (Matlin, 2009). When other streams are factored in, such as SAT subject tests and the Preliminary SAT (PSAT), the 2006 tax returns for the College Board revealed total revenues of $582.9 million. Even with expenditures of $527.8 million, the College Board still earned a $55.1 million surplus, or "excess," in the language of nonprofits (Matlin, 2009). And these numbers do not include revenues of the College Board's partner organization, Educational Testing Service (ETS), which annually receives a large portion of the Board's business for test design, scoring, and transportation. Further confusing the nonprofit versus business distinction, both organizations have in recent years created for-profit subsidiaries, such as collegeboard.com and Chauncey Group International (Matlin, 2009; Nordheimer & Frantz, 1997; Hoover, 2006). Indeed, one observer noted in 2006 that "a sense of prosperity permeates" the College Board (Hoover, 2006, p. A23).

How and why are these different, contradictory characterizations of the College Board possible? As the College Board has grown and changed during the late twentieth and early twenty-first centuries, its concerns have mirrored those of American culture in general and education in particular. The increasing democratization of the nation, in terms of education and civil rights, has compelled the Board to broaden access to its products and programs. The AP Program, in turn, has moved away from the province of elite, gifted students and toward a more diverse pool of able, motivated talent. In this institutional and intellectual history, I characterize the AP as having evolved in relation to three primary variables: rigor, access, and a charitable impartiality. The program, at its best, has promoted the liberal arts at consistently high standards; has aided in the ongoing, expanded project of democratizing education for students; and has advocated for student interests in the spirit of true educational liberalism. The initial relation between the AP Program and the liberal arts ideal is a particularly compelling story. And although AP was initially intended for the talented elite, it admirably expanded its mission to include a wider portion of the able.

However, critics of AP, a group that includes high school and college educators, watchdog groups, and even a few of the College Board's past employees, loosely characterize the same three variables of rigor, access, and charitable impartiality as gaming, growth, and greed, respectively. These critics see the game as students scoring well for mere credit's sake (as opposed to being focused on rigor, process, and critical thinking), the notion of growth as being merely for the sake of making the organization larger (as opposed to fostering access through restrained, thoughtful expansion), and the greed as increasingly evidenced in a neoliberal ethic focused on College Board revenue gains. With the last, they assert that the Board has acquiesced to a market-friendly, corporate mentality, as opposed to being true to its trusted nonprofit status.[1] From this perspective, growth by itself would seem to prove the necessity and overall success of the program. And if growth did not reveal worth, then the continued usefulness of AP to what Schrum (2009) calls the "instrumental university" would. Growth and service to universities have become the ultimate justification of AP's existence, not whether AP fostered the less useful, abstract idea of a liberal education. To critics, then, these factors have combined to create a looming sense that something has gone awry in AP's recent history.

Peculiarities exist in the historiography of the AP Program. First, while there are a great many AP-related publications, few are historical in nature. The program is rarely covered in history of education textbooks; the closest accounts are of gifted and talented programs begun during the cold war (Pulliam & Van Patten, 2003, p. 273; Urban & Wagoner, 2000, p. 325). And while many histories of AP have been published by the College Board itself, or by those with close ties to it, they are Whiggish, overly positive, and usually less-than-comprehensive assessments of the program (e.g., DiYanni, "AP Central"; Cornog, 1980; Nugent & Karnes, 2002).[2] Second, while some in-depth academic studies of AP exist, most were published before and during the 1980s. In the last twenty years, most non–College Board publications about the program have appeared in periodicals, and a great many are critical. Third, this brief history has practical limitations. It makes no attempt to comprehensively cover all types of AP courses taught and the particular AP subcultures that have evolved in relation to reading, or grading, each test. Nor does it cover many details of AP's internal workings or its less prominent employees. As such, this study is less a bottom-up social history than it is an institutional and intellectual history of AP and the College Board.

THE ANTECEDENTS OF AP

Before the creation of the College Board's AP Program in the early 1950s, advanced placement had always existed in some form in U.S. colleges, depending on a student's individual qualifications and the temperament of college administrators.

Prior to the Civil War, when a college offered advanced placement, it went only to the most gifted and highly talented students. And since a college education was available only to the nation's elite, advanced placement applied to the very best of those with access. An example of this preferential treatment is Founding Father Alexander Hamilton, who reportedly demanded that King's College (now Columbia University) grant him permission to finish his degree in one year (Rothschild, 1999). This likely qualifies as an instance of what later came to be known as flexible promotion, but there is no record of whether Hamilton finished his coursework faster than the other students.

Beginning with the Civil War, there were roughly three periods of systematic thinking about advanced placement: period 1, ca. 1867–1900; period 2, ca. 1900–1920, and period 3, ca. 1920–1949 (Elwell, 1967, pp. 1, 8, 44; Bergeson, 1966, pp. 5–6, 17; Sumption & Luecking, 1960). During this roughly eighty-year period, some of the most prominent names in educational philosophy and practice put forward their thinking on the nature of what would become advanced placement. By the late 1940s and early 1950s, their thinking would synthesize, creating the seeds for the AP Program as we know it.

The common thread in the first two post–Civil War periods of advanced placement thinking is a focus on separating talented students from their peers. The ideas of *flexible promotion* and *acceleration* characterize the period lasting from roughly 1867 to 1900. These ideas grew out of the thinking of William Torrey Harris, cofounder of the Hegelian St. Louis Philosophical Society and, according to education historian Lawrence Cremin (1988, pp. 157–164), the "best-known schoolman of his time." Sometimes called the St. Louis Plan, Harris's view of acceleration encouraged gifted students to complete grades faster without missing important subject matter (Bergeson, 1966, p. 19; Elwell, 1967, p. 8).[3]

The second period of advanced placement's progress, lasting from 1900 to 1920, focused on *enrichment* and *ability grouping* for better students. Rooted in Progressive Era thinking, this form of advanced placement embraced tracking—the sorting of students by ability (e.g., vocational, college bound)—and allowed for the development of schools for the gifted (Bergeson, 1966, p. 20; Elwell, 1967, p. 8). These themes relied on efficiency and scientific thinking founded on intelligence testing and achievement. Like the Harris period, this era saw the separation of gifted students from their peers. This approach toward advanced placement culminated with the 1918 publication of the *Cardinal Principles of Secondary*

Education, authored by the National Education Association's Commission on the Reorganization of Secondary Education (Cremin, 1988, pp. 232–234).

The third developmental period of advanced placement commenced in the 1920s and lasted through the 1940s. It correlated with the rise of the *progressive education* movement (which occurred after the Progressive Era) and required the gifted to move through the grades with their peers but to follow an enriched curriculum (Bergeson, 1966, pp. 21–22). If progressive education can be characterized by the three themes of vocationalism (career/work focus), respect for the scientific method, and social adjustment (schools as social institutions), then the third era of advanced placement reflects the full implementation of the John Dewey–inspired progressive creed (Cremin, 1988, pp. 223, 242–243). Bergeson (1966) reports that progress in advanced placement thinking was stunted by the economic woes of the Great Depression and the distractions of World War II, and those practical barriers to innovation were fed by what Hartman (2008) labels "intellectual energies" committed "to preserving the American status quo"—namely, a "relativist theory of democracy" in education that sought stability in the face of international crises (p. 4). But this consensus crumbled in the 1940s and 1950s due to a large number of students entering college, a rethinking of the idea of general education, criticisms of progressive education, and the efforts of secondary schools to better coordinate curricula with higher education.

The harbinger of change with regard to thinking about advanced placement came in the form of the 1945 Harvard Report, or "The Redbook," officially titled *General Education in a Free Society*. Commissioned by famous midcentury educator and former Harvard president James Bryant Conant, the report concerned liberal education and elite students—the subjects and ideas every bright student ought to know in order to function properly in a democracy. The issue at hand—the notion of a general education and what constitutes it—had percolated for much of the twentieth century due to what critics of progressive education perceived as an overemphasis on scientism, vocationalism, and specialization and because of students' increasing focus on their social lives while in college. Indeed, through the 1930s and 1940s, education leaders and philosophers such as Robert M. Hutchins and Mortimer J. Adler of the University of Chicago had already forwarded the Great Books idea as a solution to what would become the general education controversy of the 1940s and 1950s, even applying their solution at the high school level in the university's famous laboratory schools. However, on its publication, the much-discussed Harvard Report quickened and nationalized the general education/liberal arts controversy, expanding the discussion broadly beyond higher education into the upper tiers of secondary schools.[4] The report helped shape future discourse about advanced placement by limiting the program to survey courses that could form the core of a general education curriculum ("Education," 1945).

The best expression of the Harvard Report for secondary schools exists in a 1952 book with a similar title, *General Education in the School and College*. That work played a key role in the founding period of the AP Program but must be understood in the context of the creation of the College Board and ETS.

The College Board existed for just over a half century before taking on the AP Program in the 1950s. As noted above, it began in 1900 as small association of elite northeastern colleges. It grew, however, out of a meeting of the Association of Colleges and Secondary Schools of the Middle States and Maryland (an accrediting agency).[5] The purpose was "to bring school and college teachers together to write, administer, and score subject matter examinations for college admission," exams otherwise known as college boards (Lagemann, 1983, p. 99; Rudolph, 1965, pp. 436–438). The College Board's first president, serving from 1900 to 1925, was none other than Nicholas Murray Butler, the larger-than-life president of Columbia University from 1900 to 1945. Under Butler's leadership, the organization grew from a few institutions in 1900 to twenty-nine colleges in 1910 testing four thousand students, and then to thirty-three colleges in 1920 testing more than fifteen thousand students (Rosenthal, 2006, pp. 93–94; Lemman, 2000, pp. 28–29; Fuess, 1950; College Entrance Examination Board, 1926). In 1926 the College Board began using the SAT. The non-subject-specific SAT enabled College Board institutions to draw on a larger potential applicant population than did the college board exams that were tailored for private and public schools in the Northeast. The SAT thus enabled a less regional, more meritocratic vision of higher education to take hold in the late 1920s—and it helped elite northeastern colleges recruit more students in the midst of the Great Depression (Hoover, 2006, p. A23; Lagemann, 1983, pp, 99–100, 108; Levine, 1986, pp. 145, 152). But no matter the motivation, by the late 1940s and the early 1950s the SAT was the College Board's best-known endeavor.

The growing practical needs of the College Board led it to help found a partner organization for test development and research. Educational

Testing Service, formed in 1947 and headed by Henry Chauncey, grew out of conversations in the 1930s and 1940s among College Board test researcher and SAT inventor Carl Brigham, Carnegie Foundation for the Advancement of Teaching staffer and education expert William Learned, Columbia University educational psychologist and researcher Ben D. Wood, and Harvard president Conant (Lagemann, 1983, pp. 101, 104, 115, 117; Nordheimer & Frantz, 1997; Nairn et al., 1980, p. 2). Brigham proved to be both a practical and philosophical obstacle to the formation of ETS. He was skeptical of contemporary research into educational psychology, noting that "thinking is one of the most obscure topics in psychology and education" (Lagemann, 1983, pp. 117–118). He also feared that "the sales or service component of a large testing agency would overwhelm its research program." But Brigham's concerns over fundamentals died with him in 1943, and ETS came into being shortly thereafter. At its incorporation in 1947, ETS became the administrator of the SAT on behalf of the College Board, as well as the Graduate Record Examination (GRE), developed in the 1930s by Learned and Wood, on behalf of the Carnegie Foundation. ETS also absorbed Wood's precursor test research and development organization, the Cooperative Test Service, formed in 1930 (Lagemann, 1983, pp. 109, 111, 120). In sum, ETS was immediately a powerful nonprofit organization with a serendipitous corner on the higher education testing market. Brigham's warning about sales and greed versus research would provide fodder for future critics (Nordheimer & Frantz, 1997; Nairn et al., 1980, pp. ix–xvii).[6]

FOUNDING PERIOD, 1950–1960

The onset of the cold war and the massive influx of students taking advantage of the 1944 Servicemen's Readjustment Act, or GI Bill, and its Korean War successor, the Veterans' Readjustment Assistance Act of 1952, created an environment conducive to making U.S. higher education more efficient and popular (Cremin, 1988, p. 250; Smith & Bender, 2008, p. 394; Kerr, 1982, p. 52). This efficiency manifested itself in a number of ways, such as administrators finding means to process more applications (e.g., by using SAT scores in addition to grades), colleges creating opportunities for the talented to move along faster, and institutions like the College Board helping families save money on education costs (e.g., testing out of courses). Educators in the 1940s had understood that college would become more attractive in the post–World War II era, hence the discussion about general education, admissions tests, and other topics. And shortly after the war, school-level educators also renewed their interest in talented students. This was demonstrated by the 1950 publication of *Education of the Gifted*, a report issued jointly by the Educational Policies Commission and the National Education Association (NEA), as well as by the appearance in 1951 of the essay collection *The Gifted Child*, edited by Paul Witty on behalf of the American Association for Gifted Children (Bergeson, 1966, 23–25). Finally, two unique issues with social and political dimensions arose in this period with regard to education: the delinquent student problem, and a concern about the quantity and quality of American mathematics and science education precipitated by the Soviets' launch of Sputnik. Both made it imperative to educators and politicians to keep American students motivated and to foster the talents of the already gifted. History conspired to make education a high priority of the post–World War II and early cold war era.

The drive to establish a school-to-college transition program for the gifted in the 1950s came not primarily from the federal government but from private foundations, particularly the Ford Foundation and Carnegie Corporation. The Ford Foundation's Fund for the Advancement of Education (FAE), created by associate director Robert Hutchins and headed by Clarence H. Faust (a former dean under Hutchins at the University of Chicago), provided seed money for studies beginning in 1951. In the mid-1950s the Carnegie Corporation (not to be confused with the Carnegie Foundation) funded a study, led by James B. Conant, of high schools and gifted students that led to his famous 1959 book *The American High School Today*. Around the same time the Carnegie Corporation also supported two other efforts, the Inter-University Committee on the Superior Student and the North Central Association's Program for Superior High School Students. Both the Ford Foundation and Carnegie Corporation also cofunded education projects during the 1950s and 1960s (among them the Children's Television Workshop, which produced the much-loved *Sesame Street*).[7]

The FAE directly supported five experiments relevant to advanced placement. Two of these are well-known in AP Program lore, but the other three are less so. One of the lesser-known efforts, the Early Admissions group, began in 1951 and initially involved eleven higher education institutions and 420 first-year students. These students began college two years early, with only a few having finished high school. The experiment, which lasted until 1954 and eventually involved 1,350 Early Admissions

Scholars, was judged a success intellectually, though there were some so-cial adjustment problems for male students in particular (e.g., dating). ETS helped evaluate the data gathered on the group, and the Ford Foun-dation's 1957 publication *They Went to College Early* presents those data (Elwell, 1967, pp. 33–36; FAE, 1957, pp. 1, 7–8). A second FAE-funded experiment, the Portland Project, began in early 1952 as a cooperative effort between Reed College and Portland Public Schools. The secondary school and college faculty worked together closely to enrich the school curriculum for gifted children. By the mid-1950s the project involved more than two thousand students in twenty-one Portland area elemen-tary and high schools. It was also judged a success because nearly all of the high school students who participated went on to college (FAE, 1957, pp. 3–4; Elwell, 1967, pp. 29–32). A third FAE effort, the Atlanta Experi-ment in Articulation and Enrichment in School and College, involved intensifying the curriculum during the last two years of secondary school and the first two years of college, the grade 11–14 period. This project lasted from 1953 through the early 1960s and initially involved four At-lanta, Georgia, institutions: Westminster Schools, Oglethorpe University, Agnes Scott College, and Emory University (FAE, 1957, p. 3). These three advanced placement programs provided information that complemented or confirmed the findings of the other well-cited FAE AP programs.

The two most-cited projects related to the founding of the College Board's AP Program were exemplary for opposite reasons—one was a more philosophical exercise, and the other was weighted heavily toward the practical. Both were conceived in 1950 and received Ford's FAE monies the following year. The practical program, known widely as the Kenyon Plan for the home institution of its prime mover, Kenyon College presi-dent Gordon Keith Chalmers, also carried the official title of School and College Study of Admission with Advanced Standing (SCSAAS) (FAE, 1957, pp. 4–5; Rothschild, 1999, pp. 178–179; Elwell, 1967, pp. 46–100; DiYanni, "AP Central"). Donald Bruce Elwell argued that the Kenyon Plan provided the crucial framework for what would come. Long-time College Board employee and former executive director of the SCSAAS project Wil-liam H. Cornog agreed (Elwell, 1967, pp. ii, 43; Cornog, 1980, p. 14).

The premises and structure of the Kenyon Plan are familiar to those with knowledge of the AP Program today. The plan assumed that "gifted students can proficiently do college-level work while still in second-ary school," that appropriately trained high school teachers can deliver the subject matter, and that high school is the best social setting for adolescents (Elwell, 1967, pp. 46–47). While Chalmers cited the Harvard Report as partial inspiration for his plan, he favored the study of particular subjects—specialties—over larger, interdisciplinary endeavors (e.g., Western Civilization, Great Books, or Great Ideas courses) like those promoted in both the Harvard Report and, later, the last plank of the Ford Foundation's five studies, the *General Education in School and College* report. Chalmers believed rigor was needed as a corrective for the failures of progressive education, especially the life adjustment wing, which had been castigated by intellectuals and educators such as Richard Hofstadter, Mortimer Adler, and Robert Hutchins. But Chalmers still hoped that his program would evolve into something that served more than just the gifted.

Early participants in the Kenyon Plan included advisers such as the College Board's Frank Bowles and Cornog (who at the time was president of Philadelphia's Central High School), about dozen colleges from Kenyon in Ohio to Carleton in Minnesota and the Massachusetts Institute of Technology, and seven pilot high schools—two from New York City, two from Philadelphia, and one each from Evanston, Illinois, Newtonville, Massachusetts, and St. Louis.[8] By 1952, the plans had already become national in scope, and in the 1953–1954 academic year, participating schools increased to twenty-seven. Kenyan plan committees explored advanced placement achievement tests in history, mathematics, chemistry, biology, physics, English (composition and literature), Latin, French, and German. By May 1954, 532 students from eighteen of the twenty-seven schools took 959 exams. And during that same year college students were tested as a control group. Needless to say, the results were more than satisfactory. In October 1954 the College Board assumed responsibility for the "continuation and expansion" of the Kenyon Plan; it took full control in 1955–1956 (Elwell, 1967, pp. 73, 83–84, 88–90, 91, 94, 99, 101; Cornog, 1980, p. 15).

The other well-cited experiment related to the AP Program's founding, and the fifth study supported by FAE, derived from a committee of elite preparatory school and university faculty. The full title of the final report, published in 1952, names the principal institutions: *General Education in School and College: A Committee Report by Members of the Faculties of Andover, Exeter, Lawrenceville, Harvard, Princeton and Yale* (GESC). The GESC Committee tackled the more philosophical issues related to general education, much like the Harvard Report, which it acknowledged, but pointedly applied them to the grades 11–14 period and to "superior students." Indeed, the group relayed that there was "no intent" with their report to "call for reform of the whole American educational system for the sake of a relatively small group of students"; its concern was that elite students were not being challenged and that they were content with "mediocrity" (GESC, 1952, pp. 1–2, 8, 10, 35–36; FAE, 1957, pp. 2–3; Rothschild, 1999, p. 177; DiYanni, "AP Central"; Nugent & Karnes, 2002, p. 31).

The credentials and specialties of the GESC Committee members explain, in part, why the final report concerned itself with the humanities and the idea of a liberal education. Participants included Alan R. Blackmer, chairman and instructor in English, Phillips Academy; Henry W. Bragdon, instructor in history, Phillip Exeter Academy; McGeorge Bundy, associate professor of government, Harvard University; E. Harris Harbison, professor of history, Princeton University; Charles Seymour Jr., associate professor of art history, Yale University; Wendell H. Taylor, chairman of the science department, Lawrenceville School; and executive secretaries Robert W. Sides, Andover (before February 1952), and William H. Harding, Andover (February 1952 on). The committee held thirteen meetings and drew on outside expertise for advice, such as Columbia University history professor Jacques Barzun (GESC, 1952, pp. iv, 1–2, 5–7, 19–20). This group was patently slanted toward the humanities and liberal education, which mirrors the predominance of themes present in the GESC report.

The committee defined liberal education quite broadly. The final report included character traits such as "articulate," "thinks rationally, logically, objectively," "imaginative and creative," "perceptive, sensitive to form, and affected by beauty" (GESC, 1952, pp. 19–21). The elite nature of the institutions involved in this study probably assuaged concerns about standards among contemporary critics who might have looked askance at the possibility of secondary schools meeting collegiate standards. But the committee also countered potential charges of elitism by connecting a liberal education to the proper development of a democracy. It argued that a society of illiberal specialists was more susceptible to totalitarianism; indeed, it asserted that "liberal education and the democratic ideal are related to each other in a thousand ways. It is not too much to say that they stand and fall together" (GESC, 1952, pp. 19–21). Crusading on behalf of a liberal, or general, education gave committee members an outlet to display their concerns about war, both hot and cold, and good governance.

The committee not only enumerated and criticized the current weaknesses of grades 11–14, "conceived as a whole" period of instruction in general education, but it also proposed remedies (FAE, 1957, pp. 2–3;

GESC, 1952, p. 8). It addressed both halves of the diagnosis-prescription paradigm in terms of philosophy and practice, leaning more toward the former. Weaknesses included "conspicuous" waste through unneeded *repetition* in the subjects of English (composition and literature), history, sciences, and foreign languages. It stated that the disjointed nature of the grades 11–14 transitional period also revealed a "failure to arouse" the students due to the "failure to communicate . . . the full meaning and purpose of a liberal education" (GESC, 1952, pp. 12–15, 24, 26, 100). Further, the committee maintained that a liberal education could not be obtained through a cafeteria-style curriculum; student class choices had to be balanced by core requirements.

The GESC Committee buttressed its practical remedies with two philosophical assertions: that (a) some things must be known (similar to E. D. Hirsch's cultural literacy philosophy); (b) flexibility for individual differences must be allowed; and (c) core programs must have intelligible sequences of courses. The second assertion was also known as *progression in strength*—that you could move as far as possible in chemistry, for instance, if it was your best subject even if you were not so proficient in any foreign language. This became a linchpin of the AP Program. To this day, a student may progress in one subject as far as AP itself goes without any prerequisites in other disciplines set down by the College Board: specialization is acceptable. In accordance with the committee's concern for liberal education and the GESC's predecessor, the Harvard Report, members proposed that Great Books courses could fulfill content and programming needs in English literature (GESC, 1952, pp. 82, 85–86). Other practical remedies suggested by the committee included the recruiting of creative teachers, assigning more independent work and papers, fostering more faculty-student interaction, and instituting one year of universal military training (GESC, 1952, pp. 106, 111). As for acceleration schemes, the committee laid down several conditions: they must not create extra work for the students, grade-skipping must occur at the school-to-college transition, and subject achievement examinations must be taken at the secondary school level. Members recommended that ETS could create the exams and that advanced placement credit would be given after admission to a college or university (GESC, 1952, pp. 114, 118–119).

Contemporaries attended to the GESC report, but reactions to its philosophical assumptions and practical suggestions were mixed. Edward G. Ballard (1953) of Tulane University reviewed *General Education in School and College* for the *Journal of Higher Education* late in 1953 and noted several problems. For instance, while he agreed that the problem of "welding the last two years of high school and the first two years of college" was indeed a real one, he felt the GESC study did not "shed any new light upon it" (pp. 498–499). He felt they spent too much time thinking about content and not enough on the "really great complexities" facing institutions trying to address all needed coursework in that four-year timeframe. While the committee named the subjects important to a general education, enumerated the character traits of a liberally educated student, and asserted the existence of a "hierarchy of knowledge" (GESC, 1952, p. 122), Ballard observed that the report contained no description of the relative importance of each subject matter. He wanted more philosophy, epistemology in particular, in order for the report to properly address efficiency with regard to course offerings.

Citations of GESC and the other Ford Foundation studies increased in 1954 and 1955. Richard L. Greene (1954), writing about how to make the English major more attractive, cited GESC as "a splendid example" of school-college cooperative work and deemed the book "direct and realistic as well as earnest and cultivated" (p. 332). He thought it should be "nationally read." In the *Review of Educational Research,* Michigan State University education professor Paul Leroy Dressel (1954) surveyed the status of liberal and general education formulations in the postwar years. He cited GESC and the Ford Foundation studies. He found that the idea of a traditional "liberal education untainted by vocationalism" existed "more in the imagination of conservatives than in reality" (p. 285). At the same time, however, he noted the necessity of programs for the gifted even if "coolness" or "antipathy" were exhibited to the same by college or school faculty (pp. 289, 291). Several other citations and positive GESC references appeared in the 1953–1955 period, proving the prominence of the study (see Horn, 1953; Sparer, 1954; O'Dell, 1954; Jones & Ortner, 1954; Morse, 1955).

TRANSLATING IDEAS AND IDEALS INTO PRACTICE

Taken together, the criticisms and weaknesses of the GESC study and the Kenyon Plan reveal persistent, unresolved questions about the AP Program. Indeed, much of the criticism and praise of the program dates from its testing precursors, these two studies, and the founding period. Just as with Brigham's concerns about business and profit in relation to ETS's formation, the final report of the Kenyon Plan/SCSAAS project, published in 1956, warned that decisions "by colleges regarding advanced credit or placement must be based not only upon [test] results . . . but upon a reasonable acquaintance on the part of college teachers with the level of teaching achieved by the strong secondary schools" (Elwell, 1967, 99–100). Kenyon Plan participants believed that a "spirit of cooperation" must never degenerate into "a giving and taking of college-patented prescriptions of courses." That cooperative spirit will also never be solely "fostered by a mere advanced level examining system." It was "repeated meetings" and "cordiality" that resulted in an atmosphere of trust that, in turn, brought about real advanced placement articulation. That same spirit of cooperation seems lacking today.[9] Indeed, Elwell noted a decrease in school-college cooperation and visits as early as the mid-1960s—soon after the College Board took control.

While the charge of elitism in relation to the GESC study holds some truth, the same charge could be leveled at the Kenyon Plan at its beginning (Rothschild, 1999, 177). Even though the GESC study came out of elite preparatory schools and colleges, Chalmers's public-school-populated project favored excellence over access. He believed that only about 2 percent of secondary students were ready and willing to choose advanced placement. Although he did eventually broaden his expectations, his first inclination was to offer advanced placement to only an elite cadre of students (Elwell, 1967, pp. 52, 55). When excellence and rigor are involved, hierarchy is always in play, which means that charges of elitism will be inevitable. And in evaluating these charges, it is crucial to discern the source of that elite status: unearned privilege or merit?

At its core, the assessment of the AP Program depends on how one defines liberal education. If it is about exceeding mediocrity in terms of content and particulars, as Chalmers argued, then one would expect testing expansion and celebrate increased offerings of AP courses covering the arts, sciences, humanities, and languages (Elwell, 1967, p. 53). This happened, and the program grew steadily under the tutelage of the College Board—with continued early financial support from the Ford Foundation—in the late 1950s. In the 1955–1956 academic year, participation included 104 schools, 1,229 students taking exams, 2,199 exams taken, and 130 colleges entered. By 1959–1960 these numbers increased to 890 schools, 10,531 students, 14,158 exams, and 567 colleges (Elwell, 1967, p. 109, app. E; College Board, "Program Participation"). The next year Conant (1961) wrote that "the success of the Advanced Placement

Program in the last few years is one of the most encouraging signs of real improvement in our educational system" (p. 92; Elwell, 1967, p. 111; Di-Yanni, "AP Central"). Rigorous, liberal education in the key subjects was expanding and improving.

If we are to believe, however, that liberal education is more about exceeding mediocrity in terms of process, critical thinking, and creativity, then the AP Program either has never been needed or has never succeeded—or, at most, has been only partially successful. Few proponents of AP expansion point out the irony that truly superior—not merely talented—students are, by definition, rarely content with mediocrity; they do not need AP courses to demonstrate their drive. But even if AP mattered to exceptional students for reasons beyond excellence (e.g., practical considerations), to educators and philosophers seeking the expansion of liberal education the early numerical growth in AP mattered less than fostering some lifelong appreciation of the liberal arts. GESC participants knew that some would measure success by diffuse kinds of evidence associated with emotional development, better social adjustment, less anti-intellectualism, more affinity for democracy, and better writing and listening skills (GESC, 1952, pp. 10, 20–22, 24). But it can be argued that the AP Program succeeded in merely helping normalize survey courses at the upper secondary and lower college levels rather than aiding the promotion of liberal education as envisaged by the GESC participants. Any conveyance to students of the meaning and purpose of a general education was left entirely to the teachers of AP courses (Schrum, 2007, p. 288). If the College Board ever made any effort beyond acknowledging the liberal education issues discussed by the GESC Committee, then those efforts were never recorded or promoted through any kind of required common AP course—short or long—on philosophy that would include a consideration of one's own desires for education. Indeed, even GESC participants assumed "agreement on the essentials of a liberal education . . . is widespread in America today" (GESC, 1952, p. 19).

Few accounts of AP's formation and early years acknowledge disagreement about the fundamentals of a liberal education. Most give the basic facts, chronology, practical findings, and recommendations of the Kenyon Plan and the GESC Committee work (e.g., Bergeson, 1966; Cornog, 1980; Nugent & Karnes, 2002; DiYanni, "AP Central"). Of course, the philosophical work of GESC and Chalmers's own intellectual history are not totally neglected; they give those early accounts of AP's founding some weight. But the focus is on early leaders, practical problems, finances, a few failures, course changes, and growth—as if the last proves the necessity and overall success of the program. Nevertheless, philosophical criticism existed. In 1963 intellectual historian and cultural critic Jacques Barzun, then an administrator at Columbia University, expressed concern that the "once distinctive" liberal arts college curriculum was being squeezed out of existence between AP and preprofessional offerings for junior and senior students (Elwell, 1967, p. 247; Bell, 1966, p. 54). Sociologist Daniel Bell (1966) worried that subject-specific advanced placement courses would squeeze out classic integrative courses such as Contemporary Civilization at Columbia University (Elwell, 1967, p. 250; Bell, 1966, pp. 131–135).[10] The same concern would apply to Great Books courses at other institutions. Other early concerns related to the liberal arts, as outlined by Elwell (1967), include whether high school students possess the requisite maturity to fully absorb and understand the humanities and whether advanced placement "encourages a student to decide prematurely" on a major. Elwell did not dismiss the first but found the second to lack evidence (p. 252).

GROWTH AND BACKLASH, 1960–1975

Despite the presence of these unresolved philosophical issues, the AP Program grew between 1960 and 1975. Once the College Board had taken charge of a program, with its practical flaws corrected, the Board's job became simple: propagate. At first this meant introducing the program as widely as possible to upper- and upper-middle-class public and private schools. Indeed, the College Board did this successfully in the face of both catalytic and crimping historical events of the late 1950s through the 1970s. Despite philosophical issues with the product, students increasingly demanded AP credit, and higher education responded affirmatively.

Toward the end of AP's founding period, history intervened on behalf of the program when the Soviet Union launched the first Sputnik satellite in October 1957. This event shocked America, and the general reaction to it spurred a reevaluation of the quality of American schooling during the cold war. That reevaluation corresponded with a special moment in the history of education in which juvenile delinquency was receiving heightened, if somewhat exaggerated, attention—as evident in the popular 1955 film *Blackboard Jungle*. This came in a general U.S. social environment of conformity, consumerism, containment, and consensus about behavioral norms. In this period, education critics such as Arthur Bestor, Admiral Hyman Rickover, and James Conant continued, or began anew, individual crusades for higher standards in secondary schools, more programs for elite students, or the increased funneling of students toward mathematics and the sciences. Their work correlated with the increasing profile of research at the university level, feeding a nationwide search for talented students, especially those inclined toward mathematics and the sciences. National policy cemented this move by passing the 1958 National Defense Education Act (NDEA), which funded university-level research.[11]

These events set up the 1960s to be a decade of steady participant growth for the AP Program. To be sure, the program increased its number of partner institutions: secondary schools from 890 in the 1959–1960 academic year to 3,186 in 1970 and colleges from 567 to 1,368. Student participation grew from 10,531 to 55,442, with the number of examinations taken rising from 14,158 in 1959–1960 to 71,495 in 1970 (College Board, "Program Participation"). Research published in the 1960s generally confirmed positive feelings about the AP Program by affirming its methods and the advantages for participating students. When these studies did acknowledge criticisms, such as those raised by Barzun and others, those concerns were underplayed (Bergeson, 1966, pp. iv–vi, 88–89; Elwell, 1967, pp. ii, 276–279; Ralston, 1961, chap. 6). But despite the relatively good publicity, increased participant numbers, and the generous early seed money from the Ford Foundation, the AP Program ran annual deficits for the College Board all through the decade. In 1958 the College Board had approved a fee increase, but problems persisted. Paul Holbo, chief reader of American history from 1968 to 1971, recalled in 1995 that there were discussions of ending the program in the late 1960s. But the dramatic increase in student examinees and examinations taken during the decade made the program viable—even a moneymaker for the College Board—by the early 1970s (Rothschild, 1999, pp. 183–184, 188–189). And according to Jack Arbolino (1961), who directed the program from 1958 to 1965, the economic circumstances of the affluent early 1960s were so good for AP that even its financial losses helped by shielding the program from criticism that it operated for moneymaking reasons alone.

In the early 1970s, however, the AP Program experienced its first and only numerically evident backlash. From 1970 to 1975 growth stagnated.

The student revolts of the 1960s, which historians normally discuss in the context of higher education (e.g., in loco parentis, draft resistance, resistance to formalities), included either a backlash against programs for the gifted or a downplaying of one's gifted status. The numbers clearly indicate a flattened trend. From 3,186 secondary schools in 1969–1970, participants went to 3,342 in 1970–1971, 3,397 in 1971–1972, 3,240 in 1972–1973, and 3,357 in 1973–1974. In 1973 the 54,778 students taking exams was only 1,400 more than in 1969, and the 70,651 examinations taken in 1973 totaled only about 1,200 more than in those taken in 1969. This stagnation should be seen relative to the fact that only 14 percent of the nation's high schools offered AP exams in the spring of 1969 (College Board, "Program Participation"; Rothschild, 1999, p. 185; Brubacher & Rudy, 1976, pp. 349–353; Farber, 1994, pp. 157–160, 194–199). In addition, using a College Board study, Rothschild (1999) documents that, between 1964 and 1973, the average SAT math score fell more than twenty points and verbal more than forty points (p. 185).

But why did this occur? And was it a backlash? Rothschild suggests as much, blaming a general devaluation of educational excellence in favor of democratization rather than the reevaluation of meritocratic advancement that also took place in the period.[12] He also offered more specific evidence in relation to AP from College Board publications: "During these years . . . the number of [AP] essays including pornographic prose and attacking the country, the schools, their teachers, AP, the College Board, and/or even the readers increased sharply. By 1973, there was the first positive proof of cheating—in fifteen essays" (p. 186). These factors and the numerical stagnation in participation do suggest backlash.

No matter the causes, the College Board and others took notice. The Board offered new examinations in French, music, studio art, and art history by 1972. Both the U.S. and European history exams added document based questions in 1973 and 1975, respectively (Rothschild, 1999, p. 187). Ideas for improvement and better coordination with higher education trends also came from outside. One was offered by Edward Van Gelder (1972), who resurrected the idea of the three-year bachelor's degree by suggesting its relevance in light of the development of AP and CLEP (College Level Examination Program) and due to increasing expenses for all parties in higher education, per Earl Cheit's 1971 study *The New Depression in Higher Education* (pp. 6–8). Van Gelder saw the three-year degree as more attainable and desirable than ever before.

DEMOCRATIZATION, DIVERSITY, AND ACCESS, 1975-1999

The AP Program had resumed its steady arc of growth and democratization by 1975. During the years from 1975 to 1999, stability characterized the AP Program internally. Indeed, according to Rothschild (1999), it "became a national program to a degree which even its most fervent supporters in the early years could not have imagined" (p. 189). Outside historical factors generally favored the program's expansion and democratization, and criticism was only sporadic in this period.

In terms of numbers, the AP Program's growth was astounding. In 1973–1974 there were 3,357 schools participating, and in 1974–1975 there were 3,498. This was followed by a steady increase all through the rest of the decade and into the 1990s: 4,079 in 1977, 4,950 in 1980, 5,827 in 1983, 7,201 in 1986, 9,292 in 1990, 11,274 in 1995, and 12,886 in 1999. Anywhere from around 150 to more than 500 schools joined the program in any one year, with the 1983–1990 period standing out for averaging nearly 500 annual additions. About half of all U.S. secondary schools were involved with AP by the mid-1990s. Student participation went from 65,635 in 1974–1975 to 704,298 in 1998–1999, and the number of examinations taken increased from 85,786 to 1,149,515 in the same period. College participation increased from 1,517 to 3,007 as well (College Board, "Program Participation"; Rothschild, 1999, p. 197). In 1975 the fees were $6 for registration and $20 per exam. By 1995 the maximum exam fee was $72, although students with financial need could receive a reduction to $43, and some states even paid the students' fees (Rothschild, 1999, pp. 188, 197). Fees aside, this growth clearly fostered an expansion of AP for the able.

Student diversity in the AP Program also increased dramatically. A substantial movement toward racial, ethnic, national, and age democratization among examinees occurred during the 1980s in particular. Again, the College Board promoted this. The program's expansion included more urban and multiracial schools, allowing rising examinee numbers among African American, Mexican American, Asian American, and Native American students. Rothschild (1999) reports that 19.5 percent of all U.S. examinees in 1988 were from minority populations. The program was also internationalized in this period, beginning in 1981. At first only about 2,700 overseas students took exams, but College Board officials began soliciting foreign universities to accept AP credit during the early

1980s. By the late 1980s the Department of Defense's Dependent Schools recognized exam results, and in 1993 nearly ninety German universities began a special program where admission was granted based on AP exam results. By 1994 approximately fifty countries hosted 16,659 AP examinations. The 1975–1999 era also witnessed the emergence of more diversity in ages of AP students. The best students in biology, for instance, might take the AP exam on the subject as sophomores, or those excelling in European history might take that exam during their junior year. Indeed, by 2009 these age-level, subject-specific examination tendencies would become quite complex (DiYanni, "AP Central," "Internationalization"; Rothschild, 1999, pp. 193–194, 196–197; College Board, 2008).

There were numerous qualitative changes to the program in this period. Spanish examinations were added in 1977, as well as Drawing as a Studio Art option in 1980, Computer Science in 1984, Government and Politics (Comparative and American) in 1987, Micro- and Macroeconomics in 1989, Psychology in 1992, Statistics in 1997, and Environmental Science in 1998. Beginning 1988 the AP Biology Development Committee added laboratory exercises to the exam. Even graphing calculators were allowed in Calculus starting in 1995 (Rothschild, 1999, pp. 190, 193).

Receptivity to and knowledge of the AP Program was promoted through government and nongovernmental initiatives—and even through a popular culture phenomenon. One government program increasing AP participation at this time was South Carolina's Education Improvement Act of 1984, which mandated that AP courses and a gifted and talented program be offered statewide by August 1987. Of course, AP existed in South Carolina before the law. In 1957 Dreher High School in Columbia became the first school in the state to offer AP, and two other schools joined by 1961. But growth remained slow in rural areas; as late as 1971, no small rural high schools in South Carolina offered AP. By 1987, with the law in full effect, only thirty-five of fifty-eight small rural schools offered AP courses (Aluri, 1987, pp. x–xi, 3, 30; Rothschild, 1999, pp. 194–195). By the mid-1990s several other states promoted AP by providing funds for coursework or reimbursing exam fees. These included the District of Columbia, Florida, Georgia, Indiana, Kentucky, Minnesota, North Carolina, and Texas. Finally, in addition to these state-level programs, the Mellon and Josiah Macy foundations provided some funding for AP Programs across the nation beginning in the 1980s and continuing into the next decade (Rothschild, 1999, pp. 194–195). This newfound political and economic support seemed to point to an acknowledgment of the program's diversity and increased access, as well as serve as an impetus for other entities to cooperate with a program whose growth evidenced its success. The appearance of success in the educational market made acceptable to a growing neoliberal political consensus the AP program.

The AP Program also received a boost through cinema. In an event that may have been as helpful as government sanction or foundation money, the program became the object of a small, low-budget Hollywood film based on a true story. *Stand and Deliver* (Musca, 1988) told the inspirational story of a Los Angeles public school teacher, Jaime Escalante, portrayed by Edward James Olmos and costarring teen idol Lou Diamond Phillips and Andy Garcia. An innovative mathematics teacher, Escalante encouraged his inner-city Latino students of Garfield High School to challenge themselves with AP Calculus. In the film, all of the students pass their exams, but ETS questions the correlation of results, both for correct and incorrect answers. Escalante feels that ETS doubts the results based on race and class factors. The students retake the exam at the end of the summer and, again, all pass it. In spite of the suspicion by ETS in the film, there can be little doubt that the College Board profited from the film's success (Mast & Kawin, 1996, pp. 582–583; Rothschild, 1999, pp. 195–196; DiYanni, "AP Central").

Despite the growth and popularity of the AP Program, criticism remained. The ultimate compendium of complaints about ETS, with varied applicability to AP, came with the report by lead author Allan Nairn titled *The Reign of ETS: The Corporation That Makes Up Minds* (1980). Its opening line—right or wrong—sets the tone: "The conception for this report on the Educational Testing Service began with the victims of standardized testing" (p. ix). Slant aside, the report makes explicit the service-business conceptual fear articulated by Brigham in the 1930s—a caution rarely expressed by AP's founders and early enthusiasts. The Nairn report suggests that ETS and the College Board operated in a monopolistic environment that ignored the complaints of customers, meaning the examinees primarily, a criticism seconded by Vopat (1989). Citing a Federal Trade Commission study conducted in 1979, the report also argues that students could game the tests through coaching, garnering high scores not just by the excellence of their work in a subject. These stakes, it claims, provided more incentive to game on AP exams than in a regular class. The study also suggests, for the first time, that there was dissension within ETS on policies and recommended changes (Nairn et al., 1980, pp. x, xii-xiii, 260–261; Vopat, 1989, p. 63). This last source of criticism of AP, as well as of the College Board and ETS, would become more prominent over the next three decades.

The Nairn study, which began in 1974, also includes late-1970s revenue figures for AP and other College Board programs. In 1974–1975 AP apparently brought in $2,378,307 and spent $2,101,210, clearing roughly $277,000. It should be noted that this was one of the early years of solvency for the program, according to former AP employee Paul Holbo (Rothschild, 1999, p. 184). In subsequent years, actual and estimated profit amounted to $199,869 (1975–1976, actual), $456,000 (1976–1977, estimate), $663,522 (1977–1978, actual), $598,912 (1978–1979, actual), and $793,000 (1979–1980, estimate) (Nairn et al., 1980, pp. xi, 260–261, 469n2, 481n76, 527–528).[13] It is clear, from these figures at least, that the AP program was no longer an economic burden for the College Board by 1980.

Themes of the Nairn study recurred in the 1990s and first decade of the twenty-first century—with a few twists. In a 1998 *Chronicle of Higher Education* piece, Reisberg relayed that coaching was a concern for college professors trying to teach inadequately prepared AP students. The same article notes the use of AP courses as application enhancers apart from actual credit earned. And furthering the earlier coaching, or teaching-to-the-test, argument, in a 1999 symposium for *The History Teacher*, a student invited to contribute to this special issue devoted to AP History argued that a kind of "tunnel vision" for facts alone diminished his enthusiasm for AP U.S. History (Neutuch, 1999, pp. 245–248).

THE GASTON CAPERTON ERA, 1999–PRESENT

The year 1999 marked the beginning of an explicit move toward a neoliberal corporate ethic for the AP Program. Matlin (2009) argues that with the hiring of Gaston Caperton as its president that year, the College Board "developed a mean revenue streak." Indeed, revenue, if not profit (or excess), from AP had been building for years. But the 2009 exam fee of $86 leads Matlin to estimate that AP revenue for 2008 was more than $232 million. This provides a significant portion of the College Board's overall revenue, which in 2006 totaled $582.9 million. After idealistic eras when excellence was valued and access facilitated, it appears that the AP Program, and the College Board by extension, has devolved into an organization exhibiting a corporate mentality of actively pursuing excess revenue, or profit in the business world. As such, its motives in relation to

AP's rigor and access are left open to question. It prompts one to ask: *Are students still the focus?*

Succeeding Donald M. Stewart, Caperton arrived at the College Board with a sound record in financial management and an enthusiasm for education, but little firsthand administrative or teaching experience in secondary or higher education. His College Board biography speaks of his degree in business (from the University of North Carolina at Chapel Hill) and his hard work growing an insurance company into the nation's "tenth-largest privately owned insurance brokerage firm" (College Board, "Caperton"; Nordheimer & Frantz, 1997). Caperton parlayed this experience into two terms as the Democratic governor of West Virginia from 1988 to 1996. During his tenure he helped move the state from a $500 million debt to a $100 million surplus and created 86,000 jobs, reducing unemployment from 9.8 to 6.2 percent. He also invested approximately $800 million in programs to improve school infrastructure. Caperton did teach in a university setting for a few years, from 1996 to 1999, as a fellow with the John F. Kennedy Institute of Politics at Harvard University, and at Columbia University where he founded its Institute on Education and Government. It is clear from his record, which includes personal experience with dyslexia, that Caperton is an education advocate (College Board, "Caperton"; Hoover, 2006; Matlin, 2009).

But it is also evident that his talents lie in financial and business matters. This appears to have been highly desired at the time by the College Board trustees. Access to their deliberations is not available, but the trustees apparently felt that business was sluggish in the late 1990s and that a shake-up was needed. It could only help that, in addition to his professional qualities, Caperton was regarded as personable, respectful, engaging, energetic, and driven—the embodiment of the neoliberal ideal of melding a market orientation with a traditional, authentic liberal concern for education (College Board, "Caperton"; Hoover, 2006; Matlin, 2009).

While some positive trends have continued—more courses being offered, increased minority access to AP, greater attention paid to standards—the overall trend is toward gaining more revenue. While Caperton emphasizes that revenue growth is merely a by-product and natural consequence of increased access and growth, the specifics behind allocations and expenditures reveal the College Board as "a service organization with a corporate ethos" (Hoover, 2006, p. A23). In addition to the high annual salaries of the Board's president, vice presidents, and senior staff

($637,757 for Caperton and an average salary of $239,374 for each of the thirty-eight vice presidents and senior staff members in 2006), as well as the 2006 surplus noted above (Matlin, 2009), during his very first year Caperton initiated the creation of the College Board's for-profit spinoff, collegeboard.com. This dot.com experiment cost $30 million, and its purpose was to compete directly with Kaplan, Inc., and Princeton Review. The venture lasted three years before being transformed into a nonprofit. And the small things mattered too in developing a new ethos. For instance, Caperton would distribute copies of Jim Miller's book *From Good to Great: Why Some Companies Make the Leap . . . and Others Don't* (2001). Lastly, as is the case with many big businesses, Caperton also sought state subsidies for his institution. Under the time-honored principle of increasing access, he has obtained subsidies for AP coursework from the U.S. Department of Education and from states, such as Florida (Matlin, 2009; Hoover, 2006).

If the questionable motives of the College Board were not enough of a concern, its partner organization in AP programming, ETS, has also ventured away from its nonprofit ideal. Examples abound: in 1993 it created an allegedly anticompetitive agreement with the Sylvan franchise; in 1996 it created a for-profit subsidiary, the Chauncey Group, with clients, employees, and assets derived from ETS endeavors; and in 2007 it reported a $94 million excess, with its president earning $931,605 (Nordheimer & Frantz, 1997, Lewin, 2003). To teachers, or those toiling in underfunded humanities and social science nonprofits, these salaries and revenue excesses represent a distortion of ideals. The College Board and ETS appear more revenue driven than beholden to the idea of a liberal education—an endeavor traditionally motivated by nonmonetary priorities.

If questions of money and motivation were only raised by outside critics they would be easier to counter or dismiss. But concerns persist among former AP, College Board, and ETS employees, disgruntled and otherwise. A thirteen-year veteran of the College Board's New England regional office, Jim Montague, believes that the Board has gone from being an "education partner" to "just another vendor" selling tests. Former Board committeeman Theodore A. O' Neill believes the organization became infused with "capitalist, free-market fever." And a past director of the Board's office for academic affairs, Robert Orrill, asserts that it became sales-focused, more concerned with the education marketplace, and vigilant about the "bottom line." These complaints do not include those of education institutions that work with the College Board regularly

(Hoover, 2006, p. A23). Former ETS senior vice president Winton H. Manning recorded his disappointment "in the direction they have taken away from education and public service." In so doing, he argued, ETS was losing "the kind of affinity and loyalty and sensitivity that comes from [being] a public service operation" (Nordheimer & Frantz, 1997). A former DuPont executive, Kurt Landgraf, became ETS president in 2001 and has since been accused—per Manning's 1997 assertion—of moving ETS toward a more explicit corporate model (Lewin, 2003).

CONCLUSION

The story of the AP Program begins with high motives and high-powered intellectual conferences about excellence and general education. The program came into being as a nonprofit focused on smoothing the transition between high school and college for gifted students. Over time the program became less concerned with keeping smart students from being bored and more involved—to its credit—in the democratic ideal of increasing access to high-level coursework for able, motivated students. The College Board democratized the notion of advanced placement in the American educational system.

But recently the program has become a potentially tragic morality tale about corporate-style revenue grabbing and the subversion of AP's nonprofit ethos. The founding ideals of the College Board, ETS, and AP have become merely advertising points, students' excellence and rigor have been reduced to test-score gaming, democratization has become growth in market share, and not-for-profit public service has become an experiment in neoliberal ideology. There presently appears to be no outside encouragement to change, at least not from any person or institution with the power to force action. The story's ending, however, is uncertain. One organization, Americans for Educational Testing Reform, did recently file a complaint about ETS and the College Board with the Internal Revenue Service (Jensen, 2009)—an avenue for change that has been unsuccessfully attempted before. Some schools and colleges have exercised their consumer power to opt out or lessen their exposure to AP. Reasons vary from concerns about standards, teaching flexibility, and abuse of AP coursework in the college admissions process. There is also philosophical opposition to strengthening America's testing culture, and potential structural discrimination, because of economic class correlations with test success (Ganeshanaanthan, 2000).

To bring the story full circle, perhaps the most foundational criticism of current AP coursework is the charge that it subverts the liberal arts ideal. Katz (2006) singles out AP courses for undermining the vitality and imagination of liberal arts curriculum. He scorns AP as a mere "testing hurdle." Schools that agree with Katz's critique are eliminating AP because, for example, in its history courses it substitutes "chronological parades of facts and documents" for understanding. The cultivation of good "habits of the mind," as well as the ability to improvise and tailor are "squeezed out in the rush to swallow information" (Berger, 2006, p. 7). To critics like Katz, the AP exam, rather than the process of learning to think, drives the form and content of any given course; the course becomes training for the test. And if this is true for the AP Program in general, then neoliberal concerns about revenue and market share appear to have trumped the idealists' concerns for rigor and true democratization.

ACKNOWLEDGMENTS
I offer my thanks to the following colleagues and friends for their observations, suggestions, encouragement, and sometimes vigorous disagreement: Fred Beuttler, Andrew Hartman, Jodi Lacy, Christopher Miller, Tamara L. Smith, Gerhard Sonnert, Jason Stacy, and David Veenstra.

NOTES

1. The *American Heritage College Dictionary* (3rd ed., 1993) defines *neoliberalism* as "a political movement beginning in the 1960s that blends traditional liberal concerns for social justice with an emphasis on economic growth." Although some might debate the 1960s as the chronological starting point for neoliberalism (including David Harvey below), few will contest an explicit connection to the Democratic Party and neoliberalism's friendliness to market ideas. Indeed, neoliberalism was not a new liberalism but rather an openness to achieving midcentury liberal aims by other means. Other 1960s and 1970s liberal Democrats moved in the direction now known as neoconservatism. Their concerns grew out of unhappiness with President Johnson's social policies and liberalism in general. Neoconservatives focused on the idea of equality, favoring an emphasis on the notion of equality of opportunity over equality of outcome. Finally, although neoconservatives came out of the liberal tradition, they never explicitly attached themselves to either the Democratic or Republican parties (although a significant number would become

Republicans in the 1980s). For more on neoliberalism, see Harvey (2005); for more on neoliberalism's critics, see Boltanski and Chiapello (2005); for more on neoconservatism, see Steinfels (1979) and Blumenthal (1986).

2. My use of the College Board's literature in this chapter is restricted primarily to its quantitative reports.

3. For more on W. T. Harris and the St. Louis Hegelians, see Goetzmann (1973).

4. See Bergeson (1966, p. 24), Hartman (2008, p. 179), Elwell (1967, pp. 23–27), Cremin (1988, pp. 248–249), Smith and Bender (2008, p. 14), Ravitch (1983, p. 11), Adler (1977, p. 153), Levine (1986, pp. 89–90, 102, 105–106), Harms and DePencier (1996, chap. 4).

5. I believe the Association is the historical antecedent of today's Middle States Commission on Higher Education (http://www.msche.org/).

6. The American College Testing Program (ACT) was not formed until 1959.

7. For more see Lagemann (1989, pp. 181, 198, 232–233), Bergeson (1966, pp. 26–27), Elwell (1967, p. 27), Macdonald (1989, p. 51), Reeves (1969, pp. 13–14, 20, 58, 75), Nielsen (1972, pp. 81–82), Dzuback (1991, p. 235).

8. See Adler (1977, pp. 9–10, 163, 177–180, 214), Cornog (1980, pp. 15, 17), Dzuback (1991, pp. 125–127), Elwell (1967, pp. 52–53, 58–60, 81, 101–102), Hartman (2008, pp. 58, 132–135), Hutchins (1936).

9. Recent articles noting decreased cooperation on various topics include Glenn (2005) on colleges misusing AP results, Smydo (2007) on AP not offering the diversity of survey courses offered by colleges, and Mattimore (2009) on high school teachers speaking through the press (rather than to AP) to correct myths in higher education about the program.

10. For a more recent take on the pleasures and pains of Columbia's integrative, introductory surveys, Literature Humanities (Lit Hum) and Contemporary Civilization (CC), see Denby (1996).

11. See Cremin (1988, pp. 241–242, 270), Hartman (2008, pp. 124–130, 169–171, 175–180, 182, 185), May (1988, chap. 1), Patterson (1996, pp. 343–344, 369–371, 418–422), Urban and Wagoner (2000, pp. 288, 293–298), Pulliam and Van Patten (2003, pp. 214, 250).

12. The reevaluation of meritocratic advancement is evident in texts such as Robert Rosenthal and Lenore Jacobson's 1968 study *Pygmalion in the Classroom*.

13. I cannot confirm these revenue expense clearance numbers.

REFERENCES

Adler, M. J. (1977). *Philosopher at large: An intellectual autobiography*. New York: Macmillan.

Aluri, R. S. (1987). *The Advanced Placement Program in small rural high schools of South Carolina: An analysis.* Unpublished doctoral dissertation, University of South Carolina.

Arbolino, J. N. (1961). *What's wrong with the Advanced Placement Program?* Reston, VA: National Association of Secondary School Principals.

Ballard, E. (1953). Review of *General Education in School and College Journal of Higher Education, 24*(9), 498–499.

Bell, D. (1966). *The reforming of general education: The Columbia College experience in its national setting.* New York: Columbia University Press.

Berger, J. (2006, October 4). Demoting Advanced Placement. *The New York Times,* B7.

Bergeson, J. B. (1966). *The academic performance of Advanced Placement Program participants compared with non-participants at Northwestern University, 1965.* Unpublished doctoral dissertation, Northern Illinois University.

Blumenthal, S. (1986). *The rise of the counter-establishment.* New York: Harper & Row.

Boltanski, L., & Chiapello, E. (2005). *The new spirit of capitalism* (G. Elliott, Trans.). New York: Verso.

Brubacher, J. S., & Rudy, W. (1976). *Higher education in transition: A history of American colleges and universities, 1636–1976* (3rd ed.). New York: Harper & Row.

Cheit, E. F. (1971). *The new depression in higher education: A study of financial conditions at 41 colleges and universities.* New York: McGraw-Hill.

College Board. (n.d.). Annual AP Program participation 1956–2008. http://www.professionals.collegeboard.com

College Board. (n.d.). College Board history. http://www.collegeboard.com/about/association/history.html

College Board. (n.d.). Fact sheet. http://www.collegeboard.com/about/news_info/sat/factsheet.html

College Board. (n.d.). Gaston Caperton biography. http://www.collegeboard.com/about

College Board. (2008). Program summary report. http://www.professionals.collegeboard.com

College Entrance Examination Board. (1926). *The work of the College Entrance Examination Board, 1901–1925.* Boston: Ginn.

Conant, J. B. (1961). *Slums and suburbs: A commentary on schools in metropolitan areas.* New York: McGraw-Hill.

Cornog, W. H. (1980, Spring). The Advanced Placement Program: Reflections on its origins. *College Board Review, 115,* 14–17.

Cremin, L. A. (1988). *American education: The metropolitan experience, 1876–1980.* New York: Harper & Row.

Denby, D. (1996). *Great books*. New York: Simon & Schuster.

DiYanni, R. (n.d.) AP central—The history of the AP Program. http://apcentral.collegeboard.com/apc/public/courses-/21502.html

DiYanni, R. (n.d.). The internationalization of the Advanced Placement Program. http://apcentral.collegeboard.com

Dressel, P. L. (1954). General and liberal education. *Review of Educational Research, 24*(4), 285–294.

Dzuback, M. A. (1991). *Robert M. Hutchins: Portrait of an educator*. Chicago: University of Chicago Press.

Education: Harvard asks a question. (1945, August 13). *Time*. http://www.time.com/time/magazine/article/0,9171,792287.00.html

Elwell, D. B. (1967). *A history of the Advanced Placement Program of the College Entrance Examination Board*. Unpublished doctoral dissertation, Columbia University Teachers College.

Farber, D. (1994). *The age of great dreams: America in the 1960s*. New York: Hill & Wang.

Fuess, C. M. (1950). *The College Board: Its first fifty years*. New York: Columbia University Press.

Fund for the Advancement of Education [FAE]. (1957). *They went to college early*. New York.

Ganeshanaanthan, V. V. (2000, July 14). Advanced Placement Program faces new criticism over its testing standards. *Chronicle of Higher Education*, A45.

General Education in School and College [GESC]. (1952). *A committee report by members of the faculties of Andover, Exeter, Lawrenceville, Harvard, Princeton, and Yale*. Cambridge, MA: Harvard University Press.

Glenn, D. (2005, January 21). Scholars say college admissions offices misuse Advanced Placement data. *Chronicle of Higher Education*.

Goetzmann, W. H. (Ed.). (1973). *The American Hegelians*. New York: Knopf.

Greene, R. L. (1954). Making the English major more effective and attractive. *College English, 15*(6), 332–339.

Harms, W., & DePencier, I. (1996). *Experiencing education: 100 years of learning at the University of Chicago laboratory schools*. University of Chicago. http://www.ucls.uchicago.edu/about-lab/history/

Hartman, A. (2008). *Education and the cold war: The battle for the American school*. New York: Palgrave Macmillan.

Harvey, D. (2005). *A brief history of neoliberalism*. New York: Oxford University Press.

Hoover, E. (2006, June 30) Captain Caperton. *Chronicle of Higher Education*, A23.

Horn, F. (1953). Music in general education. *Music Educators Journal, 40*(1), 25–26.

Hutchins, R. M. (1936). *The higher learning in America*. New Haven: Yale University Press.

Jensen, D. C. (2009, June 20). Letter to IRS EO classification. http://www.aetr.org

Jones, E. S., & Ortner, G. K. (1954). Articulation of high school and college. *Review of Educational Research, 24*(4), 322–330.

Katz, S. N. (2006, March 10). The liberal arts in school and college. *Chronicle of Higher Education*, B46.

Kerr, C. (1982). *The uses of the university* (3rd ed.). Cambridge, MA: Harvard University Press.

Lagemann, E. C. (1983). *Private power for the public good: A history of the Carnegie Foundation for the Advancement of Teaching*. Middletown, CT: Wesleyan University Press.

Lagemann, E. C. (1989). *The politics of knowledge: The Carnegie Corporation, philanthropy, and public policy*. Middletown, CT: Wesleyan University Press.

Lemman, N. (2000). *The big test: The secret history of the American meritocracy*. New York: Farrar, Straus, & Giroux.

Levine, D. O. (1986). *The American college and the culture of aspiration, 1915–1940*. Ithaca, NY: Cornell University Press.

Lewin, T. (2003, January 14). Testing group ends effort to make profit on Web site. *The New York Times*.

Macdonald, D. (1989). *The Ford Foundation: The men and the millions*. New Brunswick, NJ: Transaction Publishers. (Original work published 1955)

Mast, G., & Kawin, B. F. (1996). *A short history of the movies* (6th ed.). Needham Heights, MA: Allyn & Bacon.

Matlin, C. (2009). Taking the $ATs: The big money. *Slate.com*. http://www.thebigmoney.com/articles/diploma-mill/2009/5/13/taking-sat

Mattimore, P. (2009, February 6). 5 fundamental misconceptions about AP courses. *Chronicle of Higher Education*.

May, E. T. (1988). *Homeward bound: American families in the cold war era*. New York: Basic Books.

Morse, F. A. (1955). Review of the book *The Community College in the United States*. *Journal of Higher Education, 26*(7), 396–398.

Musca, C. (Producer), & Menendez, R. (Writer/Director). (1988). *Stand and deliver* [Motion picture]. United States: Warner Brothers.

Nairn, A., et. al. (1980). *The reign of ETS: The corporation that makes up minds*. Washington, DC: Ralph Nader.

Neutuch, E. (1999). Advanced Placement United States history: A student's perspective. *The History Teacher, 32*(2), 245–248.

Nielsen, W. A. (1972). *The big foundations*. New York: Columbia University Press.

Nordheimer, J., & Frantz, D. (1997, September 30). Testing giant exceeds roots, drawing business rivals' ire. *The New York Times*. http://www.nytimes.com

Nugent, S. A., & Karnes, F. A. (2002). The Advanced Placement Program and the International Baccalaureate Programme: A history and update. *Gifted Child Today, 25*(1), 30–39.

O'Dell, S. (1954). Symposium: Responsibility for literacy, part V. *College English, 15*(7), 409–410.

Patterson, J. T. (1996). *Grand expectations: The United States, 1945–74*. New York: Oxford University Press.

Pulliam, J. D., & Van Patten, J. J. (2003). *History of education in America* (8th ed.). Upper Saddle River, NJ: Merrill Prentice Hall.

Ralston, N. C. (1961). *A study of the Advanced Placement Program in the Cincinnati Public Schools*. Unpublished doctoral dissertation, Indiana University.

Ravitch, D. (1983) *The troubled crusade: American education, 1945–1980*. New York: Basic Books.

Reeves, T. C. (1969). *Freedom and the foundation: The fund for the republic in the era of McCarthyism*. New York: Knopf.

Reisberg, L. (1998, June 26). Some professors question programs that allow high-school students to earn college credits. *Chronicle of Higher Education*, A39–40.

Rosenthal, M. (2006). *Nicholas miraculous: The amazing career of the redoubtable Dr. Nicholas Murray Butler*. New York: Farrar, Straus, & Giroux.

Rosenthal, B., & Jacobson, L. (1968). *Pygmalion in the classroom: Teacher expectations and pupils' intellectual development*. New York: Holt, Rinehart & Winston.

Rothschild, E. (1999). Four decades of the Advanced Placement Program. *The History Teacher, 32*(2), 175–176.

Rudolph, F. (1965). *The American college and university: A history*. New York: Vintage Books.

Schrum, E. (2007). Establishing a democratic religion: metaphysics and democracy in the debates over the President's Commission on Higher Education. *History of Education Quarterly, 47*(3), 277–301.

Schrum, E. (2009). *Administering American modernity: The instrumental university in the postwar United States*. Unpublished doctoral dissertation, University of Pennsylvania.

Smith, W., & Bender, T. (Eds.). (2008). *American higher education transformed, 1940–2005: Documenting the national discourse*. Baltimore: Johns Hopkins University Press.

Smydo, J. (2007, August 6). College Board cool to AP course in African-American history. *Pittsburgh Post-Gazette*.

Sparer, J. L. (1954). "Professional" book releases. *The English Journal, 43*(1), 51–52.

Steinfels, P. (1979). *The neoconservatives.* New York: Simon & Schuster.

Sumption, M. R., & Luecking, E. M. (1960). *Education of the gifted.* New York: Ronald Press.

Urban, W., & Wagoner, J. (2000). *American education: A history* (2nd ed.). New York: McGraw-Hill Higher Education.

Van Gelder, E. (1972). *The three-year B.A.: A wavering idea.* Gainesville: Institute for Higher Education, University of Florida.

Vopat, J. B. (1989). The politics of Advanced Placement English. In G. A. Olson, E. Metzger, & E. Ashton-Jones (Eds.), *Advanced Placement English: Theory, politics, and pedagogy* (pp. 52–64). Portsmouth, NH: Boynton/Cook.

PART TWO

Inside AP

CHAPTER 3

How Are AP Courses Different?

Philip M. Sadler

Advanced coursework in high school is designed to differ from regular coursework in content coverage and intellectual demand. Most high schools offer some form of advanced coursework, typically Advanced Placement, International Baccalaureate (IB), or honors courses. Enrollment in advanced science and mathematics courses has been increasing for the last two decades (see figure 3.1), except for honors biology or AP Biology, which began plateauing in the late 1990s. When compared with enrollments in regular courses, one in seven high school students is taking an advanced course in science and one in four in mathematics (Snyder, Hoffman, & Geddes, 2007, table 142).

The three types of advanced courses taught in high school differ from each other in important ways. The College Board's Advanced Placement Program encompasses thirty-seven courses in twenty-two disciplines. In the sciences, AP programs cover biology, chemistry, physics, and environmental science. In mathematics, AP courses are offered in calculus, statistics, and computer science. Each course labeled AP is now subject to an audit of its syllabus for each teacher. The College Board offers professional development for teachers, yearly exams for each subject, and a wealth of support materials. AP courses often receive higher levels of administrative support than other courses, which can include special funding from the district or state and extra compensation to teachers whose students pass the AP exam (Herr, 1992b; Baron, 2009; see also Klopfenstein & Thomas, this volume). Herr (1992a) found that AP courses were viewed by teachers as more satisfying than honors courses and that they covered a broader variety of topics in greater depth and at a faster pace.

FIGURE 3.1   Growth in advanced high school course-taking in science and mathematics

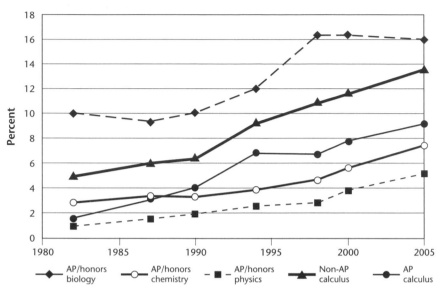

The International Baccalaureate offers a demanding two-year high school–level program with a final examination. It is offered in 2,005 schools worldwide and 672 schools in the United States (IBO, n.d.). The IB program covers all academic areas and offers teacher training and curriculum materials. A delegation visits each school that applies for participation. These courses, however, are too rare in U.S. schools to allow for inclusion in this analysis.

Honors courses are not standardized, with coverage and level of difficulty differing from school to school. Herr (1992a) found that greater curricular freedom in choosing texts, topics, and teaching methods existed in honors courses than in AP courses and that teachers noted that honors courses were less stressful to teach, allowed students more time in the laboratory, and were better at developing students' thinking skills. Honors and AP courses can serve different purposes. Typically, an honors course is taken by students as a first-year prerequisite for AP if an AP course is offered by the school (Herr, 1992b).[1] In schools without AP, honors courses are usually the highest level of course offered. When an AP course is not offered in the high school, few schools offer a second year of biology, chemistry, or physics. Only elite private schools and wealthy suburban schools have turned away from AP in some or all subjects and offer second-year honors courses that they claim are the equivalent of college-level coursework (Ramírez, 1998).[2] These schools often prepare students for the AP exam, although they do not list their courses as "AP" or subject them to a College Board audit. Several have joined together in an association that promotes the development and implementation of alternatives to "test-driven programs" such as AP or IB.

METHODS

The present study of students enrolled in introductory college science courses provides the means to compare many of the attributes of the different types of high school science courses. The study, entitled Factors Influencing College Science Success (FICSS, see chapter 13 for details), used surveys to collect data from students enrolled in fifty-five four-year colleges and universities out of an original sampling of sixty-seven institutions across all fifty states. The purpose of the study was to collect evidence that could support or refute hypotheses held by science educators about how best to prepare students for college science. Different from most other studies investigating the impact of curriculum and classroom pedagogy, FICSS was based on a large, stratified random sample of colleges and universities rather than on a single institution or single state. This made the findings more generalizable across high schools in the United States. (Details concerning the planning and implementation of this study can be found in chapter 6 of this volume.)

In formulating the analysis in this chapter, I used data from 7,491 students enrolled in first-semester introductory college biology, chemistry, or physics courses. The study examined only students who took a class in the particular subject prior to their college course and excluded students with unusual backgrounds (i.e., those who did not attend a U.S. high school or who took the college course as a special student or graduate student).

The purpose of the study was to examine differences among the three major types of high school science courses that are well represented in our sample: regular, honors, and Advanced Placement. The differences discussed concern three aspects: the characteristics of the students who are enrolled in each of these course types, the characteristics of the teachers of these course types, and the pedagogy used. It is important to note that this analysis is only of students who progressed to a college-level introductory science course in each field; lost to our sample are students who took a high school course but decided not to enroll in the corresponding college course. Strictly speaking, therefore, the data are not representative of the high school science course experience of the entire population of American high school students, but they are representative of the course experience of those high school students who go on to attend college and take a science course there.

STUDENT BACKGROUND

The students taking introductory college biology, chemistry, and physics do not have identical backgrounds. They represent the full range of levels of high school coursework as preparation. Federal statistics find that gender differences in high school course-taking are vanishing nationally for regular science courses: 51 percent females in biology, 53 percent in chemistry, and 47 percent in physics. National statistics concerning advanced coursework combine honors and AP courses and show greater gender disparities than for regular courses: 56 percent females in honors biology or AP Biology, 50 percent in honors chemistry or AP Chemistry, and 38 percent in honors physics or AP Physics (Snyder et al., 2007, table 142). Because introductory college science is typically taken by the stronger high school science students, study participants expected to find that the course-taking backgrounds of male and female students in the FICSS study would essentially be the same. Indeed, in college biology and chemistry courses, the percentages of male and female students who had taken regular, honors, and AP are similar to within 2 percent. Among the students in introductory college physics, males and females are just as likely to have taken a regular high school physics course, but 5 percent more females choose honors, and a corresponding 5 percent more males have the background of AP Physics.

How and to what extent do students who take different levels of science courses differ in other characteristics? The study found that the mathematics backgrounds of students enrolling in introductory college science courses differs considerably by science and by the type of high school course taken (figure 3.2). Students taking honors biology, chemistry, or physics in high school are more likely to have had a course in calculus during high school than students taking regular courses (i.e., non-AP calculus, AP Calculus-AB, AP Calculus-BC). Similarly, in each of the three disciplines, the likelihood of taking calculus is even higher for

FIGURE 3.2   Math background of college science students by level of
preparation in science subject

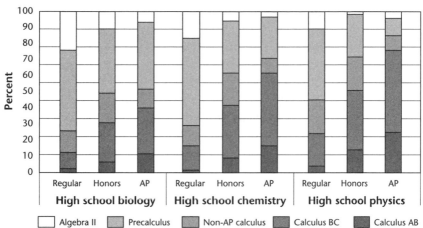

AP science students than for honors students. This may suggest that AP courses, particularly in chemistry and physics, attract students who have much stronger mathematics backgrounds than do students who take honors or regular science courses. The study found little difference in the calculus background of males and females taking college biology (38 percent of males and 34 percent of females) or college physics (48 percent of males and 47 percent of females). By contrast, there is a large gender difference in the calculus background of students taking college chemistry (47 percent of males and only 34 percent of females). Hence, females in college chemistry exhibit a weaker mathematics preparation, on average, than do male students. This is consequential because mathematics preparation, particularly calculus, is a strong predictor of introductory college chemistry grades (Tai, Ward, & Sadler, 2006). It is interesting that there is no significant difference between the average SAT Math scores earned by honors and AP students. Presumably this is because there are no items requiring calculus on the SAT.

Historically, there has been a difference in parental education levels between male and female scientists (Sonnert & Holton, 1995). There was no such disparity evident in the FICSS data, reflecting a contemporary cohort of college students. Male and female introductory college biology, chemistry, and physics students have a nearly identical distribution of parental education levels. However, parental education level tracks with the increasing rigor of high school science courses. Students with at least one parent holding a graduate degree make up about 30 percent of the students enrolled in regular high school science courses, but 35 percent of those taking honors and 40 percent taking AP science. Conversely, the percentage of students for whom neither parent has earned a four-year college degree is about 40 percent among those who took only a regular course, but it drops to 35 percent of those who took an honors course and to 30 percent of those who took an AP course. In terms of race and ethnic background, minority students are underrepresented in advanced courses, according to data collected from AP teachers, with a majority reporting fewer than 10 percent ethnic minority students (Milewski & Gillie, 2002). This study's data show similar results. Of those who took AP Biology, Chemistry, or Physics in high school, 9 percent identified themselves as Asian/Pacific Islander, 4 percent as black, and 5 percent as Hispanic.

Advanced courses in high school typically have fewer students (Milewski & Gillie, 2002). In the FICSS sample, there were no significant differences in class size between regular and honors high school science classes in biology or chemistry; all averaged 23 students. AP Biology and Chemistry classes averaged 19 students, 4 fewer than regular or honors. Regular and honors physics classes averaged 21 students with little difference between them. AP Physics courses averaged 5 fewer students. Since AP science courses have proportionally fewer students, each pupil receives a larger proportion of his or her teacher's attention (17 percent for biology and chemistry, 20 percent for physics). Hence, in terms of class size, AP courses have an advantage over honors and regular courses across all three science disciplines.

TEACHER CHARACTERISTICS

Teachers of honors high school courses report more intellectual stimulation and greater collegiality with peers than those who teach AP courses (Herr, 1992a). In the FICSS dataset, students' reports show substantial differences in observed characteristics between teachers in regular, honors, and AP courses in the sciences. The study grouped the student rating variables of their teachers into two categories: (1) the teacher's knowledge of the science subject matter and (2) various aspects of teaching ability (i.e., fairness, ability to maintain student interest, organization of lessons, and skill at explaining problems). Graphing these two categories against each other reveals distinct groupings by course type (figure 3.3).

FIGURE 3.3   Student ratings of their high school science teachers

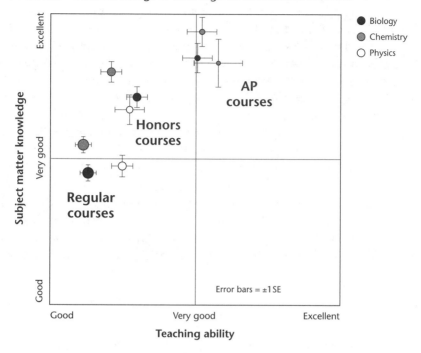

In general, students rate their science teachers more highly on subject matter knowledge than on teaching ability; average ratings range from very good to excellent on subject matter knowledge and from good to very good on teaching ability. Students' ratings of the two categories are also correlated: a teacher who receives a high rating in one category is likely to also be rated highly in the other. Additionally, the figure shows interesting details. The average teaching ability ratings of regular and honors science teachers differ somewhat, with honors teachers earning higher ratings (except in physics). The degree of subject matter knowledge is seen as much higher for honors teachers than for teachers of regular courses. In the eyes of the students, honors course teachers thus distinguish themselves from regular course teachers more in terms of greater subject matter knowledge than in terms of greater teaching ability. AP teachers are given substantially higher ratings in both subject matter knowledge and teaching ability, indicating that they may have more thorough training and more extensive teaching experience.

In examining the proportion of male and female teachers, the study noted near parity in biology and chemistry. In regular and AP courses, 45 percent of teachers are female; honors classes in biology and chemistry are taught by females 55 percent of the time. Parity has not been reached in physics, however, where only 26 percent of regular and AP Physics teachers are female, with honors courses taught by female teachers 34 percent of the time. Student disruptions of the class are reported far more frequently in regular classes than in honors classes and are very rare in AP classrooms. This could be the result of teacher experience, smaller class size, or students' overall prior academic success and interest in learning. Milewski and Gillie (2002) report in a College Board study that 81 percent of AP teachers are certified in their subject area and most are within twelve years of retirement, giving them a possible edge on experience. This is in agreement with the findings laid out in chapter 4 of this volume, where Paek, Braun, Ponte, Trapani, and Powers also conclude that AP Biology is generally taught by veteran teachers with strong academic preparation.

PEDAGOGY

On the surface, pedagogies chosen by high school teachers appear to differ little by course type. Students report very similar allocations of class time between regular, honors, and AP courses concerning, individual, small group, and whole class activities, such as lectures, test taking, and class discussion. Yet particular activities are used more often in some course types. Honors students report substantially more emphasis on carrying out their own projects than do either regular or AP students, while regular students report more involvement in community projects. AP students spend more time teaching each other and twice as much time preparing for standardized exams. Quantitative problem-solving is more central in honors and AP courses, as are exams with open-ended questions and students having to draw graphs by hand or computer. AP students spend more time on homework, reading the textbook, and studying outside of class than do honors or regular students.

Overall, students report taking two and a half to three labs each month, with little difference in frequency between subject or course level. In probing beneath that superficial similarity in terms of quantity, differences in the quality of the lab experience become apparent. The study found that honors courses exhibit a substantially greater frequency—and AP courses more still—of certain laboratory pedagogies:

- Questions about lab results appearing on exams and quizzes
- Computer use to automate data collection
- Time devoted to discussion of laboratory findings
- Lab experiments more often building on each other

Students report that they spend 26 percent more time preparing lab reports for honors and 54 percent more time for AP than for regular courses. While the frequency of the actual laboratory experience differs little, the time spent in lab-associated activities, assessment, and discussion and the use of technological aids and the more sequential nature of the labs make labs in honors and, particularly, AP courses more central to the science course.

SUMMARY

Advanced Placement science courses differ from regular and honors courses offered in most U.S. high schools. They are generally taken only by students who performed well in a prerequisite first-year course. These students have strong mathematics backgrounds and high quantitative SAT or ACT scores, and they usually graduate high school having taken calculus. AP students are also more likely to have well-educated parents. Racial minorities appear underrepresented in AP science programs.

Advanced placement courses are taught by more experienced teachers with greater subject matter knowledge and teaching ability. The classes usually have fewer students than regular or honors courses and suffer fewer classroom management issues. The teaching strategies in AP courses are used with similar frequency to those in honors or regular courses. However, the results of the laboratory work are more strongly integrated into assessment and class discussion. Labs also more frequently use computers to log data, and experiments connect more strongly to each other. The largest difference is that students report that they work much harder in AP courses preparing for the exam, writing lab reports, studying, and reading the textbook. Advanced Placement courses are more demanding of students that honors or regular courses.

AP, honors, and regular science courses thus vary in a variety of aspects, ranging from the characteristics of the students to those of the teachers

and the pedagogies employed. This finding has methodological consequences for studies that compare, for instance, outcomes for AP and non-
AP students. Making a simple comparison between those two groups is,
to some extent, like comparing apples and oranges. It behooves studies to
control, as far as possible, for other factors that are associated with course
levels if they wish to isolate specific AP effects. Without considering the
appropriateness of a range of control variables, a study including them in
data collection, and using them in data analysis, runs the risk of reaching
conclusions concerning the effectiveness of advanced coursework that
are really the result of other substantial differences among the groups examined. Particularly since AP courses are taken more often by students
with higher SAT/ACT scores, stronger mathematics backgrounds, and
more highly educated parents, the expectation is of stronger performance
in later years. But only by the careful and deliberate use of controls can
the true impact be fairly measured.

NOTES
1. The FICSS study found that an earlier high school course in the same
   science subject was taken by 94 percent of those who enrolled in AP Biology, 92 percent of those in AP Chemistry, and only 47 percent of those
   in AP Physics.
2. For example, Milton Academy in Milton, MA; Scarsdale High School in
   Scarsdale, NY; Phillips Exeter Academy, Exeter, NH; the Lawrenceville
   School in Lawrenceville, NJ.

REFERENCES

Baron, M. (2009, August 26). In AP effort, students soar—and teachers unions
   flunk. *The Boston Globe*, A12.
Herr, N. E. (1992a). Administrative policies regarding advanced placement
   and honors coursework. *NASSP Bulletin, 76*(544), 80–87.
Herr, N. E. (1992b). A comparative analysis of the perceived influence of advanced placement and honors programs upon science instruction. *Journal of Research in Science Teaching, 29*(5), 521–532.
International Baccalaureate Organization [IBO]. (n.d.). http://www.ibo.org/
   country/US/index.cfm
Milewski, G. B., & Gillie, J. M. (2002). What are the characteristics of AP teachers?
   An examination of survey results. http://professionals.collegeboard.com/
   profdownload/pdf/200210_20717.pdf

Ramírez, E. (2008, September 19). Some high schools are dropping out of the Advanced Placement Program. *U.S. News and World Report.*

Sonnert, G., & Holton, G. (1995). *Gender differences in science careers: The Project Access study.* New Brunswick, NJ: Rutgers University Press.

Snyder, T., Hoffman, C., & Geddes, C. (2007). *Digest of education statistics.* Washington, DC: U.S. Department of Education, National Center for Education Statistics.

Tai, R. H., Ward, R. B., & Sadler, P. M. (2006). High school chemistry content background of introductory college chemistry students and its association with college chemistry grades. *Journal of Chemical Education, 83*(11), 1703–1711.

CHAPTER 4

AP Biology Teacher Characteristics and Practices and Their Relationship to Student AP Exam Performance

Pamela L. Paek, Henry Braun, Eva Ponte,
Catherine Trapani, and Donald E. Powers

The potential advantages of the Advanced Placement Program are both educational and financial: high school students are intellectually stimulated and challenged by accelerated learning opportunities while saving time and money by completing entry-level college courses. However, these advantages can be realized only if the courses are taught at a level commensurate with the college standards and if the students are motivated to perform to meet those standards. Achievement of the standards is primarily determined by student performance on the exam that is administered on the completion of AP coursework.

The College Board, which runs the AP Program, puts considerable effort into defining course content, so that most colleges will give credit for AP courses; in providing curriculum materials that can be consistently implemented nationwide; and in constructing valid and reliable end-of-course assessments. Even with these ample resources, the pivotal player in this complex enterprise is the teacher, and thus we need a better understanding not only of the contexts in which teachers work but also of their teaching practices. Milewski and Gillie (2002) conducted a comprehensive study of AP teacher *characteristics*, but as yet there has been no comprehensive survey of AP teacher *practices*—how teachers successfully organize and deliver AP course content.

We thus set out to document teaching contexts and practices of AP teachers and then investigate the relationships between these documented practices and students' performance on the AP Biology exam. We chose to study AP Biology because it has a very broad and dynamic curriculum that poses many pedagogical challenges. In addition, biology is the most popular AP exam in science, as measured by the number of test-takers, and thus has the largest dataset of student AP data available for analysis.

While research has established that teachers have a measurable effect on student achievement, it has proven much more difficult to pinpoint the specific characteristics of teachers, or aspects of their pedagogy, that can be linked to higher student achievement (Olson, 2003). Nonetheless, this issue is now more relevant than ever, because current legislation, such as the No Child Left Behind Act (NCLB) and the American Recovery and Reinvestment Act (ARRA), requires more school and teacher accountability for student achievement. These two acts share a common focus on the preparation of a high-quality teaching force that will provide students with the best education possible. The underlying expectation is that improvements in the professional development of teachers will translate into positive changes in teaching practices, which will, in turn, enhance student achievement.

MEASURING TEACHING PRACTICES

This study of AP Biology focuses on a distinctive teaching milieu in which (1) the course content is more comprehensive and detailed than the usual high school course in the same subject area and in which (2) students are assessed through a national high-stakes exam. These factors create a unique environment that has not usually been the focus of research on teaching.

One important area of research on teaching focuses on factors that influence teachers' effectiveness, as determined by the performance of their students. Based on this research, we selected factors that we deemed most relevant in AP Biology courses (and that were measurable through a survey). Using these factors and their underlying theoretical assumptions, we constructed a model of teaching practices that served as the basis for the creation of our AP Biology teacher survey instrument. The model defines teaching practices in three categories: instructional and assessment practices, content coverage, and test preparation practices. We do not regard these as discrete categories but, rather, as overlapping categories that, together, provide an overall portrait of teaching practices. Additionally, measuring teacher practice is an extremely difficult task, not only because it is challenging to measure those specific elements of pedagogy reliably but also because many contextual and moderating factors ultimately affect it.

If measuring teacher practices accurately and reliably presents a number of difficulties, then linking those practices to student outcomes can prove to be an even greater challenge in terms of devising appropriate analytical techniques as well as getting access to data that relate teachers to students. We note that our study is based on teacher-reported practices and that no one should draw causal inferences from an observational study such as this.

Method

The three steps of this study included (1) developing and pilot-testing an instrument that could be used to document the practices of AP teachers; (2) summarizing teachers' responses to the survey; and (3) linking teacher survey responses with their students' AP exam performance. Data were analyzed at the teacher level.

SURVEY CONSTRUCTION

This study used a survey to create a statistical profile of a relatively large sample of AP teacher practices. To reliably identify general trends and needs among AP teachers, we chose to use a survey to gather data from a larger number of teachers rather than developing a smaller number of in-depth case studies. The survey went through several revisions before the final version was administered to the large sample in spring 2003. We started by reviewing preexisting surveys, such as those used to gather information for the National Assessment of Educational Progress (NAEP) and about AP Summer Institutes, for possible item types. Based on this review, we constructed a draft survey. We then conducted focus groups with AP teachers, asking them to respond to each item from the draft survey and indicate which items they deemed most relevant or irrelevant and to suggest what other items should be included in the survey to identify key issues that we might have overlooked. Based on the teacher feedback, we revised the survey. We then sent this revised survey to 127 AP Biology teachers as part of a pilot study. After our analysis of their responses, we made four types of changes: (1) modified the scale of some items to better obtain distributions of responses across all respective categories regarding the frequency of use, (2) combined some items, (3) eliminated some items, and (4) added some new items. Most items in the survey required answers on a five-point rating scale, though there were a few items with four-point scales and one open-ended question (see Paek, Ponte, Sigel, Braun, & Powers, 2005).

Sample

We developed a comprehensive list of AP Biology teachers representing both public and non–public high schools of widely different population sizes and in various regions of the nation.[1] Using these criteria, we sent our survey to 1,874 AP Biology teachers in spring 2003. Of those, 1,171 teachers responded (a 62 percent return rate). We used the responses of all returned surveys for our description of AP teacher characteristics and practices.

We were not able to use all of these responses in our analyses linking teachers with students, because in schools with more than one AP Biology teacher, we had no unique identifiers linking each teacher to his or her students. We also decided to eliminate classes with fewer than eight students with usable data to ensure reasonable stability of class averages. As a result of these eliminations, we had a final sample that included 473 public school teachers and 194 non-public-school teachers, for a total of 667 teachers. This sample was not representative of all the schools surveyed, since schools with only one AP Biology teacher (usually smaller schools) were overrepresented. For simplicity of reporting results, our analysis of the relationship of teachers and students for this chapter uses only the data from public school teachers.[2]

We pulled student AP Biology exam scores from the spring 2003 administration and matched PSAT scores for those students from previous years, fall 2002 or earlier; therefore, all students in this study took the PSAT prior to taking the AP Biology exam.

SURVEY VARIABLES

Given the host of factors that describe and affect teacher practices, we focused on two main dimensions for analysis: (1) contextual variables that affect teachers' practices and (2) factors that specifically measure teacher practices. In the following sections we present each dimension and its factors.

Dimension 1: Context-for-Teaching Variables

Substantive expertise and training. Substantive expertise and training refers to the teacher's experience with the content of the given course. This is a product of numerous factors, such as the educational background of the teacher, previous experience teaching courses in this subject area (AP and otherwise), and the teacher's ongoing professional development through workshops, institutes, university classes, and seminars. Presented in this light, professional development covers both further exposure to course content and experiences that bolster pedagogical knowledge. In our model for describing this factor, we include variables related to professional experience (including total years of teaching experience, years of AP teaching experience, educational level, major, teaching certificate) and AP-specific professional development (APPD) activities.

School context. School context refers to the nature of the learning environment. It measures a variety of factors related to how the school provides or does not provide a positive setting for teaching and learning. The school support factor consists of school policy for assigning teachers to AP classes, number of classes taught, number of students per class, type of teaching schedule, adequacy of different school resources, influence of AP resources.

Classroom context. Classroom context describes factors that affect the composition and organization of the classroom. The variables involved with classroom context include teacher control (including hours dedicated to preparing for AP class, teaching autonomy, school criteria for AP enrollment, school policies determining which students take the AP exam, percentage of students who take the AP exam, class size), hours of preparation, and number of classes taught.

Dimension 2: Variables Indicating Teacher's Practices

Instructional and assessment practices. Instructional and assessment practices (teachers' pedagogical practices) may be manifested through the nature of assignments and the ways teachers assess students' understanding and provide feedback to students based on those assessments. It also includes the relative role of various styles of instructional delivery the teacher uses. In addition to measuring the teacher's decisions about how to deliver instruction, this factor reflects the emphasis the teacher places on various "types" of knowledge realized through the course. For instance, it measures the relative focus that the teacher places on different kinds of knowledge and on the various strategies used by teachers, such as having students recite facts and terminology and helping them understand key concepts and develop particular types of reasoning skills. Additionally, this factor addresses teachers' use of technology in the classroom. Finally, it covers issues directly related to instructional practice that do not usually take place during instruction, such as teachers' preparation time and students' homework load. The variables that define this factor include: types of learning goals, instructional methods, assessment, feedback, and student activities/tasks.

Content coverage. Content coverage addresses the manner in which teachers cover topics in the AP Biology course. The first issue addressed is how teachers negotiate depth of course concepts relative to breadth of course content. Second, teachers are asked to report on the specific topics and themes that they find most relevant, and thus tend to emphasize, and to rank those topics and themes regarding the degree of difficulty students have learning them. Finally, this also refers to the extent to which the content of the AP class is aligned with the content of the AP exam. To examine such alignment, we used the information teachers gave about the emphasis they place on topics and themes and about topic difficulty and compared that information with the number of questions per topic/theme included in the AP exam, which covers three main areas: molecules and cells (typically constituting 25 percent of the exam questions), heredity and evolution (25 percent), and organisms and populations (50 percent).

AP exam–specific instructional activities and practices. AP exam-specific instructional activities and practices are those that teachers use specifically because they are teaching an AP class. This factor addresses teachers' instructional decisions, both inside and outside of class time, related to getting students ready to take and pass the AP exam. It also considers the extent to which the teacher encourages or requires students to participate in extracurricular activities, such as districtwide competitions, in as much as these activities relate to gaining knowledge about course content and preparing for the AP exam. The variables in our model include AP exam preparation techniques (focus on multiple choice, free response, or both portions of the test; percentage of class time dedicated to preparing for the exam during the year; percentage of class time dedicated to preparing for the exam during the month prior to the exam; type and frequency of review activities implemented to prepare for exam).

Additional data. In addition to the factors listed above, we gathered other background information about the teachers, such as age, ethnicity, and gender. This data is summarized only in the first part of the study where we provide a profile of teacher characteristics and practices. Demographic data of teachers were not controlled for or used in our analysis linking teacher reported practices with student performance on the AP exam, as our preliminary study searched for possible relationships between teachers and students. These analyses were not based on teacher demographics, which could be conducted in future analyses.

RELATING TEACHING AND CONTEXTUAL VARIABLES WITH STUDENT OUTCOMES

Since higher AP performance is to be expected among those students with well-developed academic ability, we wanted to find a workable proxy for prior student achievement. We chose the PSAT based on previous research that showed a strong relationship between PSAT and AP performances (Camara, 1997; Camara & Millsap, 1998). In addition, the College Board refers to the PSAT as a reasoning test designed to measure critical thinking and reasoning skills, which corroborates our categorization of PSAT as a measure of prior academic achievement.

We employed two definitions of a successful student performance on the AP exam: an AP score of 3 or better and an AP score of 4 or better. The reason for choosing these two definitions is because of how colleges and universities use AP exam results for college credit. An AP score of 3 is generally accepted by colleges and universities as equivalent to a C in a college-level course and can be used toward college credit. An AP score of 4 is generally considered equivalent to a B in a college-level course and is sometimes used as the more stringent credit transfer criterion in various colleges and universities (see Paek, Braun, Trapani, Ponte, & Powers, 2007).

Through logistic regression techniques, we devised a residual, which is basically the difference between the predicted and actual AP score that student received. This residual can be viewed as analogous to a gain score for the student. We believe that the residual is a more sensitive criterion than the raw AP score (which has a five-point scale) in determining possible contributions of teacher-reported context and practices to students' AP achievement, because the residual controls for students' prior achievement.

We carried out a systematic series of exploratory unweighted regression analyses using the general linear models (GLM) methodology. The independent variables were organized into groups of AP teacher practices, as described earlier. The dependent variables were the two student success criteria (residuals). Moreover, because of the presumed importance of the overall quality of a school, all regressions included the five-year mean PSAT score for the school in which the class was located. This variable included all students who took a PSAT at a given school, regardless of whether the students participated in the AP program.[3]

In grouping variables that addressed similar aspects of teaching practice, we relied on the theoretical framework we created to guide the construction and analysis of the survey (Paek et al., 2005). Every regression was run with the mean school PSAT entered first. Data from each group of substantively related questions was then entered on its own. Individual questions were included in the analysis as separate variables. For example, the first survey question related to teaching objectives. This was a multipart question that asked how much emphasis was placed on each of five possible objectives. The responses were measured on a five-point Likert scale ranging from "Less than average emphasis" to "More than average emphasis." These five objectives were entered into the regression as a group of variables, after the mean school-level PSAT score was included in the model.

At each stage, the significant effects were identified using the partial sums of squares (Type III[4]), generally using as a criterion a p-value of 0.15 for inclusion in subsequent models rather than the usual 0.05 p-value. This moderately liberal p-value was chosen because we did not want to eliminate any possible variables of interest too rashly by choosing a very stringent significance value criterion. The variables at our disposal fell into the two general categories of context for teaching and teacher practice.

The significant variables ($p \leq 0.15$) that emerged from each group were then entered together in a regression model that included mean school PSAT as a covariate. Those variables that *again* achieved significance ($p \leq 0.15$) were retained to form a parsimonious context-for-teaching model.

A similar sequence was carried out for the teacher practice variables: all the significant teacher practice variables were entered in a new regression with mean school PSAT as a covariate, and those that attained significance were retained in a parsimonious teacher practices model.

To construct the final model,[5] the mean school PSAT was again entered first because of the need to take into account its strong statistical relationship to the criterion. Next, the parsimonious teacher context variables were entered into the model to account for contextual differences among teachers. Lastly, the parsimonious teacher practices variables were entered. Thus, after accounting for individual prior student achievement (by means of the preliminary logistic regression), mean school PSAT, and other context variables, we were able to estimate the incremental contribution of teaching practices to AP exam performance. These steps created a very stringent standard for identifying reported teaching context and practices that may be related to higher student achievement.

Results

The analyses we offer answer two main questions: (1) What are the potentially salient differences in AP teachers' characteristics, situational contexts, and teaching practices, and (2) Which of these characteristics and practices are related to higher student achievement on the AP exam?

Teacher Characteristics

The teachers tended to be *veteran* teachers, to have a higher level of teaching experience than the average U.S. teacher and a higher level of academic preparation (both in degrees and certification). For instance, 71 percent of the AP Biology teachers had taught for more than ten years, which is higher than the 61 percent of public school teachers teaching for this same length of time (NCES, 2002). Most teachers in the sample had taught AP Biology for fewer than ten years, and the majority of teachers (more than 80 percent) had taught AP Biology in the previous three years.

AP Biology teachers tended to have a high level of academic preparation, with 85 percent having obtained at least a master's degree. NCES (2006) data indicates that only 47 percent of public school teachers had this level of education. Similarly, while the vast majority (84 percent) of AP Biology teachers had a degree in biology and held a standard state teaching certificate, just 59 percent of U.S. high school teachers have attained this same level of preparation.

Demographic data indicate that most teachers in this survey are thirty-six years or older (79 percent), Caucasian (93 percent), and female (56 percent). Compared to national trends, our sample has fewer minorities than are present in comparable U.S. teacher populations.[6] In addition, there were more males in our sample (44 percent) than in the current population of secondary school–level teachers (35 percent) (NEA, 2003).

The most common AP-related professional development *activities* in which teachers participated were the review of the released AP exams (87 percent), course descriptions (80 percent), and the *AP Biology Teacher's Guide* (77 percent). AP teachers said that they valued the professional development offered by the College Board and pointed to some areas in which they would like to see further professional development opportunities, such as integrating technology and dealing with students who may lack some skills that they deemed to be general study skills and extraneous to the subject matter being taught, such as performing well in class and on tests.[7] A major concern reported by the teachers was the vast amount of material covered in the course and their need to use strategies to select the areas on which to focus.

Teachers indicated that the *resources* that had the most influence in their teaching of AP Biology were lab manuals (68 percent) and previously administered AP essay topics and/or the accompanying free response scoring rubrics (64 percent). The area in which teachers noted having the most critical *training need* (78 percent) was "covering the course content in the time available" or "knowing what can be dropped or modified" (see Paek et al., 2007).

School Context

The majority of teachers (68 percent) said they had *volunteered* to teach the AP class, and most reported having to teach only one AP Biology class (70 percent). With regard to the *AP teaching schedule*, more than half of the teachers (52 percent) reported teaching a 30-to-60-minute session every school day throughout the academic year. The other teachers were mainly divided into two subgroups: some teachers reported teaching a 61-to-110-minute session every day (25 percent) or every other school day throughout the academic year, or block scheduling (19 percent).

Most teachers (76 percent) indicated that their schools had special procedures or criteria for students' enrollment in AP Biology classes, the most common being the completion of a prerequisite course (72 percent) and the achievement of required grades in prior courses (63 percent). This indicates that AP Biology classes are relatively selective regarding enrollment and that departments offering AP Biology may need to have some kind of screening process that ensures that students have taken a basic science class in the subject matter. In fact, 51 percent of the AP Biology students who took the exam in 2003 were high school seniors. This finding reveals that students most likely take this AP Biology course as an additional science course in their final year of high school rather than as a graduation requirement, indicating the high academic motivation of those students taking the course.

Regarding the school *procedures for students to take the AP Biology exam*, 41 percent of teachers noted that in their schools all students who took the AP course were required to take the exam, while 38 percent of teachers reported that all students who took the course were encouraged to take the exam. As a result of these policies, the most common scenario (75 percent) was for 75 percent or more of the students in a class to take the AP exam.

Classroom Context

In response to questions about the degree of control teachers had over various classroom aspects, 97 percent of teachers indicated they had "substantial" or "complete" control over selecting their teaching techniques. They also noted that they had "substantial" or "complete" control in determining what textbooks to use (63 percent), what supplementary materials to use (86 percent), and what content to teach (89 percent). However, some teachers shared their feeling that this autonomy at the high school level was limited by the prescriptive nature of the AP curriculum and exam.

In terms of *class size*, a majority of AP Biology teachers (71 percent) reported having twenty or fewer students per class. Gruber and colleagues (2003) found that average class size in traditional secondary public school classes with departmentalized instruction was twenty-three students per class. Therefore, the AP Biology classes in our sample are smaller than the average high school class.

Instructional and Assessment Practices

When asked about the main objective of their classes, the most frequent teacher response (67 percent) was students' "understanding key concepts." The teachers also said they used "lecture" as the most common instructional method (92 percent indicated using this method more than once or twice per week) and frequently asked students to engage in activities in which they had to explain their reasoning or thinking (59 percent reported using this activity more than once or twice per week). Other methods included working on biology exercises (49 percent), conducting an experiment (34 percent), and applying biology concepts to real or simulated real-world problems (39 percent). The *assessment* method that teachers most frequently used was multiple-choice tests (95 percent indicated using this method at least once or twice a month). The type of *feedback* most utilized by teachers was providing students with numerical or letter grades (64 percent provided this kind of feedback more than once or twice a week).

All these descriptions of teacher practices point to one common thread: teachers preferred using strategies that helped them cover the material in the most efficient way. Teachers noted using a number of practices—such as lecturing, using multiple choice tests, and giving reduced feedback in the form of letter grades or numbers—because they felt the methods were effective in helping students pass the AP exam. However, some teachers felt that the use of these practices limited their teaching in ways that were not in line with current visions of how students learn (e.g., using more project-based instruction, implementing more complicated assessments such as portfolios, or giving more detailed feedback as a strategy to improve student learning). Teachers noted that while they thought all these strategies were key in promoting useful and lasting learning, the amount of material to cover and the demands posed by the exam prevented them from using them as often as they would like.

Nearly half of the teachers indicated spending at least ten hours of their time each week *preparing* for their AP Biology class(es) outside of the classroom and their allocated preparation time, indicating their dedication of a substantial amount of time to preparing for their AP classes. The majority of teachers (81 percent) required their students to devote between five and ten hours per week to AP homework, demonstrating that they expected high student involvement.

Content Coverage

More than half of the teachers (57 percent) stated that their primary concern in preparing students for the AP exam was to cover some topics very thoroughly, even if that meant not covering other topics at all. The remaining teachers (43 percent) said that they preferred to cover each potential topic on the examination, even if only briefly. Teachers expressed a desire for some guidance on which was the best way to proceed, wondering if the content load could be reduced either by splitting the class or by giving specific guidelines about which areas to highlight and which to touch on only slightly, or if the exam could be moved to a later date to allow teachers and students more time to cover and review all necessary content.[8]

Test-Specific Instructional Activities and Practice

Most teachers (68 percent) said that in helping their students *prepare for the AP exam,* they focused on both the multiple choice and the free response portions of the test. Throughout the year, a large proportion of teachers (62 percent) claimed that they dedicated less than 20 percent of their instructional time to helping students pass the AP exam. This number tends to increase in the month before the AP exam, when the majority of the teachers (55 percent) tend to dedicate more than 40 percent of their time to this end.

Teachers reported a variety of exam preparation strategies taking place in the month before the exam. Most commonly (66 percent), teachers reported that students take responsibility for their preparation and dedicate more than four hours a week studying course material on their own. Among the strategies used by teachers to help students prepare of the exam, the most widespread one is using old AP exams as practice tests; 49 percent of teachers indicated using this strategy more than four hours a week.

LINKING TEACHER PRACTICES AND STUDENT PERFORMANCE

The following results address which teacher practices and characteristics are related to higher student achievement. All variables from the context-for-teaching and teacher-practice profile models were subjected to the analyses described earlier to create a model for each outcome criterion.

The variables from the survey listed in table 4.1 are the ones that differentiated more successful AP Biology public school teachers from less successful teachers. The first variables listed are the ones that were significant in both models, followed by the significant variables in either the model with AP scores greater than 3 or the one with AP scores greater than 4, but not in both. It should be noted that all omitted variables were not significant. This could be due to one or more of the following reasons: (1) there is no association between the variable and the criterion; (2) the variable was highly correlated with other variables included in the

TABLE 4.1   Public school models: Statistically significant (p < .10) variables

Variables	AP score ≥ 3	AP score ≥ 4
Percentage of students who took the exam	+	+
Influence of resources: Frequency of class meetings	+	+
Influence of resources: AP exam topics and/or scoring rubrics	+	+
Number of years teaching	+	
Participation in AP professional development activities attending an AP Institute	−	
Reviewing *AP Biology Teacher's Guide*	−	
Class size	−	
Objective: Learn scientific methods	+	
Assessment: Tests requiring lengthy written responses	+	
Influence of resources: Frequency of using exemplary syllabi from other AP Biology classes		−
Type and frequency of review activities: Teacher estimate of student time dedicated to studying course material on their own		+
Teaching test-taking strategies		X
Computer use: Teacher researching information on the Internet		−
Focus of attention on preparing students for AP exam		X
Percentage of class time dedicated to preparing for the AP exam during the month prior to the exam		X

Notes: Response choices to the variables are listed in increasing order unless the variable is listed as nominal. The symbol + represents a positive relationship with the variable; − represents an inverse relationship with the variable; and X represents a nonlinear relationship with the variable (e.g., the variable either is not ordinal or the relationship is neither positive nor negative).

model; (3) there is little heterogeneity among teachers on the variable; or (4) there is insufficient power in the analysis, since too many degrees of freedom were required to code the response categories. For all models, the exclusion of a variable does not mean it is unimportant but, rather, that it does not account for differences in mean student outcomes among teachers given the other variables in the model.

We were interested in how much more of the criterion variance we could account for with context and teacher practice variables. For the model with AP exam scores of 3 or better, the initial regression using only mean school PSAT score as a predictor yielded an R-square of 0.06. Our final model has an R-square of .27. Thus, the selected survey variables do predict a modest amount of (residual) student performance, accounting for an additional 21 percent of the variance over mean school PSAT alone. Similarly, for the model with AP exam scores of 4 or better, the initial regression yielded an R-square of 0.06 with the final model having an R-square of .33. The context and teacher practices variables account for an additional 27 percent of the variance over the PSAT alone. In contrast to the fitted model for AP scores of 3 or better, the model with the more stringent success criterion includes more teacher practice variables, possibly indicating that teacher practices are more important at higher performance levels.

Three variables linked teachers' context and practices with student outcomes in both models. The variables were frequency of class meetings, percentage of students who took the exam, and the use of AP exam topics and/or rubrics. Students whose AP Biology classes met every day—whether for 30–60 minutes or 61–110 minutes—performed better throughout the school year than did those students whose classes met less frequently. The proportion of students who took the AP exam also had an effect: classes in which fewer than 50 percent of students took the exam tended to perform significantly worse than classes with 75–100 percent of the students taking the exam. In other words, the higher the percentage of students in the class taking the exam, the better the classes tended to do. Lastly, most teachers said that they found the use of AP exam topics and/or rubrics to be between "somewhat" and "extremely" influential. For AP scores of 3 or better, the more useful the teacher found this resource, the better his or her classes performed. In general, the more often teachers found these resources to be useful, the better their classes performed.

The variables that were significant only for the model with AP scores greater than 3 were mainly teaching related (e.g., professional development and teaching experience): overall teaching experience, the use of essay topics and/or rubrics as a resource, AP Institute attendance, use of the AP Biology Teacher's Guide, and class size. As expected, classes of beginning teachers (teaching fewer than three years) performed less well than did the classes of more experienced teachers. This finding is not surprising, as studies on beginning teachers indicate that teachers need at least three years to become adept in their teaching (Darling-Hammond, 1997; Feiman-Nemser, 2001). It may be that experienced teachers, who are more familiar with the course content and the exam, can fine-tune their teaching, thus resulting in better class performance. An interesting aside is that the teachers were much more experienced in teaching biology than teaching AP Biology. In fact, 75 percent of teachers had ten or more years' experience teaching biology, which may imply that teachers do not teach AP Biology until they have substantial teaching experience.

Two variables dealt with AP professional development, the first of which was attending an AP Institute. AP Institutes are usually weeklong gatherings where teachers work together on different lessons. Fifty percent of teachers claimed they had never attended an Institute, while 40 percent of teachers had attended just once. The classes of these two groups of teachers tended to perform similarly on the AP exam. The remaining 10 percent had attended an AP Institute more than once, though their classes tended to perform worse than the classes of the other two groups. However, it would be rash to conclude that the attendance at AP Institutes had a deleterious effect. Rather, this result might indicate that the teachers who attended more than one Institute were sent by their supervisors to attend an additional Institute because their classes did not perform adequately on the AP exam the first time. These teachers may not have been as effective in the classroom, regardless of the number of times they had attended an Institute.

The *AP Biology Teacher's Guide* provides sample course outlines designed by successful AP Biology teachers at seven diverse schools. Each of the detailed outlines includes a description of the school environment, the objectives of the course, prerequisites, student selection, a timeline for topics, and assignments. Most teachers used this guide to inform their teaching. A small number of teachers who had taught for longer than ten years indicated they did not use the *AP Biology Teacher's Guide*, yet their classes performed much better than classes of less-experienced teachers. It may be that these teachers had developed their own guide or no longer needed to use the AP guide given their extensive experience teaching the course. Finally, larger classes were more likely to underperform on the AP exam; classes of fifteen or fewer students performed significantly better than all other larger classes.

The two remaining variables for this model are related to teacher practices: teaching students the scientific method and assessing them using tests requiring lengthy responses. Most teachers (68 percent) regarded their students' learning the scientific method as a teaching goal of average or slightly above-average emphasis. In general, the more a teacher emphasized this learning objective, the better his or her classes tended to perform. Teachers who employed at least average emphasis had classes performing better than those who stressed learning the scientific method with less-than-average emphasis. In terms of assessment methods, teachers who used tests requiring lengthy written responses at least once or twice a month had classes that performed significantly better on the AP exam than those who did this only several times per year or rarely.

The variables in the model for AP scores of 4 or better are mostly related to teacher practices: teachers estimating the time students dedicate to studying course material on their own, their teaching of test-taking strategies, their researching information on the Internet, and their focusing on preparing students for the AP exam, as well as the percentage of time teachers spent directly helping students pass the AP exam the month before the exam. The use of exemplary syllabi as a resource was the one remaining variable included in this model for measuring teaching context. The more often teachers used this resource, the lower the predicted student success. It appears that teachers who relied less on this resource had classes that performed better than those who relied on it more heavily. This may be related to experience and degree of comfort with the course content (e.g., teachers who were more familiar with the course probably needed to consult the syllabi less often).

Regarding teachers' estimates of the time students spent studying AP material, about 67 percent of teachers believed their students studied for the AP exam on their own at least four to nine hours per week. A small number of teachers claimed that their students studied more than twenty hours per week, and those classrooms of students performed significantly better than the classrooms that, according to the teachers' estimates, collectively studied less often.

Analysis of teachers' use of the Internet indicates that most teachers (92 percent) sought out information on the Internet and that teachers who did not use the Internet had classes that performed better than those teachers who did. It would be interesting to see where on the Internet these teachers obtained their information. In terms of preparing students for the exam, most teachers prepared their students equally for both parts. It appears, however, that teachers who focused on the multiple choice section of the exam produced significantly higher-performing classes.

The last variable included in the model is the percentage of time dedicated to preparing students in the month before the AP exam date. The distribution of this variable was roughly uniform across the five choices. Intriguingly, the most successful strategies appeared to be at either extreme. Teachers spending less than 20 percent of their time the month before the exam in preparing their students obtained the best results, but they were followed by those who spent more than 80 percent. Teachers who spent less than 20 percent of their time may not have needed that extra preparation time because they felt confident in how they had prepared their students over the course of the year. By contrast, high-volume exam preparation the month before (80 percent or more) also appeared to pay off. Teachers may have had students take practice tests and work specifically with released exams, which would give the students familiarity with the exam format.

CONCLUSIONS

In the first part of our study, we examined the profiles of AP Biology teachers and documented their characteristics, contexts, and practices. The results showed definite trends in reported teaching contexts and practices, and this information was then used in the second part of our study to answer the following question: What are the differences in the characteristics, contexts, and practices between teachers of "more successful" and "less successful" students, as evidenced by AP exam performance?

When looking at the context and teaching practices related to student performance, we found evidence of a relationship between teacher practices and student achievement in AP classes once we had adjusted for the student achievement proxy (PSAT) and teacher context variables. These teacher practices differed depending on the criterion variable used (an AP exam score of 3 or better or 4 or better). For instance, there are more teacher practice variables unique to the model of AP scores of 4 or better. This finding may indicate that teaching practices have a stronger effect when the criterion for achievement is more stringent.

There are more differences than similarities between these two models; however, each provides a unique view of the relationship between teacher practices and student performance. Because the models contain teaching contexts and practices that are related to student exam performance, it seems reasonable to conclude that we have identified some variables that are likely to differentiate more and less successful practices. In general, our results suggest that there are teaching practices related to higher student achievement in AP Biology. Even in a relatively standardized and uniform setting such as the AP Biology course, the teacher still makes a difference and has a substantial impact on students' performance.

LIMITATIONS

This study reveals some of the challenges in linking teacher practices to student achievement. Those challenges include obtaining representative samples of teachers, accurately characterizing the teaching context and teacher practices, condensing that information into a form suitable for quantitative analysis, developing criteria related to student learning, and dealing with collinearity among predictors. Although we targeted a nationally representative sample of AP Biology teachers and students, we obtained a nonrandom sample, and thus our application of findings to the general population must be made tentatively.

Researchers in this field also recommended looking at multiple years of data. Since this study is the first in a possible series, our analyses used only the data we had, which was a single year of AP exam data mapped to teachers' accounts of their practices. Further research into the cumulative and residual effects of teacher practices could be carried out when additional years of student exam results for a single teacher taking this survey have been compiled.

IMPLICATIONS

Schools, districts, teachers, and administrators often adopt or continue educational practices without evidence of whether the practices are really helping to improve their students' achievement. Our study of AP teacher practices sheds light on what needs to be done to uncover meaningful information about practices, gauge their success, and determine how to adapt and incorporate such successful practices in classrooms nationwide.

Our description of teacher practices can benefit the AP Program in several ways. First, by providing an assessment of teacher needs, it has the potential to inform the AP Program in its development of professional development services to meet the most reported and essential needs of AP teachers. Second, the program will be able to identify effective teacher practices that are underutilized by AP teachers and then offer professional development that supports those practices. Third, the description of teacher practices can serve as a baseline for the evaluation of professional development services and other AP Program interventions to improve such practices. Without knowing the nature of current practices, it is difficult to know how they may change following any intervention. Additionally, linking these practices to student performance allows us to identify practices related to higher student achievement. By identifying what practices are related to higher learning, professional development can be refined to support and encourage those practices.

In addition to being of assistance to the AP Program, the description of teacher practices can directly assist AP teachers. Teachers can use the information from the study to compare their practices to those of their colleagues and find out which of their own practices are typical of AP teachers as a group. They can also revisit their own pedagogical practices and consider incorporating strategies and techniques that have proven to be beneficial for student performance. Finally, by revealing a relationship between AP teachers and students, the results of this study can suggest to the College Board areas that may warrant further study in understanding AP teacher practices and their influence on student learning and performance.

NOTES

1. We originally planned to analyze public, private, and parochial schools. This was under the assumption that "private" schools were secular and "parochial" schools were religious. However, parochial schools can also be classified as "private," so we decided to combine private and parochial schools into one category called *non-public-schools*.
2. For analyses of non-public-school teachers, please refer to the report by Paek, Braun, Trapani, Ponte, and Powers (2007).
3. One drawback to using the mean PSAT at the school level is that it is not uniformly administered across states. For instance, some districts require all students—not just college-bound students—to take the PSAT. Scores from these districts will be lower overall than scores from districts where the PSAT is optional.
4. This method calculates the sums of squares of an effect in the design as sums of squares adjust for any other effects that do not contain it and orthogonal to effects (if any).
5. Variables were included in the final model if their p-value was ≤ 0.10.
6. NCES (2002) table 68 (which aggregates public and private and elementary and secondary school teachers) indicates that 84.3 percent of teachers are Caucasian while the rest (15.7 percent) are minorities.

7. Teachers were asked, "Do you have any comments for us regarding your experience as an AP Biology teacher? Is there anything you do as an AP Biology teacher that you feel is especially noteworthy?" Since the questions allow for an infinite number of possible responses, this analysis tried to combine the data into themes to report trends about areas that AP teachers found important to mention.
8. More specific information about AP Biology topics can be found in the report by Paek et al. (2005).

REFERENCES

Camara, W. J. (1997). *The relationship of PSAT/NMSQT scores and AP examination grades* (RN-02). New York: College Board.

Camara, W. J., & Millsap, R. (1998). *Using the PSAT/NMSQT and course grades in predicting success in the Advanced Placement Program* (College Board Report No. 98-4). New York: College Board.

Darling-Hammond, Linda. (1997). *The right to learn: A blueprint for creating schools that work.* San Francisco: Jossey-Bass.

Feiman-Nemser, Sharon. (2001). From preparation to practice: Designing a continuum to strengthen and sustain teaching. *Teachers College Record, 103*(6), 1013–1055.

Gruber, K. J., Wiley, S. D., Broughman, S. P., Strizek, G. A., & Burian-Fitzgerald, M. (2003). Schools and staffing survey, 1999–2000: Overview of the data for public, private, public charter, and Bureau of Indian Affairs elementary and secondary schools. *Education Statistics Quarterly, 4*(3). http://nces.ed.gov/programs/quarterly/vol_4/4_3/2_1.asp

Milewski, G. B., & Gillie, J. M. (2002). *What are the characteristics of AP Teachers? An examination of survey results.* New York: College Board.

National Education Association [NEA]. (2003). Wanted: More male teachers. http://www.nea.org/teachershortage/03malefactsheet.html

National Center for Education Statistics [NCES]. (2002). Schools and staffing survey, 1999–2000: *Overview of the public, private, public charter, and Bureau of Indian Affairs elementary and secondary schools* (NCES Publication No. 2002-313). Washington, DC: U.S. Department of Education.

National Center for Education Statistics [NCES]. (2006). *Schools and staffing survey: Characteristics of schools, districts, teachers, principals, and school libraries in the United States 2003–2004* (NCES 2006-313 Revised). Washington, DC: U.S. Department of Education.

Olson, Lynn. (2003). The great divide. *Education Week, 22*, 9–10, 13–14, 16, 18.

Paek, P. L., Ponte, E., Sigel, I., Braun, H., & Powers, D. (2005). *A portrait of advanced placement teachers' practices* (College Board Report No. 2005-7). New York: College Board.

Paek, P. L., Braun, H., Trapani, C., Ponte, E., & Powers, D. (2007). *The relationship of AP teacher practices and student achievement* (College Board Report No. 2007-5). New York: College Board.

CHAPTER 5

Validating AP Exam Scores
Current Research and New Directions

Maureen Ewing, Kristen Huff,
and Pamela Kaliski

INTRODUCTION

For more than fifty years, the AP Program has offered high school students the opportunity to take advanced-level coursework while still in high school and to demonstrate proficiency by taking the corresponding end-of-course exams. Students who perform well on the exams may earn credit for the equivalent college course or placement into higher level courses, depending on the policies at their colleges or universities. The AP Program grew out of thinking in the early 1950s that centered on ways of improving American education by strengthening the connection between secondary and postsecondary education. A committee of educators from elite secondary prep schools and prestigious colleges, among them Harvard, Princeton, and Yale, met to consider ways of improving students' experiences in their last two years of high school and their first two years of college. The committee ultimately recommended that high schools and colleges forge partnerships with one another and conceive of themselves as "two halves of a common enterprise" (College Board, 2009d). The Committee on Admission with Advanced Standing was formed around the same time and advocated for the development of rigorous, college-level course materials that could be taught by high school teachers. This committee enacted its recommendations by creating pilot course curricula and examinations, and in 1952 it launched a pilot program involving seven secondary schools and eleven initial subjects (College Board, 2009d). Today there are thirty-three AP exams, and the number of students and schools participating in the program continues to grow. In 2009 close to 1.7 million students took one or more AP exams worldwide, and the number of schools participating in the AP Program exceeded 17,000 (College Board, 2009b).

Extensive research, test development, and psychometric work are conducted annually to support and maintain the large and diverse set of AP courses and exams. The purpose of this chapter is to highlight the theory and principles of educational measurement that guide not only the development of AP exams but also the valid score interpretation and use of exam scores. For example, what does it mean to say test scores are reliable and valid, and what evidence is needed to support such claims? We begin by defining key measurement principles and then move on to describe the evidence that has been accumulated to support reliable and valid interpretations of AP exam scores. Although the focus of this chapter is on AP science courses and exams, the process used to develop AP exams and validate exam scores is generally consistent across all subjects. We will review the nature and quality of evidence collected to support inferences about AP science exam scores in relation to Kane's (2006) argument-based approach to validity, which represents the most contemporary thinking about test score validation and draws from a rich history of validity theory development (e.g., Cronbach & Meehl, 1955; Cronbach, 1988; Messick, 1988). As Kane (2006) puts it, "A mature testing program is expected to stand up to criticism, and the accumulated evidence is expected to be evaluated in an evenhanded way" (p. 17). Our conclusion is that the validity evidence that will be described in this chapter supports the stated purpose of AP exam scores for course credit and placement.

Although the AP Program is certainly an example of an established testing program, even established testing programs must be periodically refined or even redesigned to reflect changes and advancements in learning theory, curriculum, and assessment. The AP Program is no different; it must respond to the changing needs of American education. In this spirit, in the final section of this chapter we describe work that has recently been undertaken by the AP Program to conduct an intensive review of its science courses and exams beyond the standard operational work that is regularly conducted to ensure quality. The impetus for the work stems from a desire not only to develop AP science courses that emphasize deep conceptual understanding but also to develop exams with multiple choice (MC) questions that measure more complex scientific reasoning practices, which traditionally have been assessed only by free response (FR) questions. MC questions require the examinee to select a response from a set of options, whereas FR questions require the examinee to create the response to the question and are often referred to as constructed-response or open-ended questions. Evidence-centered assessment design (ECD) was the primary methodology used for the AP science course and exam revision (Mislevy, Almond, & Lukas, 2004; Steinberg et al., 2003), and this chapter describes more fully what ECD entails, how it was implemented, and the benefits and challenges of its use in the context of the AP program. We pay particular attention to describing how the use of ECD strengthens the validity argument for test score use and interpretation.

WHAT IS TEST SCORE RELIABILITY AND WHY IS IT IMPORTANT?

The usefulness of tests rests on the premise that individuals exhibit some degree of stability in their measurements over a specified period of time depending on the purpose and context of the testing situation (AERA, APA, & NCME, 1999). Statistical measures of reliability, often referred to as reliability coefficients, quantify the degree of stability or replicability of examinee scores over repeated measurements of the same or parallel test questions. It is important to note that reliability is a property of the test scores, not a property of the test. Obviously, lack of precision in the measurement of a particular construct reduces the usefulness of the scores that result from that measurement.

Generally, three primary conceptions of score consistency can be considered when estimating reliability, including: (1) parallel forms reliability, (2) test-retest reliability, and (3) internal consistency. Estimates of reliability involving parallel forms require that two interchangeable test forms be available for administration to the same group of examinees over a reasonable time interval. Determining a reasonable time interval is not a trivial task because too short an interval may introduce errors of measurement related to examinee fatigue and motivation while too long an interval may allow scores to be influenced by learning or maturation. Once scores are obtained on both forms of the test for the same group of examinees, the estimate of reliability is computed by calculating the correlation between the two sets of scores. The resulting statistical values range from zero to one, with higher values indicating greater reliability.

Test-retest reliability is similar to parallel forms reliability, except that the repeated use of same test form is used in the design rather than two separate, but interchangeable test forms. The test-retest design faces the same challenges as the parallel form design plus an added one, given that the design relies on the use of the exact same test questions. That is, the reliability estimate may be artificially inflated because there is the potential that examinee responses will be influenced by their recollection of the previously administered test questions (Haertel, 2006, p. 70).

Internal consistency represents the third method of estimating reliability and is estimated using question response data from a single administration of a test by either dividing the test into two or more equivalent parts (and calculating split-half reliability) or by computing Cronbach's alpha, which summarizes the average of all possible inter-item correlations and measures the extent to which the questions measure the same underlying construct. An advantage of internal consistency measures over other measures of reliability is that they do not require multiple administrations of the test—something that is impractical in most educational settings. Later sections of this chapter summarize results from AP reliability studies, which rely on internal consistency measures of reliability. Additional reliability evidence collected for AP exams involves degree of classification consistency and reader-reliability estimates, both of which will be discussed later, as will the use of generalizability theory as a promising method for conducting future research on the reliability of AP exam scores.

WHAT IS VALIDITY AND WHY IS IT IMPORTANT?

While the reliability of test scores is a necessary condition for supporting valid inferences of test scores, it is not a sufficient one. For example, a measure may be reliable but not valid for its intended purpose. Validity is concerned with the appropriateness of test score interpretations and uses and, like reliability, is a property of the test scores, not a property of the test itself. In other words, it is not the case that a test is valid or invalid, but, rather, the accumulation of evidence may (or may not) support various intended interpretations and uses of test scores. The Standards for Educational and Psychological Testing (AERA, APA, & NCME, 1999) define validity as the "degree to which evidence and theory support the interpretations of test scores entailed by proposed uses of tests" and further note that validity is "the most fundamental consideration in developing and evaluating tests" (p. 9).

Kane's (2006) argument-based approach to validity offers a practical framework for thinking about and evaluating the proposed uses and interpretations of test scores. Kane's approach involves two types of arguments: an interpretive argument and a validation argument. The interpretive argument indicates the proposed interpretations and uses of test scores, while the validation argument offers an evaluation of what is proposed in the interpretive argument. The validation argument is often empirically based but may also be judgment based according to the particular interpretive argument. Kane's framework encompasses a broad definition of validity and includes all of the inferences that lead one from the observed performances on individual test questions to decisions and conclusions based on the total test score. In this modern conceptualization, reliability evidence is actually subsumed under the larger umbrella of validity evidence and associated with a specific interpretative argument. The idea that reliability evidence is a subcomponent of the validity argument makes sense given that the reliability of test scores is a necessary, but not sufficient, condition for supporting valid inferences about test scores.

Kane's interpretive argument for placement tests includes four inferences: (1) scoring, (2) generalization, (3) extrapolation, and (4) decision. The scoring inference is concerned with moving from performance on individual questions to the observed total test score and involves the accuracy of the scoring rule, whether it is the answer key, as in the case of multiple choice questions, or the rubric, as with open-ended or performance-based questions. In the context of AP, for example, evidence of rater agreement in applying the rubrics to score the free response questions would lend support to the scoring inference. The generalization inference is focused on the reliability of the observed score (e.g., AP Physics exam score), while the extrapolation inference focuses on the appropriateness of that score as a representation of the level of required content knowledge and skill needed for mastery in a particular course (e.g., introductory college-level physics). Finally, the decision inference evaluates the appropriateness of the credit or placement decision.

CURRENT RESEARCH AND RESULTS FROM AP RELIABILITY STUDIES

Gathering evidence of *test score reliability* is essential for testing programs. The AP program gathers reliability evidence for all AP exam test scores. Moreover, the program has promising proposals for future research that incorporates an additional sophisticated measurement methodology known as generalizability theory.

What Reliability Evidence Is Collected for AP?

The majority of AP exams are mixed-format exams; that is, they are comprised of a multiple choice question section and a free response question section. The composite score is the total score, which is created by combining the appropriately weighted MC and FR section scores. This composite score is then converted to the examinee's final reported AP score of either 1, 2, 3, 4, or 5 using cut scores on the composite. Separate reliability evidence is collected for the MC section, the FR section, the composite score, and the final AP exam score.

After each AP exam administration, several reliability values are estimated for the AP test scores of that particular year (i.e., Kane's generalization inference). The reliability coefficient estimated for the MC section, the FR section, and the composite score is known as coefficient alpha. Coefficient alpha is a measure of internal consistency reliability, which is the degree that the questions are homogeneous and therefore measuring the same construct (e.g., Devillis, 2003; Haertel, 2006). The value ranges from 0 to 1, with 1 representing perfectly reliable test scores. The coefficient alpha value for the MC section reflects the internal consistency of only the MC questions; the closer the value is to 1.0, the more homogeneous the MC questions are. Similarly, the coefficient alpha value for the FR section reflects the internal consistency of only the FR questions and their degree of homogeneity. The coefficient alpha value for the composite score reflects the internal consistency of all the questions (MC questions and FR questions) on the exam. Homogeneity may seem like an undesirable characteristic. Homogeneity of questions indicates that all of the questions are measuring the same domain of interest (e.g., biology, calculus). Although we include questions that measure many different aspects of the domain of interest (e.g., evolution, energy transfer), we are interested in ensuring homogeneity, because lack of it would suggest that the questions are requiring skills or knowledge that is not germane to the targeted domain. For example, in tests of mathematics, a test developer strives to avoid including questions that require a substantial amount of reading to ensure that those who are highly skilled at reading are not benefited on the mathematics test, given that the goal is to assess mathematics rather than reading.

Additionally, the reliability of classification for the final AP scores (1, 2, 3, 4, 5) is estimated after every administration, following the methods of Livingston and Lewis (1995). Whenever cut scores along the composite scores are used to classify examinees into performance categories represented by the final AP scores, estimating the reliability of classification is important. There are two types of reliability of classification: consistency and accuracy. The consistency classification index estimates the agreement of the AP score classifications overall and at score boundaries (e.g., 2/3) across parallel forms of the exam (nonoverlapping and equally difficult), whereas the accuracy classification index estimates the agreement of the observed AP score classifications overall and at score boundaries (e.g., 2/3) with the examinee's *true* classification, if the true classification could be known. A true classification is thought of as the examinee's average classification on all possible forms of the exam. These classification reliability values also range from 0 to 1, with a 1 indicating exact agreement between all possible parallel forms (for consistency) and between examinees' observed and true scores (for accuracy).

These various reliability coefficients are estimated for AP exam scores every year. In addition, *reader-reliability studies* are conducted for each AP exam on a routine basis every few years to estimate the reliability of FR question scores (i.e., Kane's scoring inference). Before explaining reader-reliability studies, a brief description of the training procedures used with AP readers who read student responses to the FR questions and assign a score to the response using a scoring rubric is necessary. Note that because *readers* are defined as *raters* when discussing reliability, *rater* will be used for the remainder of the chapter. Prior to reading examinee responses and assigning scores to the responses, the raters are trained to ensure fairness. Specifically, each FR question is assigned a question leader, and the raters meet within groups for each question. The question leader facilitates a discussion of the question, acceptable responses, and scoring guidelines. Examples of prescored responses that reflect all levels of ability are reviewed and discussed within the group. Then, additional prescored responses are administered, but this time with the scores removed from the papers. The groups then discuss and assign a score to the response. Additional papers are examined, and the discussion continues until all members of the group are consistently scoring the responses with the scores that align with the previous scores assigned to the responses. This ensures that the raters are applying the scoring rubrics in the same manner and that rater variability is minimized. Once conver-gence is reached among raters at the training, the operational reading is conducted (College Board, 2009c).

When reader-reliability studies are conducted, two sets of FR scores are obtained from readers at the operational reading of the exams for a sam-ple of the examinees' scores. After raters assign scores, reliability across the two raters is computed, with a value of 1 indicating perfect reliability or consistency across the two raters' scores. These studies are important to ensure that the scores being assigned to AP FR questions are not de-pendent on the rater scoring the response.

What Does the Evidence Suggest About the Reliability of AP Exam Scores?

When examining the reliability evidence gathered for the science exams (Biology, Chemistry, Environmental Science, Physics B, Physics C: Me-chanics, and Physics C: Electricity and Magnetism) from 2004 to 2008 for the various AP exams (ETS, 2008), we can draw several conclusions about the reliability of AP exam scores (see table 5.1 for the coefficient alphas from 2007 and 2008). First, for all types of reliability described above that are estimated annually, the reliability of these AP exam scores is remarkably stable across these years. That is, the reliability coefficients do not fluctuate with different administrations of the exams. Second, the reliability of the MC section scores (i.e., coefficient alpha) is generally very high (larger than 0.80 and in many cases 0.90), which indicates that the MC questions on the AP exams are homogeneous and measuring the same phenomenon. The coefficient alpha values for the FR section scores is not as high in coefficient alpha values as the MC questions for all ex-ams; this is not surprising, given that reliability coefficients increase as the number of test questions increase (e.g., Traub, 1994) and that the AP exams have more MC than FR questions. However, the values still dem-onstrate acceptable internal consistency reliability for the FR questions. The high coefficient alphas for the composite scores indicate that both the MC questions and FR questions together are homogeneous. Third, the classification of the reliability of AP reported scores is high for both consistency and accuracy and each cut score level. Fourth, the reader reli-ability coefficients vary depending on the exam subject, with the values being generally acceptable. In short, there is an adequate amount of reli-ability evidence for the AP exam scores, and the program is continuously striving to improve the reliability of exam scores.

TABLE 5.1   Coefficient alpha for AP science exams

AP exam	Multiple choice 2008	2007	Free response 2008	2007	Composite 2008	2007
Biology	0.94	0.94	0.78	0.80	0.94	0.94
Chemistry	0.93	0.93	0.86	0.90	0.95	0.95
Environmental Science	0.93	0.93	0.73	0.75	0.93	0.92
Physics B	0.92	0.92	0.86	0.85	0.94	0.94
Physics C: Mechanics	0.86	0.88	0.77	0.76	0.90	0.91
Physics C: Electricity and Magnetism	0.88	0.87	0.81	0.79	0.92	0.91

Role of Generalizability Theory in Future Reliability Work for AP

Although the various types of reliability evidence provide useful information about the reliability of AP exam scores, there are limitations with these estimated reliability coefficients that are important to consider. The limitations are the result of the calculations not taking into account the raters' and students' interactions with the tasks or with each other; rather, the reliability coefficients focus on only one source of measurement error (e.g., Webb, Rowley, & Shavelson, 1988). For example, coefficient alpha quantifies the measurement error that is due to heterogeneous test questions, and rater reliability quantifies the measurement error that is due to rater variability in scores. The different sources of error, as quantified by the reliability coefficients, cannot be compared within this framework, and there is no way to utilize these values to design the most efficient measurement procedures (e.g., number of questions, number of raters, number of forms) for future assessment design.

Generalizability theory is a sophisticated psychometric tool that can be applied to educational testing programs to design efficient assessment and measurement procedures (e.g., Hendrickson & Yin, 2009; Shavelson & Webb, 1991). The use of generalizability theory allows for multiple sources of measurement error variance to be simultaneously estimated. And accounting for multiple sources of measurement error simultaneously provides a more complete picture of the reliability of test scores. In turn, test developers can use these error variance components to estimate reliability for different testing conditions (e.g., two raters, twelve questions) in order to determine which testing conditions are most efficient. Because of the potential of generalizability theory to inform efficient measurement procedures and improve the reliability of test scores, the AP program is currently working to incorporate generalizability theory analyses in future research with AP exam scores.

CURRENT RESEARCH AND RESULTS FROM AP VALIDITY STUDIES

Various types of evidence are collected to evaluate the validity of AP score uses and interpretations. Some evidence provides support for the appropriateness of the exam score as a representation of the level of content knowledge and skill needed for mastery in a particular course (i.e., Kane's extrapolation inference), while other studies evaluate the appropriateness of the credit or placement decision (i.e., Kane's decision inference). For example, the processes used to develop AP courses and exams can be analyzed to determine the reasonableness of the inference that AP exam scores appropriately represent the level of content knowledge and skill achieved in a particular content domain and that the exam measures content and skill that are required in the course. In addition, empirical studies that evaluate the relationship between AP exam scores and college success outcomes can be analyzed to evaluate whether appropriate credit and placement decisions are made based on AP exam scores as well as the positive and negative consequences of such decisions.

How are AP courses and exams developed?

In the context of AP, the processes used to determine the content knowledge and skill to be taught in the course and measured on the exam include two main components, and the outcomes of each component contribute to evidence suggesting that an AP exam score is representative of the degree of content knowledge and skill achieved in the target domain. First, the AP course and exam development process requires the expert judgment of content experts, including well-regarded college faculty and experienced AP high school teachers. These experts meet regularly to review course materials and exams and engage in rich discussions about the content and skill that are most appropriate to include, knowing that a primary goal of AP is that students who perform well on the

AP exam should be adequately prepared for subsequent study in the discipline. Second, college curriculum studies are conducted on a periodic basis to collect data from colleges and universities regarding the content knowledge and skills being taught in the comparable introductory college courses at their institutions. These data play an important role in defining and revising the content knowledge and skill to be taught in AP courses and measured by AP exams. By heavily involving college faculty through committee work and participation in the college curriculum studies, efforts are made to ensure the strongest possible alignment between AP courses' learning objectives and those of comparable college courses. In the final section of this chapter, we elaborate on the processes for developing AP courses and exams with a focus on the use of ECD in the redesign of AP science courses and exams.

What Does the Evidence Suggest About the Validity of AP Exam Scores?

Ewing (2006) summarized the various research studies that have been conducted to evaluate the impact of the AP Program on student outcomes and noted that studies differ in terms of the characteristics or features of the AP experience that are investigated. For example, in terms of the AP experience, there may be students who take an AP course but never take the corresponding AP exam, or students who take the course and exam and then differ in the scores they receive on the exam. As a result, there are various student subgroups and research questions of interest to consider when evaluating the broader impact of AP course and exam participation and performance on student outcomes. The primary focus here is on reviewing studies that have investigated whether AP exam scores are valid indicators for credit and placement decisions at the postsecondary level as well as the positive and negative consequences of such decisions. It is important to note that these studies were not attempts to demonstrate that the experience of taking the AP course itself caused or impacted a student's college success; instead, the studies were designed to investigate whether AP exam scores were valid indicators of a student's readiness for placement into a course beyond the introductory college course. For a review of AP research that investigates the broader impact of AP course and exam participation and performance on student outcomes, see Ewing (2006) as well as work recently conducted by Hargrove, Godin, and Dodd (2008).

A key aspect of the validity argument for AP exam scores involves the notion that AP exam scores are useful in making credit and placement decisions. Toward this end, several studies have investigated the degree to which the use of AP exam scores are valid indicators for credit and course placement, and all have generally found positive results for students who were exempted from the introductory course as a result of high AP exam scores (Burnham & Hewitt, 1971; Dodd, Fitzpatrick, De Ayala, & Jennings, 2002; Morgan & Crone, 1993; Morgan & Ramist, 1998; Morgan & Klaric, 2007). Morgan and Ramist (1998) conducted an extensive study of this kind by collecting official transcript data at twenty-one colleges and universities that varied in terms of location, selectivity, and curriculum emphasis. For twenty-five AP exams they compared the subsequent course grades of students with AP exam scores of 3, 4, or 5 who were exempted from the introductory course to the subsequent course grades of all students who took the introductory course (as matriculated college students) before taking the subsequent course. When grades in the second-level subsequent course were investigated, results showed that the majority of students who were exempted from the introductory science courses because of successful AP exam scores did at least as well, if not better, in the subsequent course than those who took the introductory course. More specifically, results showed that students who earned a 4 or 5 on the relevant AP exam received higher second-level course grades, on average, than students who took the introductory science courses. Students who earned a 3 on the relevant AP exam received higher second-level course grades, on average, in all areas except biology. A more recent follow-up by Morgan and Klaric (2007) using data from twenty-seven institutions examined the subsequent course performance in biology and chemistry and found that even after controlling for general academic ability, students who earned a 3, 4, or 5 on the AP Biology or Chemistry exam earned the same (i.e., no statistical difference) or higher course grades in the subsequent course as compared to students who took the introductory course on the college campus. Data from AP Physics and Environmental Science exams were not studied.

Additional studies using data from a single university (Burnham and Hewitt, 1971; Dodd et al., 2002) or system (Morgan and Crone, 1993) have also addressed this same research question. For example, Dodd and colleagues (2002) investigated how students at the University of Texas at Austin who were exempted from introductory courses in English, calculus, or biology because of successful AP exam scores (called the "AP-exempt group" in the study) performed in relation to non-AP students who took the introductory course at the university. The AP-exempt group was also compared to AP students who took the introductory course because they did not earn satisfactory exam scores according to the university's AP credit and placement policy. Analyses were conducted separately for four different entering freshman classes. To control for the possibility that AP students might perform better in subsequent college courses because of greater academic preparation in general, the non-AP student group was matched to the AP-exempt group using high school rank and admissions test scores. This matching process resulted in a non-AP comparison group that was of similar academic ability to the AP-exempt group. For biology, the AP-exempt group was comprised of students who earned a 3 or 4 on the AP Biology exam, because the AP credit and placement policy in effect at the time this research was conducted provided credit to students who earned a 5 on the AP Biology exam for the entire sequence of introductory courses (total of three courses), and thus AP 5 students did not have grades for the subsequent course included in the analyses. Results showed that the AP-exempt students in biology earned, on average, the same grades in the subsequent course compared to the matched non-AP group in all but one year of the data analyzed.

Keng and Dodd (2008) conducted a follow-up study using more recent data from the University of Texas at Austin that compared the college performance of AP students to non-AP students of similar academic ability in ten high-volume AP subjects across four cohorts of entering freshmen (1998–2001). The two high-volume AP science exams that were included in the analyses were AP Biology and AP Chemistry. For both AP Biology and AP Chemistry, the results were generally consistent across cohorts and showed that students who placed out of the introductory course as a result of AP exam performance earned the same or higher first- and fourth-year credit hours, the same or higher first- and fourth-year overall GPA, and the same or higher course grades in the subject area of the AP exam. These results suggest that the broader consequences of granting AP credit and placement at the University of Texas at Austin are positive.

REDESIGNING AP SCIENCE COURSES AND EXAMS

In August 2001 the National Research Council sponsored the Committee on Programs for Advanced Study of Mathematics and Science in American High Schools. The committee was charged with making recommendations for improving advanced science and mathematics study in U.S. secondary education. In 2002 it published its findings and recommendations in the report *Learning and Understanding: Improving Advanced Study of Mathematics and Science in U.S. High Schools*. Specific recommendations to the AP Program by the committee included:

- Monitor and govern the use of the AP trademark, including specific guidelines for what courses can be labeled as AP on official high school transcripts
- Base AP courses and exams on entry-level college courses that foster deep conceptual understanding (pp. 14–15)

The College Board responded to the first recommendation by establishing the AP Course Audit in 2007, a new process that requires College Board authorization of any course labeled "AP" on student transcripts (College Board, 2009a). The authorization process requires teachers to provide course-specific information, namely the syllabus for the course and a thorough description of the course content and materials (e.g., textbooks, hands-on lab experiences) used for the course. Criteria for both the course syllabi and classroom materials are posted online. Teachers must have a school administrator sign to verify that the information provided by the teacher is correct and that the school will provide the necessary resources for the teacher to deliver the course as described in the syllabus. Next, the submitted information is reviewed independently by trained college faculty who have taught the comparable college course within the last three years. Only after the teacher's course has been authorized is the school allowed to label the course "AP" on transcripts sent to colleges and universities. In this way, the College Board not only monitors the use of the AP label but also provides clear expectations about the course content and curricular resources as well as providing evidence to postsecondary institutions that AP courses are aligned with rigorous, entry-level college courses.

In 2006 the College Board, with support from the National Science Foundation (NSF Award #ESI-0525575), initiated an ambitious redesign of all four AP science courses and exams (Biology, Chemistry, Physics, and Environmental Science) with the overarching goals being to:

- Limit breadth of content and increase depth of scientific inquiry and reasoning
- Base instruction and assessment on carefully designed claims of student performance and appropriate evidence to support these claims

- Embed cutting-edge scientific research and emerging issues as contextual exemplars
- Increase access by underserved students by inclusion of culturally-sensitive content and support success of all students by defining prior knowledge and essential instructional resources
- Leverage the professional development potential of the existing AP Program (College Board, 2007, p. 2)

The first step in this process was to collect and analyze detailed curricular data from postsecondary institutions known for the rigor and success of their entry-level college courses. These curricular data—including the content, skills, and instructional practices—were used as input for the redesign of the AP science courses and exams. By selecting only rigorous entry-level college courses, rather than a representative sample, the aim was to base AP courses and exams on the best practices of teaching and learning in each discipline. Details of the sampling, instrument development, data collection, analyses, and results are documented by Conley and colleagues (2006). Results from the study indicated that rigorous courses focused on the integration of key science concepts and science practices and facilitated active, hands-on classroom environments that fostered habits of mind associated with college success.

Two additional recommendations from the NRC (2002) were for the College Board to:

- Provide more detailed information about what knowledge, skills, and abilities should be taught in the course, as well as information on instructional and other classroom practices to support advanced study in the discipline
- Ensure that the assessment measures deep conceptual understanding and complex reasoning skills (pp. 14–15)

These recommendations were addressed through the use of evidence-centered assessment design (Mislevy & Haertel, 2006; Steinberg et al., 2003), an approach that supports a thorough and comprehensive framework for the valid interpretation of AP exam scores.

ECD and the Valid Interpretation of AP Exam Performance

To ensure that the knowledge and skills identified for the redesigned courses and exams were articulated in a manner that will serve as a strong foundation for both curriculum and assessment design, we leveraged principles and tools from backward design (see Wiggins & McTighe,

2005). We charged nationally renowned committees of disciplinary experts from postsecondary and secondary education to reach consensus on the concepts, content, skills, and practices that should be the focus of rigorous, entry-level college science courses. To help them in this unwieldy task of articulation and prioritization, we developed the following approach based on the backward-design framework. We asked each committee to work iteratively through three levels of specificity, each requiring multiple rounds of consensus building. First we asked the members to identify the organizing principles, or the *big ideas*, of the discipline. Next, for each big idea they identified *enduring understandings*, the primary learning objectives for the course. These are the concepts that students should retain after the course as a foundation for further study in the discipline. The last step was to identify the *supporting understandings*, which are features of each enduring understanding expressed at a level of specificity sufficient to define explicitly the bounds of the course while emphasizing depth of understanding over breadth of coverage. This process resulted in an organizing framework for the course material structured around the major concepts in the discipline. See figure 5.1 for an example from the physics committee.

The next step was to integrate the content with scientific practices (which were developed through a similar process as the content) through articulating specific *claims* we want to make about students at the end

FIGURE 5.1 An example content outline in physics

Big Idea: Changes that occur as a result of interactions are constrained by conservation laws.

Enduring understanding: The energy of a system is conserved.

Supporting understandings (selection):

A.1   Classically, an object can only have kinetic energy since potential energy requires an interaction between two or more objects.

A.2   A system with internal structure can have internal energy, and changes in a system's internal structure can result in changes in internal energy.

A.3   A system with internal structure can have potential energy. Potential energy exists within a system if the objects within that system interact with "conservative forces."

A.4   The internal energy of a system includes the kinetic energy of the objects comprising the system and the potential energy of the configuration of the objects comprising the system.

A.5   Energy transfer can be caused by a force acting through a distance; this energy transfer is called work.

of their successful completion of the AP course. Then, for each claim, the committee articulated the *observable evidence* required to support the claim. See figure 5.2 for an example of a claim and its associated observable evidence from the physics committee.

By expressing the desired content and practices as integrated, rather than discrete lists, and by articulating how teachers can observe complex reasoning within a specific content area, the AP course descriptions and other curricular support materials will provide an unprecedented amount of detail about the expected learning outcomes from each course.

FIGURE 5.2   An example of claim and evidence from physics

Big idea: Changes that occur as a result of interactions are constrained by conservation laws.

Enduring understanding: The energy of a system is conserved.

Supporting understanding:
A.5   Energy transfer can be caused by a force acting through a distance; this energy transfer is called work.

Scientific   The student can design a plan for collecting data to answer a
practices: particular scientific question.

The student can analyze data to identify patterns or relationships.

Claim: The student is able to design and analyze an experiment to examine how a force exerted through a distance on an object or system does work on the object or system.

Observable evidence:
- Accuracy of representation that the amount of work done on or by the system can be measured or calculated in terms of the changes in energy of the system.
- Appropriateness of experimental design that is practical with defined, measurable parameters that allow calculation of work and/or changes in energy.
- Appropriateness of experimental design that appropriately isolates the independent and dependent variables. Accuracy of identification of what unmeasured quantities play a significant role in the experiment. Systematicity of the record of data.
- Appropriateness of level of precision of measurements (with units, if appropriate).
- Appropriateness of number of data sets collected. Adequacy of description of how systematic error in measurements can be avoided and how specific measurements affect the final calculations.
- Appropriateness of selection of measurement tools to the purpose. Correctness of usage of terms in the analysis (heat transfer, work, kinetic energy).
- Appropriateness of the selection of the mathematical routine for calculations of unknown quantities.
- Correctness of calculations of unknown variables from measured quantities.
- Discussion of sources of uncertainty in the experiment.

Similarly, such detail will provide an unequivocal foundation for alignment between what is taught in the course and measured on the exam.

Two additional innovative features of the redesigned courses and exams that emerge from the use of ECD are: (1) each claim is associated with an *achievement level* or *performance category* that corresponds to a final AP score (e.g., 3, 4 or 5); and (2) each question on the redesigned exam will be associated with a *task model* that describes the features of MC and FR questions that need to be present to ensure that the targeted observable evidence is either engaged and/or produced by the examinee. In this way, performance on specific AP exam questions has a direct link to the claims that are the learning objectives of the course and to the scores that are provided to postsecondary institutions, secondary teachers, and the students.

Kane (2006) defines assessment as a process of reasoning from evidence; the validity of the inferences about student performance must be evaluated on the merits of the argument connecting what is observed (through the assessment) to the claims (or inferences) we make about students. ECD explicates a transparent *evidentiary argument* to warrant the inferences we make from student test performance through the use of *task models*, which are the blueprints for the development of test questions and which are designed from the *claims* we want to make about students and the *observable evidence* required to warrant those claims. The claims are aligned along the hypothesized performance continuum represented by the achievement levels; the achievement levels directly inform the placement of cut-points along the composite score scale and the resulting score interpretation of the final, reported AP scores. Consequently, the explicit relationships among claims, evidence, task models, questions, and achievement levels provide an evidentiary argument for valid inferences about student test performance (Ewing, Packman, Hamen, & Thurber, in press; Hendrickson, Huff, & Luecht, in press; Huff, Steinberg, & Matts, in press; Plake, Huff, & Reshetar, in press).

CONCLUDING REMARKS

The AP Program has grown tremendously since its original inception in the early 1950s. Large bodies of reliability and validity evidence have been gathered over the years to aid in the interpretation of exam scores, and the purpose of this chapter is to provide an overview of the nature and quality of that evidence. The review suggests that consumers of AP exam scores (i.e., students, parents, teachers, postsecondary institutions, etc.) can be confident in the reliability and validity of AP exam scores when using them to make credit and placement decisions. There is also much to be excited about in terms of the future of AP. The use of ECD to redesign the AP science courses and exams makes available an unprecedented amount of detailed curricular material about the expected learning outcomes for each course, provides tighter alignment between what is taught in the course and assessed on the exam, and further strengthens the validation argument for AP exam scores.

REFERENCES

American Educational Research Association [AERA], American Psychological Association [APA], & National Council on Measurement in Education [NCME]. (1999). Standards for educational and psychological testing. Washington, DC: American Educational Research Association.

Burnham, P. S., & Hewitt, B. A. (1971). Advanced Placement scores: Their predictive validity. *Educational and Psychological Measurement, 31*(4),939–945.

College Board. (2007, July). From research to practice: Redesigning AP science courses to advance science literacy and support learning with understanding. NSF Award # ESI-0525575. Annual report to NSF. Washington, DC: National Academies Press.

College Board. (2009a). AP course audit. http://www.collegeboard.com/html/apcourseaudit/review_process.html

College Board (2009b). AP data 2009. http://professionals.collegeboard.com/data-reports-research/ap/data

College Board (2009c). AP exam scoring. http://apcentral.collegeboard.com/apc/public/courses/1994.html

College Board (2009d). The history of the AP Program. http://apcentral.collegeboard.com/apc/public/program/history/8019.html

Conley, D. T., Aspengren, K., Gallagher, K. V., Stout, O., Veach, D., & Stutz, D. (2006). *College Board Advanced Placement best practices course study* [Research report]. Eugene, OR: Center for Educational Policy Research.

Cronbach, L. J. (1988). Five perspectives on the validity argument. In H. Wainer & H. Braun (Eds.), *Test validity* (pp. 3–17). Hillsdale, NJ: Erlbaum.

Cronbach, L. J., & Meehl, P. E. (1955). Construct validity in psychological tests. *Psychological Bulletin, 52*(4), 281–302.

Devillis, R. F. (2003). *Scale development: Theory and applications* (2nd ed.). Thousand Oaks, CA: Sage.

Dodd, B. G., Fitzpatrick, S. J., De Ayala, R. J., & Jennings, J. A. (2002). *An investigation of the validity of AP grades of 3 and a comparison of AP and non-AP student groups* (College Board Research Report No. 2002-9). New York: College Board.

Educational Testing Service [ETS]. (2008). *College Board 2008 Advanced Placement Program analyses forms 4EBP* [Unpublished statistical report].

Ewing, M. (2006). *AP Program and student outcomes: A summary of research* (College Board Research Note No. 29). New York: College Board.

Ewing, M., Packman, S., Hamen, C., & Thurber, A. (in press). Representing targets of measurement within ECD. *Applied Measurement in Education.*

Haertel, E. (2006). Reliability. In R. L. Brennan (Ed.), *Educational measurement (4th ed.; pp. 65–110).* Washington, DC: American Council on Education.

Hargrove, L., Godin, D., & Dodd, B. (2008). *College outcomes comparisons by AP and non-AP high school experiences* (College Board Research Report No. 2008-3). New York: College Board.

Hendrickson, A., Huff, K., & Luecht, R. M. (in press). Claims, evidence, and achievement level descriptions as a foundation for test specifications and item design. *Applied Measurement in Education.*

Hendrickson, A., & Yin, P. (2009). Generalizability theory. In G. R. Hancock & R. O. Mueller (Eds.), *The reviewer's guide to quantitative methods in the social sciences* (pp. 157–167). New York: Routledge.

Huff, K., Steinberg, L., & Matts, T. (in press). The promises and challenges of implementing evidence-centered design in large scale assessment. *Applied Measurement in Education.*

Kane, M. (2006). Validation. In R. L. Brennan (Ed.), *Educational measurement (4th ed.; pp. 17–64).* Washington, DC: American Council on Education.

Keng. L., & Dodd, B. G. (2008). A comparison of college performances of AP and non-AP student groups in 10 subject areas (College Board Research Report No. 2008-7). New York: College Board.

Livingston, S. A., & Lewis, C. (1995). Estimating the consistency and accuracy of classification based on test scores. *Journal of Educational Measurement, 32*(2), 179–197.

Messick, S. (1988). The once and future issues of validity: Assessing the meaning and consequences of measurement. In H. Wainer & H. Braun (Eds.), *Test validity* (pp. 3–17). Hillsdale, NJ: Erlbaum.

Mislevy, R. J., Almond, R. G., & Lukas J. (2004). *A brief introduction to evidence-centered design* (CRESST Technical Report 632). Los Angeles: Center for the Study of Evaluation, CRESST, UCLA.

Mislevy, R. J., & Haertel, G. (2006). Implications for evidence-centered design for educational assessment. *Educational measurement: Issues and practice, 25*(4), 6–20.

Morgan, R., & Crone, C. (1993). *Advanced Placement examinees at the University of California: An investigation of the freshman-year courses and grades of examinees in Biology, Calculus AB, and Chemistry* (ETS Statistical Report 93-210). Princeton, NJ: Educational Testing Service.

Morgan, R., & Klaric, J. (2007) *AP students in college: An analysis of five-year academic careers* (College Board Research Report No. 2007-4). New York: College Board.

Morgan, R., & Ramist, L. (1998). *Advanced Placement students in college: An investigation of course grades at 21 colleges* (ETS Statistical Report No. 98-13). Princeton, NJ: Educational Testing Service.

National Research Council [NRC]. (2002). *Learning with understanding: Improving advanced study of mathematics and science in U.S. high schools*. Washington, DC: National Academies Press.

Plake, B. S., Huff, K., & Reshetar, R. (in press). Evidence-centered design as a foundation for achievement level descriptor development and for standard setting. *Applied Measurement in Education*.

Shavelson, R. J., & Webb, N. M. (1991). *Generalizability theory: A primer*. Thousand Oaks, CA: Sage.

Steinberg, L. S., Mislevy, R. J., Almond, R. G., Baird, A. B., Cahallan, C., DiBello, L. V., Senturk, D., Yan, D., Chernick, H., & Kindfield, A. C. H. (2003). *Introduction to the Biomass project: An illustration of evidence-centered assessment design and delivery capability* (CRESST Technical Report 609). Los Angeles: Center for the Study of Evaluation, CRESST, UCLA.

Traub, R. E. (1994). *Reliability for the social sciences: Theory and applications* (Vol. 3). Thousand Oaks, CA: Sage.

Webb, N., Rowley, G., & Shavelson, R. (1988). Using generalizability theory in counseling and development. *Measurement and Evaluation in Counseling and Development, 21*(2), 81–90.

Wiggins, G., & McTighe, J. (2005). *Understanding by design* (2nd ed.). Alexandria, VA: Association for Supervision and Curriculum Development.

PART THREE

Correlates of
AP Participation

CHAPTER 6

Advanced Placement Course Enrollment and Long-Range Educational Outcomes

Robert H. Tai, Christine Qi Liu,
John T. Almarode, and Xitao Fan

INTRODUCTION

Concerns regarding the scientific workforce in the United States have been crystallized in reports such as National Research Council's *Rising Above the Gathering Storm* (2007), the RAND Corporation's report to the National Defense Research Institute entitled *U.S. Competitiveness in Science and Technology* (Galama & Hosek, 2008), and the American Competitiveness Initiative launched in 2006 under the auspices of President George W. Bush. And now under the Obama administration, concerns about the future of the United States maintaining its leadership role in science and technology or STEM (science, technology, engineering, math[1]) have not abated. In fact, in a speech before the National Academy of Sciences, President Obama articulated major goals for STEM education over the next decade as well as individual initiatives for each of the fifty states, making STEM education a top priority (National Academies, 2009).

Not surprisingly, the national policy discussion on curbing the shrinkage in the STEM workforce has come to include the Advanced Placement Program. This program epitomizes attainable excellence in high school instruction, especially in science and mathematics.[2] Educational quality notwithstanding, STEM policy recommendations appeared to assume that participation in AP coursework would increase the likelihood of students entering the STEM workforce or would, at the very least, enhance the achievement of American students in STEM areas. Whereas the mechanism at play in this scenario is unclear, this assumption about workforce-relevant benefits of AP participation has been widespread. A key qualification necessary for most STEM-related careers is a college degree in a STEM discipline. Thus, the question we address here is, are AP students more likely to earn STEM-related college degrees than students who do not participate in the AP Program? Of course, any analysis of this type must account for students' level of academic achievement, because AP students tend to be top-achieving students, and students of high academic achievement may be more likely than the average student to earn a STEM degree whether they participate in AP or not. In other words, our study must control for the level of achievement of each student, and it must further control for other student background variables that are also likely to influence a student's educational outcomes.

While some concerns associated with this type of analysis arise from the structure of the dataset used, others stem from the circumstances of time and place. Prior to the exponential growth in the number of AP courses in U.S. high schools beginning in 1997 (Klopfenstein, 2003), the quality of the AP program had few critics (Lichten, 2000). Critics of the expanded AP program argue that its success is now gauged solely by test performance, whether the student passes the AP exam (i.e., earns a score of 3 or higher), rather than by more long-range and remote outcomes, such as selecting an undergraduate college major (Lichten & Wainer, 2007) or graduating with a bachelor's degree. In this chapter we look at the association of AP participation and college degree attainment under the circumstances prevailing prior to the broad-based expansion of the program. Using longitudinal data spanning the years 1988–2000 from the National Educational Longitudinal Study of 1988, the data include variables from as early as grade 8 and as late as six years after most participants were in grade 12. If an association could not be detected here (during a period when the AP participants were a small and highly qualified group), we would be reasonably certain that such an association was absent in today's educational environment in light of the teacher quality questions associated with the AP Program's explosive growth (Lichten & Wainer, 2007).

The use of a large-scale nationally representative longitudinal dataset allows us to test the hypothesis that AP Program participation—defined in this study as students who take an AP Exam in science or mathematics—leads to greater likelihoods of students earning college degrees in STEM-related concentrations, as compared with students who do not participate in the AP Program. Until students have taken an AP exam, they have not participated in a College Board–controlled activity and therefore are not considered AP Program participants in this analysis. This heeds the fact that even though the College Board makes curricular recommendations and provides examples of exam questions, the design of the AP courses and the quality of the AP course instructors are entirely controlled at the local level.

METHODOLOGY

Designed and conducted by the National Center for Educational Statistics (NCES, 1994) of the U.S. Department of Education, the *National Educational Longitudinal Study of 1988* (NELS:88) began with a cohort of about 25,000 students attending eighth grade in 1988. Over the course of the next twelve years, researchers conducted four additional follow-up surveys, collected in 1988, 1990, 1992, 1994, and 2000. The overall sample size after five waves was 12,144 participants. In our analysis we focus on students who graduated from four-year colleges or universities during that time, reducing the survey sample to 4,097 participants. The sample was further reduced to a final size of 3,938 participants, since 159 participants were missing data on variables used in the analysis. The survey included achievement tests in science and mathematics designed by Educational Testing Service (ETS) that were administered to the students in the first three waves of data collection, when they were mostly enrolled in eighth, tenth, and twelfth grades. The survey also included students' self-reported SAT/ACT scores. Other questionnaires covering a wide range of topics were administered in all five waves.[3]

For the purpose of this analysis, the "baccalaureate degree" was operationally defined by the area in which the participants earned their first baccalaureate degree by 2000, and the concentrations or majors were coded into three categories—physical science or engineering, life science, and nonscience—based on Biglan's classification of university academic fields (Hativa & Marincovich, 1995). This resulted in a categorical outcome or dependent variable.[4]

There are a variety of independent variables that make sense to include in the analysis as controls. To account for students' previous academic achievement, a concordance score of SAT/ACT was included in the analyses as a covariate (Dorans, Pommerich, & Holland, 2007). In cases when the test score was not available, a rescaled score from previous IRT scores was used instead. To account for students' background differences, demographic variables (gender, ethnicity, parental education background, and socioeconomic status) as well as eighth graders' expectations of what careers they would have at age thirty are included in the analyses. The major question of this study was whether the high school AP math or AP science exams are useful in predicting students' completion of a baccalaureate in science/engineering fields. Here the variable "AP math exam" includes those who took AP Calculus AB or BC; and the variable "AP science exam" includes those who took AP Biology, Chemistry, Physics B, C: E&M, or C: Mechanics

The structure of the data was conducive to a multinomial logistic regression analysis, a statistical technique designed to handle categorical dependent variables with more than two outcomes. This analysis technique allows for the results to be transformed into odds-ratios (or relative risk ratios), which are more straightforward in their interpretation. Our results offer two points of comparison: (1) life sciences baccalaureate degrees with nonscience degrees and (2) physical sciences/engineering with nonscience degrees.

RESULTS AND DISCUSSION

The descriptive statistics of the categorical outcome variable and the predictors are shown in tables 6.1 and 6.2. For the continuous variable SAT/ACT concordance scores, the mean was 995 (N=3938, min=410, max=1539). The independent variables analyzed in table 6.1 are grouped into five categories: demographics, parental education background, previous academic achievement, career expectation, and AP mathematics or science exam status. Table 6.2 shows the numbers of participants in various cross-tabulated categories. Note that while the overall data set is very large, the number of students in particular categories is comparatively small. For example, thirty-one students fall into the category Physical Science/Engineering Graduates who participated in AP science in high school. The statistical techniques we chose to apply in this analysis

TABLE 6.1   Summary of outcome variable and predictors used in analysis (N=3938)

Name of variable	Values	Frequency	Percent
College concentration	Physical science or engineering	498	12.6
	Life science	662	16.8
	Nonscience	2778	70.5
Career expectation	Science/engineering-related field at age 30	380	9.6
	Nonscience/engineering-related field at age 30	3558	90.4
AP Calculus	Took AP Calculus exam	282	7.2
	Did not take AP Calculus exam	3656	92.8
AP science	Took AP science exam	189	4.8
	Did not take AP science exam	3749	95.2

TABLE 6.2   Cross-tabulation of degree concentration and predictor variables (N=3938)

Predictors		Degree concentration			
		Physical science/ engineering	Life science	Nonscience	Total
Career expectation	Science/ engineering	103	83	194	380
	Nonscience/ engineering	395	579	2584	3558
AP Calculus	Took AP Calculus exam	83	59	140	282
	Did not take AP Calculus exam	415	603	2638	3656
AP science	Took AP science exam	31	61	97	189
	Did not take AP science exam	467	601	2681	3749

account for survey design and sampling effects by using survey and sampling weights provided in the NELS:88 data.[5]

The results of the multinomial logistic regression analysis are reported as odds ratios and their associated 95 percent confidence intervals in table 6.3. The purpose of logistic regression models is to produce an estimated likelihood for prototypical individuals with particular background characteristics and experiences to be in one particular "state." In this analysis, only students who had earned baccalaureate degrees twelve years after being enrolled in the eighth grade, or, commensurately, eight years after the usual high school graduation date, are included. The three states used as the outcomes are: (1) individual earned baccalaureate degrees in life sciences, (2) individual earned baccalaureate degree in physical sciences/engineering, or (3) individual earned baccalaureate degree in nonscience areas.

The odds ratios included in table 6.3 show two important results. The odds for students who participated in the AP Calculus were roughly four times (estimated 4.12 times in Model 2c) as high as the odds for students who did not participate in AP Calculus to earn degrees in physical science/ engineering concentrations (rather than in a nonscience area). However, the effect is not found with respect to degree earners in the life sciences concentrations.

For students who participated in AP programs in science (covering the disciplines of biology, chemistry, and physics), our findings indicate that their odds to earn degrees in life science concentrations (rather than in a nonscience area) are more than twice (estimated 2.24 times in Model 2c) as high as those odds for students who did not participate in AP science. This AP science effect is not found with respect to degree earners in the physical science/engineering concentrations. In the end, these results are striking. There appears to be a strong positive effect associated with AP Program participation in mathematics and science. The differential association between the physical sciences/engineering and the life sciences is not surprising given that knowledge of calculus is a prerequisite for enrollment in physical science/engineering concentrations and thus considered a strong foundational requirement for success in those areas. Interestingly, the association of AP science participation with a greater likelihood of earning a baccalaureate in life sciences seems to be associated with the preponderance of AP science participants taking the AP Biology exam, a less mathematically intensive science.

TABLE 6.3 Odds ratios from nested logistic models of Advanced Placement Program participation predicting likelihood to earn life and physical science–related baccalaureate degrees (Total N = 3938)

Independent variables	Life and physical science– or engineering-related coefficients			
	Model 1 (baseline)	Model 2a	Model 2b	Model 2c
Demographic background	Included	Included	Included	Included
Parental background	Included	Included	Included	Included
Academic achievement[a]	Included	Included	Included	Included
Career expectation	Included	Included	Included	Included
AP Calculus (took exam)				
Odds ratio[b]: Physical science[c]		3.52**		4.12**
Life science[c]		1.37		1.06
AP science (took exam)				
Odds ratio: Physical science[c]			0.94	0.51
Life science[c]			2.29**	2.24**
χ^2	384.16	408.95	406.22	436.82
$\Delta\chi^2$		24.79	22.06	52.66
Df	16	18	18	20
ΔDf		2	2	4
pseudo R^2	0.116	0.123	0.122	0.131
Δ pseudo R^2		0.007**	0.006**	0.015**

Notes: *: $p<0.05$; **: $p<0.01$.

[a] Academic achievement: available equated SAT/ACT test score or rescaled IRT score.

[b] Odds ratio (OR) or relative risk ratio (RRR).

[c] Physical sciences/engineering (dependent variable: physical sciences/engineering = 1; nonscience = 0); life sciences (dependent variable: life sciences = 1; nonscience = 0).

CONCLUSION

Proponents of the AP Program may construe the findings in this study as the "smoking gun" for policies supporting the proliferation of AP Program participation as a means of improving the U.S. STEM workforce. And, frankly, the results do support such a conclusion. However, we should not overlook two very important characteristics of this analysis. First, as noted earlier in this study, the data used in this analysis come from a period of time preceding the major expansion of the AP Program. Therefore, these findings might simply no longer be reflected in the current population of students participating in the AP Program. The numerical expansion of the AP Program to include more students is not the only reason for the possible change in the population characteristics. The recent initiatives to provide AP courses to previously underserved constituencies, namely minorities and all levels of socioeconomic status, make it necessary that we now look at the impact on the multiple subgroupings and the long-range impact on their educational decisions (Klopfenstein, 2004). Second, while the sample sizes shown in this study are "good enough," they are small in some important categories. As a result, it is imperative to perform a similar analysis with post–AP expansion data that contains a more robust representation of the student population. This present analysis provides a supportive glimpse at a program that may be responding to the national initiative of increasing the STEM workforce. However, more work in this area is needed to characterize the impact of the current Advanced Placement program on long-range educational outcomes.

NOTES

1. No importance is ascribed to the order of the listed disciplines.
2. The movie *Stand and Deliver* (1988) came to symbolize this aspect of the AP Program.
3. Technical details concerning NELS:88 may be found in NCES publications (e.g., NCES, 1994; Rock & Pollack, 1991).
4. A list of college degree concentrations under the three categories was used in a previously published research study and is available online at http://www.sciencemag.org/cgi/content/full/sci;312/5777/1143/DC1. (Tai, Liu, Maltese, & Fan, 2006).
5. The sampling design of NELS:88 requires special attention to the following analytical issues: (1) the effect of purposeful oversampling of some

ethnic/minority groups and (2) the effect of multistage cluster sampling on standard error estimation. In our analyses, we followed the guidelines of using appropriate sampling weights for statistical analyses as detailed in NCES publications (NCES, 1994). We accounted for the complex sampling design by using the statistical software STATA 10.0, which provided appropriate standard error estimates in our analysis.

REFERENCES

Dorans, N. J., Pommerich, M., & Holland, P. W. (Eds.). (2007). *Linking and aligning scores and scales.* New York: Springer Science + Business Media.

Galama, T., & Hosek, J. (2008). *U.S. competitiveness in science and technology.* Santa Monica, CA: RAND.

Hativa, N., & Marincovich, M. (1995). *Disciplinary differences in teaching and learning: Implications for practice.* San Francisco, CA: Jossey-Bass.

Klopfenstein, K. (2003). Recommendations for maintaining the quality of advanced placement programs. *American Secondary Education, 32*(1), 39–48.

Klopfenstein, K. (2004). Advanced placement: Do minorities have equal opportunity? *Economics of Education Review, 23*(2), 115–131.

Lichten, W. (2000). Whither Advanced Placement? *Education Policy Analysis Archives, 8*(29). http://epaa.asu.edu/epaa/v8n29.html

Lichten, W., & Wainer, H. (2007). The aptitude-achievement function: An aid for allocating educational resources, with an Advanced Placement example. *Educational Psychology Review, 12*(2), 201–228.

Musca, T. (Producer), & Menendez, R. (Director). (1988). *Stand and Deliver* [Motion picture]. United States: Warner Brothers.

National Academies. (2009). President Obama addresses NAS annual meeting. http://www.nas.edu/morenews/20090428.html

National Center for Educational Statistics [NCES]. (1994). User's manual: National Educational Longitudinal Study of 1988. Washington, DC: Author.

National Research Council. (2007). *Rising above the gathering storm.* Washington, DC: National Academies Press.

Rock, D. A., & Pollack, J. M. (1991). Psychometric report for the NELS:88 base text battery (Technical Report NCES 91-468). Washington, DC: National Center for Educational Statistics.

Tai, R. H., Liu, C. Q., Maltese, A. V., & Fan, X. (2006). Planning early for careers in science. *Science, 312*(5777), 1143–1144.

Vickers, J. M. (2000). Justice and truth in grades and their averages. *Research in Higher Education, 41*(2), 141–164.

Woodruff, D., & Ziomek, R. (2004). *High school grade inflation from 1991 to 2003*. ACT Research Report Series 2004-4. Iowa City, IA: ACT.

Ziomek, R., & Svec, J. (1997). High school grades and achievement: Evidence of grade inflation. *NASSP Bulletin, 81*(587): 105–113.

CHAPTER 7

High School Advanced Placement and Success in College Coursework in the Sciences

Philip M. Sadler and Gerhard Sonnert

To what degree can the performance of students in college courses be attributed to the AP courses they took in high school?

Students enrolling in Advanced Placement courses expect an experience that replicates the content and rigor of an introductory college course in that discipline. They—and their parents—assume that the AP course will be both challenging and rewarding, deepening their understanding of a subject beyond that which can be gained from the regular or even honors high school courses. For many, regular or honors courses in a subject constitute prerequisites for AP study. Students and their parents are also attracted by the economic advantage of earning college credit while still in high school (MacVicar, 1988; Pushkin, 1995). The benefits of a deeper understanding of an interesting subject and official recognition of mastery of college-level material have helped fuel the dramatic expansion of the AP program.

Evidence for the equivalence of AP and college courses is elusive, since it is impossible to carry out a controlled experiment in which students are randomly assigned to AP courses or not. Yet, the opinion that the AP experience is valuable is widespread. For the students, taking a challenging course in high school certainly requires a great deal of work, but any promise of equivalence to the type and amount of work required by a college course is something they cannot yet judge themselves. No doubt they learn much from a year of advanced study, perhaps the hardest course in their school experience; yet the particular value that the students themselves place on their learning is far too subjective to offer any clear picture of the worth of their AP experience. Any judgment of the quantity and quality of knowledge gained from an AP course, and any assurance of its equivalence to a college course, must come from a more neutral examination. There is a surprising lack of consensus about the value of AP courses, with some educators even hypothesizing that "it is possible that AP students were at a disadvantage in some classes or at some colleges" (NRC, 2002, p. 194). College professors also express concern about not being able to attract academically gifted students into their field when students may choose to use their AP credits and never take another course in the subject during college (NRC, 2002, p. 59).

The decision to take an AP course in high school is a form of self-selection. The most highly motivated and most academically successful high school students are drawn to these challenging courses. There is little reason to doubt that they will perform well in their later college coursework. It is difficult to ascertain whether later performance is the result of taking an AP course or of particular personal student characteristics (Dougherty, Mellor, & Shuling, 2006) or of academic preparation in other areas (Sadler & Tai, 2007). For example, the rigor of the high school course in a science subject, letter grade earned, SAT math score, level of high school math completed, last high school math grade, along with AP exam score, all predict college science grades (Sadler & Tai, 2007). Moreover, AP courses are more prevalent in wealthier communities, are typically taught by more experienced teachers (Burdman, 2000; Paek et al., this volume), and are prevalent in schools that emphasize college preparation (Willingham & Morris, 1986). Accounting for such differences is essential in any attempt to attribute the "added-value" of AP coursework.

Prior research on the effectiveness of AP coursework has focused mainly on predicting freshman grade point average or persistence to graduation. These are rather broad measures that may dilute the impact of taking specific AP courses. Other researchers have studied those students who move directly to a second- or third-semester college course, using AP credit to bypass introductory coursework, and have compared them with students who take the introductory course. This can also be problematic, because later coursework often has little relation to an introductory course (e.g., second-semester physics usually entails a study of electricity, magnetism, and light, topics distant from first-semester kinematics and mechanics). Most research studies have examined the performance of students at a single college or university or within a single state—samples that have been too specialized to generalize about the effectiveness of AP courses at large. But the most serious weakness of existing AP studies is that very few pay adequate attention to control variables.

Among the studies with the strongest methodologies, results do not offer uniform support for AP. Two recent studies found that the number of AP courses taken in high school has little relation to the GPA of college freshmen or their persistence to their sophomore college year when controlling for high school performance and socioeconomic status (Geiser & Santelices, 2004; Klopfenstein & Thomas, 2005). However, low-income students who take AP courses in high school do graduate college at a greater rate (Dougherty, Mellor, & Shuling, 2006). Geiser and Santelices (2004) did find that AP exam scores were a much better predictor. Dodd, Fitzpatrick, and Jennings (2002) studied the performance of students in second-semester college biology, matching students by high school class rank and SAT and ACT scores. Those who had been granted credit for their high AP scores and placed ahead performed adequately when compared with those who had taken the first-semester course.

Our review of these earlier studies impressed on us the importance of controlling for many plausible covariates to address the potential issue of AP students being different in many ways from those who do not enroll in AP courses. We designed a study, Factors Influencing College Science Success (FICSS), to collect data from students enrolled in introductory college science courses concerning their backgrounds, academic experiences, and performance, measures closely associated with high school science coursework that might predict their performance in introductory college science classes. In addition, at the end of the course, their college professor reported each student's course grade.

Here we examine the evidence for the equivalence of AP coursework in the sciences and performance in introductory college science courses in the three major fields: biology, chemistry, and physics. Such courses are often prerequisites for majors in science, engineering, and premedicine. Our AP analysis is only possible because many college students enroll in introductory college science courses for which their performance in AP courses could earn them college credit. Through our contact with these college students, we learned that there were three common reasons that they gave for retaking these courses at the college level:

- College requirements are more stringent for credit than the College Board's recommendation of scoring a 3 or better (out of 5) on the AP exam. Some colleges only offer credit for scores of 4 or even 5, while others do not allow students to place out of courses.
- An academic adviser or major in a science field advised them to start with the introductory course and discouraged them from placing into more advanced courses.
- They made a personal decision to take the college course in order to strengthen their mastery of basic concepts.

DATA AND METHODS

The FICSS project gathered survey data from students in 124 different first-semester introductory college biology, chemistry, and physics courses in fifty-five randomly chosen colleges and universities reflecting a nationally representative distribution of institutional size and selectivity, from small liberal arts colleges to large state universities. We chose to analyze only undergraduate students who were educated in the United States and who took the first course of an introductory sequence in the fall semester. Importantly, we also limited our sample to students from high schools that offered both general and AP courses, so as to control for the opportunity of taking an AP course. Slightly more than one-half (57 percent) of the students in our sample attended high schools in which a general course (regular or honors) and an AP course in the particular science were available. This resulted in a sample of 4,907 undergraduates of which 700 were missing data on at least one of the variables under consideration (primarily SAT or ACT scores). Thus, 4,207 undergraduates formed the sample analyzed in this chapter. Of the sample, 20 percent reported having taken an AP course in the subject in high school in which they were currently enrolled in college. Of these students, about half reported not taking the AP exam in the subject, one-third earning a passing score of 3 or higher, and one-sixth earning a score of 1 or 2. Regarding disciplines, 35 percent of the students in the sample were enrolled in biology, 45 percent in chemistry, and about 20 percent in physics. Females made up 60 percent of the biology students, 53 percent of the chemistry, and 44 percent of the physics students. In terms of race, 79 percent of the students identified themselves as white, 8 percent as Asian/Pacific Islander, 5 percent as black, 5 percent as multiracial, and 3 percent as other or reported no race. The question about Hispanic origin was answered in the affirmative by 5 percent.

Regarding the students' course-taking experiences, we formed the following six cohorts. "Not taken" indicates that no course in the particular subject was taken in high school; "Regular" signifies that the highest level of course taken in high school was neither AP nor honors level; and "Honors" signifies that an honors course was taken. The remaining three cohorts all consist of students who took an AP course in that subject: students who received AP exam scores of ≤2 (not passing); students choosing not to take an AP examination even though they took the course; and students who earned exam scores of ≥3 (passing). Figure 7.1 displays the distribution across these cohorts used in multivariate analyses in this chapter.

Because of our concern that measures of prior academic achievement correlate with taking an AP course and with AP exam scores, we calculated key measures based for the different cohorts of interest (see table 7.1). Means are reported for the SAT math and SAT verbal scores or the equivalent from the ACT using a concordance table (Dorans, Lyu, Pommerich, & Houston 1997), an estimate of high school GPA (from math, English, and science grades), the percentages of completing any type of calculus course and an AP calculus course in high school, and the percentage of parents in the cohort who had earned a four-year college degree.

In the various measures, AP students, as hypothesized, generally have an advantage over honors students, who in turn are advantaged over regular students, who in turn are advantaged over students with no high school coursework in the corresponding college science discipline. Within the AP group we see a clear pattern of higher performance corresponding

FIGURE 7.1 Distribution of students across disciplines and cohorts

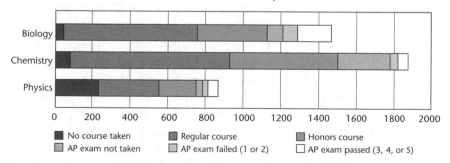

TABLE 7.1   Comparison of high school performance and background measures by cohort

Cohort	Math SAT	Verbal SAT	HS GPA	HS calculus	AP calculus	Parents with four years of college
Not taken	577	556	3.33	27%	17%	59%
Regular	576	557	3.43	32%	17%	60%
Honors	616	585	3.58	60%	41%	65%
AP exam ≤ 2	601	561	3.50	52%	42%	64%
AP exam not taken	628	594	3.58	70%	58%	67%
AP exam ≥ 3	646	628	3.68	65%	56%	76%

to passing the AP exam, and students who choose not to take the AP exam appear to have stronger backgrounds than those who fail it. These patterns complicate any effort to explain college performance from the students' AP experiences. Because test scores and grades are different for AP and non-AP students, one cannot exclude the possibility that some other factor, like verbal performance or math ability, may be the cause of any better college performance of AP students, rather than the fact that they had taken an AP course.

A statistically sophisticated way to deal with the issue of the background of students in different cohorts being rather dissimilar is to employ propensity score weighting. This method compensates for systematic differences in the cohorts, reducing the effects of covariates (Rosenbaum & Rubin, 1983). It creates, through statistical means, cohorts (e.g., students who took AP Biology and students who did not take AP Biology) that are similar on relevant characteristics by weighting some subjects more heavily than others in the analysis. This serves the goal of controlling for these characteristics. This method offers an advantage over ordinary multiple regression in that it reduces collinearities between the cohorts (i.e., not taken, regular, honors, and AP groupings) and those other characteristics.[1]

Propensity weights are then used in building hierarchical linear models (HLM) that account for variance in college grades at three different levels: students, course (or professor), and institution. HLM allows the model to take into account different levels of grading stringency by professor and institution as well as differences in overall background measures at institutions and within courses. It neatly deals with the issue of private colleges and universities generally awarding higher grades than public institutions. We report here on only the student level variables, while the HLM controls for higher level variables.[2]

RESULTS

The two kinds of results we present here can be easily confused. The first answers the question, How do students perform in their college science courses based on their level of preparation? The second answers the question, How effective are high school science courses of various levels of rigor if one accounts for differences in student background?

Predicting Student Performance in College

To predict student performance in college science, we need only graph the mean college grades for students in different cohorts (figure 7.2). We plot each with error bars. Nonintersecting error bars show a significance difference (at $p \leq 0.05$).

FIGURE 7.2   Grades earned by students in college science grouped by preparation

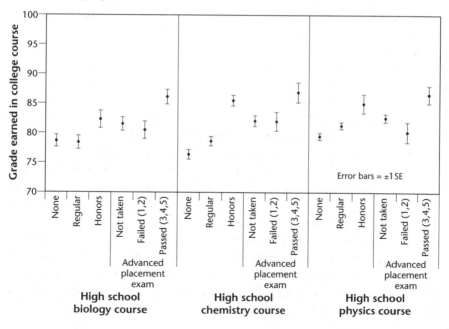

In introductory college biology, we found no significant difference in the grades between students who had taken a regular high school biology course or no course at all. Honors students did significantly better than those with regular courses. AP biology students who did not take or failed (i.e., with a score of 1 or 2) the AP biology exam earned similar grades in college to those who took an honors biology course. Those students who passed the AP biology exam performed significantly better than all other biology groups. This is evidence that students who pass an AP biology exam have more knowledge at the end of their college course.

In introductory college chemistry, significant differences are found between students who took a regular high school chemistry course and those who did not take any, although the differences are small. As in biology, students who passed the AP chemistry exam have the highest grade estimate of the cohorts, but students who took an honors chemistry course in high school earned similar college grades as those who passed the AP chemistry exam. Those who failed the AP exam and those who chose not to take it both had lower scores, on average, than the AP exam passers. For college chemistry professors considering granting course credit for a passing AP exam score, it would only be fair to grant an equal course credit to students who have had an honors course in chemistry.

For introductory college physics, results are similar to those for chemistry. Those students who had a regular high school physics course outperformed those without any high school physics. Students who enrolled in an honors physics course appeared to do as well in college physics as those who passed the AP physics exam. As in chemistry, those who failed the AP exam and those who chose not to take it both had lower scores, on average, than the AP exam passers.

In general, the performance (passing or failing) on AP science exams does a good job discriminating between students who earn a grade in the C+ to B− range in introductory college science and those who earn in the B to B+ range. We can thus summarize an answer to our first question. In all three subjects, students who had passed the AP exam performed better, on average, in introductory college courses than did their counterparts who had either failed or chosen not to take the AP exam. They also did better in all three subjects than students who had taken no high school course in the subject or only a regular course. However, only in biology did they outperform students who had taken an honors course in biology. In chemistry and physics the honors students performed at a comparable level with the AP passers.

Assessing the Effectiveness of High School Science Courses

To gauge the effect of taking different high school courses in preparation for college science, we must account for differences in student
background.

We include in our analysis variables that plausibly might affect students' performance in college introductory science classes. Through
dummy variables, we account for the year in which students take their
college science course, because maturity and experience may be related
to course performance. We have noticed that many students wait until
their senior year to fulfill science requirements, often preferring to hone
their math skills before taking science. We do not include the college-year
variables for college physics because we had difficulty estimating propensity weights for physics and because these variables, in separate analyses,
were found to make no difference in the outcome in physics. Leaving out
these relatively minor variables helped the propensity model converge.
Race and gender are dummy variables (0=other, 1=black; and 1=male,
2=female). Parental education is an average of both parents' educational
level measured on a scale ranging from "did not finish high school" to
"graduate school." High school type is a dummy (0=other, 1=public).
Community socioeconomic status (SES) is estimated from U.S. Census
data; it is a composite of the average per capita income and the average
adult education level in the student's home zip code. Students' verbal
proficiency is estimated using the SAT verbal score and last grade in high
school English (on a 4-point scale). Math ability is measured using the
SAT math score, dummy variables indicating whether AP and/or regular
calculus was taken, as well as the last grade earned in high school mathematics (on a 4-point scale).

Our initial presentation (figure 7.2) did not control for student backgrounds or academic performance prior to, and independent of, any AP
course experiences. Our propensity-weighted HLM model, presented in
table 7.2, does.[3] We can see in that table that the college year in which
students take biology does not appear to impact their course grade. In
chemistry, sophomores and juniors do significantly worse than freshmen. Race is a significant predictor of grade in both biology and physics
but not in chemistry. Females do equally well as males in all three introductory courses. Parental education level is significant for biology and
physics but not for chemistry. Former public school students are at a disadvantage only in college chemistry. Only in chemistry does the average

TABLE 7.2 HLM model explaining variance in college science grade

Control variables	Biology	Effect size	Chemistry	Effect size	Physics	Effect size
Intercept	42.77(3.38)***		43.29(2.72)		41.27(3.93)***	
Sophomore	-0.51(0.63)		-2.24(0.59)***			
Junior	-0.14(0.79)		-2.25(0.81)**			
Senior	1.61(1.21)		-1.46(1.16)			
Race	-3.33(1.20)**		-1.74(1.01)		-5.39(1.93)**	
Gender (female)	-0.65(0.52)		0.16(0.45)		-1.29(0.69)	
Parent education	0.39(0.27)		0.23(0.23)		0.76(0.36)*	
HS type (public)	-0.39(0.68)		-1.31(0.61)*		-0.78(0.94)	
Community SES	-0.01(0.14)		0.42(0.13)**		0.22(0.18)	
SAT math	0.01(0.00)**		0.02(0.00)***		0.02(0.00)***	
SAT verbal	0.01(0.00)***		0.01(0.00)*		0.00(0.00)	
HS English grade	2.25(0.47)***		1.59(0.39)***		2.67(0.53)***	
AP calculus	3.46(0.64)***		2.92(0.54)***		3.00(0.83)***	
Other calculus	1.73(0.79)*		1.36(0.67)*		1.31(1.01)	
HS math grade	3.13(0.35)***		3.04(0.31)***		3.15(0.47)***	
Effect size		Effect size		Effect size		Effect size
Cohort						
Regular course	0.36(1.56)	0.03(0.14)	2.71(1.04)*	0.25(0.10)	1.59(0.81)	0.14(0.07)
Honors	1.83(1.60)	0.17(0.15)	4.29(1.07)***	0.40(0.10)	1.44(0.90)	0.12(0.08)
No AP exam taken	2.27(1.82)	0.21(0.17)	6.88(1.15)***	0.64(0.11)	4.99(1.82)**	0.43(0.16)
Fail AP exam	1.61(1.85)	0.15(0.17)	6.43(1.74)***	0.60(0.16)	-1.40(2.02)	-0.12(0.18)
Pass AP exam	5.58(1.68)**	0.51(0.15)	8.39(1.71)***	0.78(0.16)	7.10(1.65)***	0.62(0.14)
Model descriptors						
N	1466		1875		866	
Mean college grade	79.95		80.23		81.26	
Pooled SD	10.89		10.75		11.51	
Pseudo-R^2	34.00%		32.10%		38.70%	

Note: *: $p<0.05$; **: $p<0.01$; ***: $p<0.001$.

SES level in the community appear to have an effect. Math SAT scores, along with English and math grades, are significant and strong predictors of college science grades. Verbal SAT scores predict college performance in biology and chemistry but not in physics. AP Calculus enrollment has a strong relationship to college science grades. Taking a regular calculus course is significant only for biology and chemistry. Overall, the included measures of academic success in high school and of student background characteristics are highly predictive of later success in college science.

Studies of educational impact that do not account for these variables may err in attributing too much credit to taking AP coursework for students' later success in college. Sadler and Tai (2007) found that when demographics and prior academic achievement are accounted for, the apparent advantage held by students with AP coursework is reduced by half. Willingham and Morris (1986) also found that half of the "AP advantage" was accounted for by matching students by background. This reduction is similar to findings by Dougherty and colleagues (2006) in which the introduction of two control variables (mathematics achievement and high school characteristics) in their regression analysis resulted in a one-third reduction in predicted impact of passing an AP exam. Our study extends these findings by comparing AP to other high school course offerings, by examining patterning in three different science fields, and by comparing students who differ in their AP exam performance.

Whereas cohort results in figure 7.2 presented the expected college grade (on a 100-point scale where there are ten points between each letter grade) for each of the cohorts, figure 7.3 compares the various cohorts of students who had some kind of exposure to a particular high school science subject with the baseline cohort of students who had not taken any preparatory course in that science in high school. We also choose another metric for displaying these differences in figure 7.3. Although estimates of raw grade points are useful, interpreting differences between cohorts on that scale is somewhat subjective. A more appropriate measure is effect size, which standardizes the differences among the cohorts in units of standard deviation of course grade. (For each discipline, a pooled standard deviation of college course grade earned was calculated.) Effect size has the advantage of being a common measure of the success of educational interventions and is often used in making generalizations from large numbers of research studies in meta-analyses (Cohen 1988). Another benefit is that results expressed as effect sizes can be deemed small, medium, or large, corresponding to common definitions used in

FIGURE 7.3   Effect sizes of high school science course-taking conditions

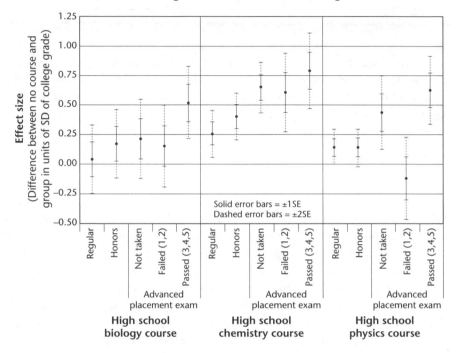

well-known research studies on student achievement. Cohen (1969) describes a small effect size as 0.2 SD, a medium effect size as 0.5 SD, which is "large enough to be visible to the naked eye," and a large effect size as 0.8 SD, which is "grossly perceptible" (p. 23). In figure 7.3 we also show error bars of both one and two standard errors. If one is interested in whether cohorts are statistically different from the baseline cohort ("no course"), using the longer error bar is appropriate, whereas the shorter error bar is of use for comparing the nonbaseline cohorts among one another.

Using Cohen's definition, we can categorize the magnitude of effect sizes that appear significant for each science. In biology we find no significant difference between students who did not take a high school biology course (the zero condition) and those who took a regular or honors biology course. For those taking an AP biology course, only students who passed the AP exam with a score of 3, 4, or 5 show a medium effect size. Hence, we have no evidence that the biology courses taken in high school impact the later success of introductory college biology students, save for those passing the AP biology exam. In particular, students who take AP biology and do not pass the exam appear to experience no benefit. This is troubling because, for most students, AP biology is their second year of study in the subject. If there is no advantage to taking a second year of biology in high school for these students, this questions the value of an AP biology course for the sizable group of students who do not pass the AP exam. For chemistry the results are strikingly different. Regular and honors high school chemistry courses have a "small" positive effect on how well students do in introductory college chemistry. AP chemistry courses appear quite effective in that students who choose not to take the AP exam and those who fail it still experience a "medium" positive effect. Students who pass the AP chemistry exam experience a "large" positive effect. AP chemistry thus appears to be beneficial for students even if they fail the AP exam or choose not to take it. In physics the effects are not significant for those in the regular, honors, or AP fail cohorts. Those taking an AP Physics course and either not taking the exam or passing it experience a "medium" positive effect, on average. Taken together, these results show a considerable difference in the effectiveness of high school coursework in preparing students for success in college science, after one accounts for the differing backgrounds of students who take these courses.

In our study, only 5 percent of those taking introductory college biology had not taken biology in high school. In the United States, 92 percent of high school students take biology, with 16 percent enrolling in AP or honors biology (Snyder, Dillow, & Hoffman, 2008, table 142). The small effect size could be the result of comparison with students in the baseline cohort who get their biology knowledge from integrated or general science courses. However, the lack of any significant difference between the regular and honors cohorts and the AP non-test-takers and AP test-failers in biology demonstrates that the significant differences seen in figure 7.2 for these cohorts are accounted for by demographic and background differences. Honors and AP courses do not have any statistically significant effect on preparing students for college biology unless students pass the AP exam. This appears to be the case in spite of views that coverage in high school biology of more advanced material and at a greater rate may convey an advantage per se in later study.

All high school chemistry courses significantly boost students' chances for success in introductory college chemistry. In our study we found that 6 percent of introductory college chemistry students had not taken any high school chemistry, a similar percentage to those who had not taken high school biology. Yet those students who took no chemistry in high school were at a distinct disadvantage when taking college chemistry.

Physics results are interesting. Of our subjects in college physics, 32 percent had not taken physics in high school. Compared with the sizable advantage seen in raw grades in figure 7.2 for students taking honors physics or passing their AP Physics exam, the effect is seen to be only moderate for AP passers and those who chose not to take the exam and not significant at all for regular, honors, or AP students who failed their exam. Students' backgrounds, primarily their mathematics achievement and course-taking, appear to have a much larger effect on their college physics success than the kind of physics course taken (or not taken) in high school.

These findings differ somewhat from the ideas many students and their parents have about the value of AP coursework. Student background and educational experiences outside of AP play a large role in the apparent success of students in college science courses. Yet caution should be exercised due to possible limitations in our analysis.

- *Sample size of the current study.* Students taking AP courses in high school are a small fraction of those in our sample. While this study is smaller than several concerning Advanced Placement, it is the largest investigation of its kind that controls for relevant background factors such as prior mathematics and science course-taking and performance.

- *Imputing causality.* Our study is not experimental. Even though we have worked hard to address alternative hypotheses that account for college science success, and though we have used a quasi-experimental approach that statistically equalizes the cohorts, we understand that this research cannot prove causal connections between variables and outcomes. However, we are able to test simultaneously the strength of many hypotheses for which empirical trials would be difficult to perform. The relationships revealed by this kind of study are then worthy of controlled, experimental studies that may establish, with increasing certainty, the postulated causal connections.

CONCLUSIONS

In this chapter we untangle two issues: the role of AP science courses as predictors of college science performance and the "value-added" of taking

AP science courses in high school. We chose to examine the performance of college students taking introductory college biology, chemistry, and physics. These students have varied academic backgrounds that suggest the use of statistical methods to model the degree to which specific variables explain differences in college performance.

We find that the students in our sample who reported passing their AP exam earned college grades that were significantly higher than those of students with other experiences. The exception is that students taking honors chemistry or honors physics performed equally well in their college science courses. However, even the grades earned by AP exam passers in college were only averaged in the B to B+ range after experiencing another semester of introductory biology, chemistry, or physics. Given that high school AP courses are intended to stand in place of college courses, it can be argued that AP students have taken the introductory college course twice; and despite this clear advantage, their performance, as a group, is by no means indicative of mastery. Perhaps we should also account for the fact that, over time, students (like everybody else) tend to forget what they have learned if they do not use it. Any knowledge acquired "ahead of time" cannot be stored perfectly, as if on a memory stick, but is subject to deterioration. While many students in our sample feel that AP is a good preparation for college science, many also feel they benefited from retaking the actual college science course. Hence, students passing an AP exam might well consider retaking introductory courses in college to more completely master the content, as many colleges and universities already require.

When we examined the value-added of taking AP courses, we needed to control for the academic abilities and experiences possessed by AP students prior to, or independent of, their AP course experiences. These characteristics contributed substantially to the students' performance in college science courses—and they also differed considerably from cohort to cohort. Therefore, we used a propensity-weighting approach to equalize the cohorts. After thus controlling for these student characteristics, passing an AP exam still boosted students' subsequent performance in introductory college courses in physics, chemistry, and biology. However, we found that students who take and fail their AP Biology exam or do not take the exam appear to have garnered no advantage when they later take a college biology course. In contrast, those students who take and fail their AP chemistry exam or do not take the exam still exhibit a considerable advantage when taking college chemistry. In physics, an AP exam score of 1 or 2 offered little evidence of any benefit derived from the AP coursework done by the students in high school, whereas those who passed the AP exam or chose not to take it had an advantage.

For high schools seeking to evaluate their AP science courses, a preponderance of AP exam scores of 1 or 2—outside of chemistry—may be interpreted to mean that the AP course in their school offered little or no benefit to students beyond regular or honors science courses. Schools in which the majority of students score in this range should examine whether exposure to AP-level rigor holds any benefits or whether more effort should be directed toward improving student background in other areas.

Advanced Placement is a popular program nationwide that is certainly of value to many students. Yet, on average, the advantage of passing an AP exam before taking the corresponding college course is not so substantial that it makes taking that course superfluous. AP courses may not be equal in academic rigor to introductory college and university courses in science. Colleges and universities should exercise caution in accepting a passing AP exam score in science as evidence that students have mastered introductory college course content. They may wish to use additional criteria in making their decision, such as the grade earned in the AP course and evidence of superior math or verbal ability, or they may choose to require a higher AP exam score before granting credit for introductory courses or placement into a higher level college course.

ACKNOWLEDGMENTS

We thank the people who helped make this large research project possible: Janice M. Earle, Finbarr C. Sloane, and Larry E. Suter of the National Science Foundation for their insight and support; James H. Wandersee, Joel J. Mintzes, Lillian C, McDermott, Eric Mazur, Dudley R. Herschbach, Brian Alters, and Jason Wiles of the FICSS advisory board for their guidance; and Nancy Cianchetta, Susan Matthews, Dan Record, and Tim Reed of our high school advisory board for their time and wisdom. This research has resulted from the tireless efforts of many on our research team: Michael Filisky, Hal Coyle, Cynthia Crockett, Bruce Ward, Judith Peritz, Annette Trenga, Freeman Deutsch, Nancy Cook, Zahra Hazari, Jaimie Miller, Marc Schwartz and graduate students Adam Maltese, Vanessa Wyss, John Loehr, and Kirsten Dexter. Matthew H. Schneps, Nancy Finkelstein, Alex Griswold, Tobias McElheny, Yael Bowman, and Alexia Prichard of our Science Media Group constructed our dissemination Web site (www.ficss.org). We also appreciate advice and interest from several colleagues in the field: Michael Neuschatz of the American Institute of Physics; William Lichten of Yale University; Trevor Packer of the College Board; Saul Geiser of the University of California at Berkeley; Paul Hickman of Northeastern University; William Fitzsimmons, Marlyn McGrath Lewis, Georgene Herschbach, and Rory Browne of Harvard University; and Kristin Klopfenstein of Texas Christian University. We are indebted to the professors at universities and colleges nationwide who felt that this project was worth contributing a piece of their valuable class time to administer our surveys and to their students for their willingness to answer our questions.

This work has been carried out under a grant from the Interagency Educational Research Initiative (NSF-REC 0115649). Any opinions, findings, and conclusions or recommendations expressed in this material are those of the authors and do not necessarily reflect the views of the National Science Foundation, the U.S. Department of Education, or the National Institutes of Health. This chapter draws from research by Sadler in Sadler and Tai (2007).

NOTES

1. Propensity score weighting is achieved by first carrying out a polytomous logistic regression of the cohort variable on other variables that appear relevant (e.g., parental education, community socioeconomic status, institutional type of high school, gender, race, etc.). This logistic regression results in a propensity score for each student (ranging from 0 to 1), indicating the student's probability of being in a particular cohort, based on his or her characteristics that were included as independent variables. Using these propensity scores, the subjects in different cohorts are then weighted to produce cohorts that all have similar group averages of the characteristics included in the logistic regression. For instance, in the propensity-matched sample, the "AP pass" cohort of students is very similar to the "regular" cohort, even though originally these two cohorts were rather different in terms of the characteristics that entered into the logistic regression. The propensity weighting carried out in this chapter follows the methodological approach described by Leslie and Thiebaud (2007), who also published sample code for the SAS statistical package that was modified and used in our study.

    As an indicator of how successful the propensity weighting was in making the cohorts similar to each other, we used analyses of variance (ANOVAs) for each of the independent variables to determine if there was any overall statistically significant difference between the cohorts. Whereas in the unweighted sample of the biology students, the cohorts differed in 8 of the 14 independent variables at the 0.05 significance level, the weighted sample contained no independent variable on which the cohorts differed significantly. Similarly, propensity weighting was able to reduce the number of significantly different variables from 13 (out of 14) to 1 for the chemistry students, and from 8 (out of 11) to zero for the physics students. This indicates that the propensity weighting method successfully equalized the cohorts to a high degree.

2. Whereas in ordinary regression the R^2 statistic—the proportion of outcome variation explained by the independent variables—is a convenient and intuitive measure of how well a particular model accounts for the dependent variable, the situation is more complicated with HLM, because here the total outcome variation is partitioned into several components. Statisticians still debate what measure should take the place of the R^2 statistic in HLM. We used a pseudo-R^2 statistic that is based on the total outcome variation (across all levels) and thus is closely analogous to the R^2 statistic in ordinary regression (Singer & Willett, 2003, pp. 102–103). One way of computing the R^2 statistic in ordinary regression is to square the sample correlation between the observed and the predicted values of the dependent variable, and we use this method to calculate the pseudo-R^2 statistic for our HLM models.

3. Our data have a three-level theoretical structure: students nested in classes nested in institutions. We examined whether a three-level HLM was necessary empirically and found that in biology and chemistry the class-level variance was not significant in a three-level HLM (student-class-institution). Hence, we report two-level models (student-institution) in table 7.2. In physics the three-level HLM contained no variance attributable to the school level. Hence, we report a two-level model (student-class) for physics in the table.

REFERENCES

Burdman, P. (2000). Extra credit, extra criticism. *Black Issues in Higher Education, 17*(18), 28–33.

Cohen, J. (1969) *Statistical power analysis for the behavioural sciences*. New York: Academic Press.

Cohen, J. (1988). Statistical power analysis for the behavioral sciences (2nd ed.). Hillsdale, NJ: Erlbaum.

College Board. (2004). *Interpreting and using AP grades*. New York.

Dodd, B., Fitzpatrick, R., & Jennings, J. (2002). *An investigation of the validity of AP grades of 3 and a comparison of AP and non-AP student groups*. New York: College Board.

Dorans, N. J., Lyu, C. F., Pommerich, M., & Houston, W. M. (1997). Concordance between ACT assessment and recentered SAT I sum scores. *College and University, 73*(2), 24–34.

Dougherty, C., Mellor, L., & Shuling, J. (2006). *The relationship between Advanced Placement and college graduation.* Austin, TX: National Center for Educational Accountability.

Geiser, S., & Santelices, V. (2004). *The role of Advanced Placement and honors courses in college admissions.* Center for Studies in Higher Education. http://repositories.cdlib.org/cshe/CSHE-4-04/

Klopfenstein, K., & Thomas, K. (2005). *The Advanced Placement performance advantage: Fact or fiction?* American Economic Association. http://www.aeaweb.org/annual_mtg_papers/2005/0108_1015_0302.pdf

Leslie, S., & Thiebaud, P. (2007). Using propensity scores to adjust for treatment selection bias. Paper presented at the SAS Global Forum. http://www2.sas.com/proceedings/forum2007/184-2007.pdf

Lichten, W. (2000). Whither Advanced Placement? *Education Policy Analysis Archives, 8*(29). http://epaa.asu.edu/epaa/v8n29.html

MacVicar, R. (1988). *Advanced Placement: Increasing efficiency in high school–university articulation.* Phoenix: Arizona Board of Regents. (ERIC Document Reproduction Service No. ED306835)

National Research Council. (2002). *Learning and understanding: Improving advanced study of mathematics and science in US high schools.* Committee on Programs for Advanced Study of Mathematics and Science in American High Schools. J. P. Gollub, M. W. Bertenthal, J. B. Labov, & P. C. Curtis Jr. (Eds.). Center for Education. Division of Behavioral and Social Sciences and Education. Washington, DC: National Academies Press.

Pushkin, D. (1995). The AP exam and the introductory college course. *The Physics Teacher, 33*(8), 532–535.

Rosenbaum, P. R., & Rubin, D. B. (1983). The central role of the propensity score in observational studies for causal effects. *Biometrika, 70*(1), 41–55

Sadler, P. M., & Tai, R. H. (2007). Advanced Placement exam scores as a predictor of performance in introductory college biology, chemistry, and physics courses. *Science Educator, 16*(1), 1–19.

Singer, J. D., & Willett, J. B. (2003). *Applied longitudinal data analysis.* New York: Oxford University Press.

Snyder, T. D., Dillow, S. A., & Hoffman, C. M. (2008). *Digest of education statistics.* Washington, DC: National Center for Educational Statistics.

Willingham, W., & Morris, M. (1986). *Four years later: A longitudinal study of Advanced Placement students in college.* New York: College Board.

CHAPTER 8

Persistence and Performance at a Four-Year University

The Relationship with Advanced Coursework During High School

William R. Duffy II

INTRODUCTION

Efforts to smooth the transition between high school and college have involved a variety of state, local, and private agencies (Bailey, Hughes, & Karp, 2002; National Commission on the High School Senior Year, 2001; Treat, 2002; Van de Water & Rainwater, 2001; WICHE, 2006). These efforts often consist of affording high school students the opportunity to do college-level coursework. In this chapter, I use the term *dual credit program* in an all-encompassing sense to cover a variety of high school and college courses. Some dual credit programs claim to have a positive impact on college persistence and performance (Burham & Hewitt, 1967; Casserly, 1986; Chatman & Smith, 1998; Dodd, Fitzpatrick, De Ayala, & Jennings, 2002; Lively, 1993; Lord, 2000; Willingham & Morris, 1986; Windham, 1997). In this analysis, I examine this claim for two types of dual credit programs: credit-based college courses programs that enable high school students to simultaneously receive both college and high school credit by completing a single college course, and examination-based high school courses that enable high school students to receive both high school credit (e.g., AP or IB courses) and, in some cases, college credit by completing an exam. This study focuses specifically on one type of examination-based high school courses, the College Board's AP Program.

The preponderance of dual credit research focuses on explaining, promoting, reviewing, and evaluating programs, which has resulted in a dearth of articles and publications in this emerging field (Andrews, 2000, 2001; Bailey & Karp, 2003; Clark, 2001; Johnstone & Del Genio, 2001; McMannon, 2000; NCES, 2005a, 2005b; WICHE, 2006). In the research that does exist, dual credit students typically exceed persistence and performance norms when compared to non–dual credit students in college. This characteristic is not entirely surprising, since the majority of students who participate in dual credit programs are academically above average. The preentry college characteristics of dual credit students typically reflect above-average ACT/SAT scores, high school GPA, and high school class ranking (Chatman & Smith, 1998; Delicath, 1999; Lord Fairfax Community College, 1995; Nelson, 1997; Rothschild, 1999; Viadaro, 2000; Willingham & Morris, 1986; Windham, 1996).

While the demand for AP and credit-based college course programs continues to grow at a rapid rate, controversy still surrounds them. In a nationwide survey of 451 postsecondary institutions, nearly one-third of the respondents indicated that they were suspicious of college credits earned in high school, and many refused to grant credit for those courses (Cambra, 2000; Clark, 2001; Flores, 2002; Johnstone & Del Genio, 2001; McMannon, 2000; Reisberg, 1998).

The potential impact and influence of these programs on all stakeholders cannot be overstated. During the 2002–2003 school year, there were approximately 1.8 million AP enrollments in high schools and an estimated 1.2 million credit-based college course high school enrollments (NCES, 2005b). Approximately 71 percent of public high schools offered courses for dual credit, and 57 percent of all Title IV degree-granting institutions had high school students taking courses for college credit (NCES, 2005a, 2005b). Considering current federal and state policies pertaining to dual credit (Karp, Bailey, Hughes, & Fermin, 2004), a major investment of public funding (Lively, 1993), and revenue/tuition, as well as the potential impact on student learning, recruitment, enrollment, and retention, the question becomes, Why has more serious attention not been devoted to this topic? Part of the problem may come from the tremendous growth of dual credit enrollment in high schools being too recent a phenomenon for researchers to have caught up with it. Additionally, varying terminology at all levels hinders the proper collection and analysis of data for in-depth research (Clark, 2001; Fincher-Ford, 1997; Hoffman, 2005; Johnstone & Del Genio, 2001; McMannon, 2000).

This chapter investigates whether significant differences exist in persistence and performance among students attending a four-year university who have completed AP courses, credit-based college courses, and regular college courses , while controlling for pre-entry attributes. For the purposes of this analysis, I chose to operationalize persistence and performance in the following manner. Persistence is measured in two ways: (1) by subsequent fall reenrollment as sophomores by first-time, full-time freshman students and (2) by students who attained a degree within five years. Performance is gauged by (1) freshman-year GPA and (2) graduation GPA.

The chapter also seeks to clarify terminology pertaining to dual credit and thus establish a framework for future research in the field. No standard set of terms has yet evolved. A testament to the terminological diversity is that other chapters in the present volume (e.g., Klopfenstein) use *dual credit* in a more restrictive sense, meaning only what I call credit-based college courses.

TERMINOLOGY AND DEFINITIONS

A review of the literature on dual credit reveals that currently there does not exist a common set of terminology to describe various aspects of these programs, with two exceptions: the AP Program (College Board, n.d.) and the IB program (IBO, n.d.). Despite repeated recommendations to standardize terminology, ambiguity remains. In the 2006 comprehensive dual credit study conducted by the Western Interstate Commission for Higher Education (WICHE, 2006), the first recommendation was a familiar one: "A national effort is needed to establish consistency in collecting, analyzing, and reporting data" (p. vii).

Yet researchers continue to use a variety of conflicting terminologies to describe dual credit. The most frequently used terms include: *accelerated learning programs* (WICHE, 2006), *college-level learning in high schools* (Johnstone & Del Genio, 2001), *credit-based transition programs* (Bailey & Karp, 2003; Plucker, Chien, & Zaman, 2006), *dual enrollment* (Hoffman, 2005; Hoffman & Robbins, 2005; NCES, 2005a), *concurrent enrollment* (NACEP, n.d.), *dual credit* (Clark, 2001; McMannon, 2000; NCES, 2005b), and *joint enrollment,* a term primarily used in Georgia.

Throughout the literature, depending on the agency conducting a given study, similar terms may have different definitions and different terms may have similar definitions. For example, the National Alliance for Concurrent Enrollment Partnerships utilizes the term *concurrent enrollment* and defines it as "high school instructors [who] teach the college courses during the normal school day" (NACEP, n.d.). NACEP restricts this definition to colleges and universities that offer courses taught only in the high school facility by college-approved high school teachers.

In contrast, the National Center for Education Statistics (NCES) uses the following definitions from two comprehensive national surveys:

1. Dual credit is "a course or program where high school students can earn both high school and postsecondary credits for the same course. Dual credit courses could be located on the high school campus or the campus of a postsecondary institution, or taught through distance education." (2005b, p. 1)
2. Dual enrollment is "an organized system with special guidelines that allows high school students to take college level courses . . . Credit for courses may be earned at both the high school and college level simultaneously or only at the college level . . . Courses may be taught on a college campus, on a high school campus, or at some other location." (2005a, p. B3).

Surprisingly, the NCES terminology also differs within its own organization, referring to dual credit as both *dual credit* and *dual enrollment*. Additionally, the NCES definitions of dual credit are far more inclusive in comparison to those of the NACEP, which restricts the definition of dual credit programs by instructor and physical location of the course.

A review of the dual credit literature indicates that the primary intent of dual credit programs is the simultaneous attainment of both high school and college academic credit, regardless of location, instructor, or delivery medium—a very simple concept for all stakeholders to understand. For the purposes of this study, dual credit is defined as courses offered during high school that enable high school students to receive simultaneous credit toward both high school graduation and postsecondary education, regardless of delivery medium, instructor, or location. Using this definition, I investigate the following research questions:

*   When controlling for preentry attributes, are there significant differences in first-year college persistence among AP, credit-based college

course, and regular college course students (who took neither AP nor credit-based college courses)?

- When controlling for preentry attributes, are there significant differences in degree completion within five years among AP, credit-based college course, and regular college course students?

- When controlling for preentry attributes, are there significant differences in first-year college cumulative GPA among AP, credit-based college course, and regular college course students?

- When controlling for preentry attributes, are there significant differences in degree cumulative GPAs among AP, credit-based college course, and regular college course students?

EXISTING LITERATURE

Adelman (1999, 2006) found that the strongest predictor for completing a bachelor's degree was the intensity and quality of the student's high school curriculum. Numerous studies on dual credit cite Adelman's studies as strong justification for establishing dual credit programs in high schools (Bailey & Karp, 2003; Hoffman, 2003; WICHE, 2006). Colleges frequently establish credit-based college course policies and procedures within their institutions and then offer these courses in local or regional high schools (ECS, 2006). Two national studies indicated that during the 2002–2003 school year, forty-two states had policies pertaining to credit-based college course programs, 71 percent of public high schools offered courses for college credit, and there were approximately 1.2 million high school students enrolled in credit-based college courses (ECS, 2006; NCES, 2005b). According to the ECS study, many of these same states provide minimal restrictions or guidelines for credit-based college course programs.

Bailey, Hughes, and Karp (2002) suggest that credit-based college course programs have the potential to expand access, success, and academic rigor from the narrow base of only higher achieving students to a much wider range of students, especially those from minority and low-income groups. In 2004 Florida showed a significant increase in minority student participation in community college credit-based college course programs (referred to as dual enrollment), with an increase of 49 percent for black students and 67 percent for Hispanic students. The students' subsequent college enrollment also reflected a substantial difference, with 69.7 percent of black credit-based college course students enrolling in colleges, while only 44.9 percent of the total black student population enrolled, and with 68.5 percent of Hispanic credit-based college course students enrolling, while only 54.3 percent of the total Hispanic student population enrolled (Florida Department of Education, 2004).

CONCERNS ABOUT AP AND CREDIT-BASED COLLEGE COURSE PROGRAMS

Despite their continued growth, dual credit programs have generated concerns and criticisms about college learning in high school from both inside and outside higher education that usually center around two fundamental issues:

1. *Turf.* Who should be entitled to say what standards should be used to evaluate college-level learning, and to what degree would these answers be corrupted by self-interest?
2. *Credibility.* Is the learning truly at the college level, and what can this mean given the enormous range of academic standards in U.S. higher education (Johnstone & Del Genio, 2001, p. 11)?

When it comes to turf issues, the potential for stakeholder bias is great. An AP student gaining credit for ten freshman-level college courses at Stanford will have paid less than $1,000 to take all ten AP exams, saving approximately $25,000 in tuition (forty-five quarter units is the maximum allowed for entering freshmen; twelve quarter units may be equivalent to four three-credit hour courses). Interestingly, Stanford University (n.d.) accepts AP credit but not credit-based college course credit.

Other issues pertaining to AP include access, availability of these programs to the average/lower ability groups, and high school scheduling (Cocking, 1990; Gamoran, 1992; Santoli, 2002). AP courses are not available in many high schools, creating a disadvantage for minority and low-income high school students applying to colleges that ascribe added value to AP courses in the admissions process (see Sadler, this volume). This perceived disparity resulted in lawsuits in California (Dupuis, 1999; Santoli, 2002). Growing concerns have also resulted from block scheduling in high schools, which often require fall semester AP students to wait four to five months to take AP exams, since the exams are only administered in the spring semester (Cocking, 1990; Hansen, Gutman, & Smith, 2000; Mendels, 1999; Santoli, 2002).

In addition, consistency in standards has become a significant concern, since many decisions about AP course content are determined at the high school level. This issue drew national attention when Harvard University announced it would award academic credit only for AP exam scores of a 5, expressing concern over the lack of academic preparedness of Harvard students who had received academic credit with an AP exam score of 4 and who subsequently performed well below the class norm in those subject areas (Lewin, 2002). Other colleges across the country are raising similar concerns (Lichten, 2000; Russo, 2000). The National Research Council released a report criticizing the high school AP courses in math and science, which it characterized as relying too much on rote memorization of facts with minimal emphasis on problem solving and discussion (Flores, 2002).

Research on AP programs and their impact on college persistence and performance, while controlling for student preentry attributes, remains uncertain. Bergeson (1968) found that AP exam scores were not related to college grades. Geiser and Santelices (2004) also found that AP and honors courses taken in high school had minimal or no relationship to college performance. Additionally, Klopfenstein and Thomas (2005) found that when controlling for student preentry attributes, no significant difference existed between AP students and non-AP students in college persistence and performance. The researchers asserted that AP students are generally no more likely to persist to the second year of college or to have higher first semester GPAs than non-AP students: "the effectiveness of the AP Program at improving early college outcomes has not been rigorously tested. Research from the College Board and ETS is fundamentally flawed because it fails to account for the nature of the typical AP student, who is particularly bright and motivated and likely to experience positive college outcomes even in the absence of AP experience" (Klopfenstein & Thomas, 2005, p. 2).

With the ongoing concerns over AP, credit-based college course programs have become an increasingly popular option for high school students, parents, faculty, and administrators. However, there have been growing concerns related to credit-based college course program standards, policies, program quality, learning, the benefits of high school students taking college courses, and the increasing number of students entering college with previously earned college credits. Most state and college representatives responding to a national survey painted a bleak picture of the state of evaluations for credit-based college course programs. Specifically, the most frequently expressed concerns were academic quality, transferability of grades, faculty credentials, course experience for students, student maturity, state funding, and the suspected negative impact credit-based college courses might have on a student's academic performance and social integration after entering college (Clark, 2001).

In spite of the popularity and rapid growth of dual credit programs, Bailey and Karp (2003) reviewed forty-five articles and reports on dual credit and found little or no evidence that linked dual credit enrollment to students' academic or college success. Their research found that most studies failed to take into account and control for college students' preentry attributes and achievements. Most research on this topic has focused on policies and trends (Hoffman, 2005; NCES 2005a, 2005b) and failed to validate the effectiveness of dual credit as it relates to persistence and performance outcomes in college.

CORRELATES OF COLLEGE STUDENTS' PERSISTENCE AND PERFORMANCE

According to Tinto (2006), "Student retention is one of the most widely studied areas in higher education . . . that now spans more than four decades" (p. 1). Yet, in the majority of studies conducted on dual credit, little reference is made to the body of existing research on persistence and performance (Bailey & Karp, 2003; Barth, 2003; Clark, 2001; ECS, 2004; Hoffman & Robbins, 2005; Johnstone & Del Genio, 2001; McMannon, 2000; Plucker et al., 2006; WICHE, 2006).

Tinto's (1993) longitudinal model of institutional departure (figure 8.1), intended for single-institution application, starts with the fact that students enter college with preentry attributes. It is well documented that preentry attributes directly and indirectly influence students' initial commitments as well as college persistence and degree attainment (Braxton, Sullivan, & Johnson, 1997; Ethington, 1990; Pantages & Creedon, 1978; Pascarella, Smart, & Ethington, 1986; Pascarella & Terenzini, 1983). In addition, the study of the preentry attributes, or background characteristics, within Tinto's model is useful for better understanding how students adjust to college (Hurtado, 2000). Tinto (1993) asserted that "improved pre-entry information aimed at the needs of future students can be an effective tool in reducing, over the long run, student departure from

FIGURE 8.1 Tinto's model of institutional departure

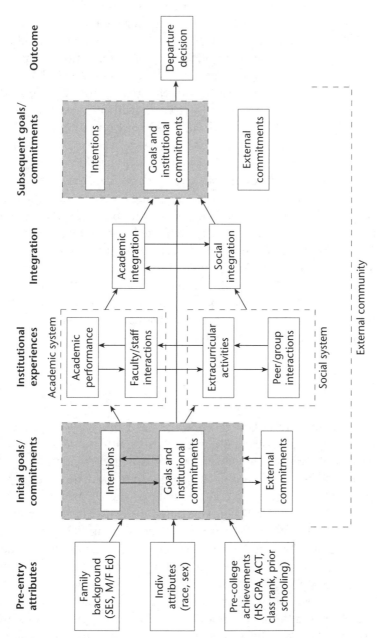

Source: Tinto (1993, p. 114).

institutions of higher education" (p. 156). The theory hypothesizes that students' preentry attributes influence their commitments to both an institution and to the goal of graduation from college. Once students arrive at an institution, their initial commitments affect their levels of academic and social integration, or lack thereof, which ultimately impacts their decisions to remain at any given institution. The greater the social and academic integration within the institution, the greater the likelihood the individual will remain committed to that institution, and the greater the likelihood of goal attainment through degree completion.

In predicting academic performance in college, the two most important preentry attributes are high school GPA and standardized test scores. Note that high school grades are the strongest predictor of degree completion and that they correlate with college grades twice as strongly as aptitude tests do (Astin, 2001). Thus, the student's high school GPA has long been considered the strongest preentry attribute in predicting postsecondary persistence, undergraduate GPA, and degree completion (Astin, 2001; Pantages & Creedon, 1978; Tinto, 1993). It has also been noted that the results of persistence studies showing lower correlations of these outcomes with high school GPA might likely be attributed to the duration of the particular study and to the intentions of the individuals (e.g., voluntary versus involuntary dropout) (Pantages & Creedon, 1978; Tinto, 1993).

METHOD

Sample

The sample for this study was taken from the University of Tennessee at Martin (UTM), a four-year public university with moderate selectivity and a Carnegie Master's M classification (Carnegie Foundation for the Advancement of Teaching, n.d.). The study compared three groups of participants: (1) regular college course students, the control group, who received no UTM credit for either AP or credit-based college courses; (2) AP students, who received UTM credit for AP courses; and (3) credit-based college course students, who received UTM credit for credit-based college courses on entering UTM. A total of 6,033 first-time, full-time freshmen entered UTM (5,398 regular college course students, 237 AP students, and 398 credit-based college course students) from fall 2000 through fall 2006. A frequency analysis on the 6,033 participants determined that 4,713 participants had valid values recorded in the university database for all study variables. This process further reduced the group sample sizes to 4,227 regular college course students, 181 AP, and 305 credit-based college course-takers. From the 4,227 regular college course control group, 300 participants were randomly selected to establish reasonably similar sample group sizes for the analyses described later in this study. Therefore, the total number of participants used for this study was 786: 300 regular college course participants, 181 AP participants, and 305 credit-based college course participants.

Variables Included in the Analysis

The analytical approach I selected for this study included independent variables falling into four categories:

1. Family income and mother and father's education combined into a single socioeconomic (SES) composite variable representing family background (SESscale) (Adelman, 2006; Astin, 1975; Attinasi, 1992; Pantages & Creedon, 1978; Pascarella & Terenzini, 1991; Tinto, 1987, 1993).[1]

2. ACT composite score, high school GPA, and high school class rank were also combined into a single composite variable, high school academic achievement (ACHscale) (Astin, 2001; Pantages & Creedon, 1978; Tinto, 1987, 1993). ACH was computed using the same procedure as SES.

3. Personal attribute variables are represented by gender and race (Astin, 2001; Pantages & Creedon, 1978; Pascarella & Terenzini, 1991; Schwartz & Washington, 2002; Tinto, 1993).

4. Student type (Stutyp) is defined by participation or nonparticipation in dual credit programs (Burham & Hewitt, 1967; Casserly, 1986; Dodd et al., 2002; Morgan & Crone, 1993; Morgan & Ramist, 1998; Santoli, 2002; Willingham & Morris, 1986).

I selected the following four variables as the outcomes: first- year persistence, degree completion within five years, first-year cumulative GPA, and final degree cumulative GPA. Table 8.1 provides a detailed listing of each variable and its definition and coding.

Analysis

I used multiple linear regression analysis and applied relative weights to account for variations in measurements within all the independent and

TABLE 8.1   Listing of initial variables, definitions, and coding

Independent variables	
Income	Family combined income (Income); original values
Mother's education	Mother's education (MOed): less than high school = 1; high school diploma = 2; college degree = 3; unknown (declared as missing value) = 4
Father's education	Father's education (FAed): less than high school = 1; high school diploma = 2; college degree = 3; unknown (declared as missing value) = 4
ACT	Composite of ACT score (ACT)
HS GPA	High school grade point average (HS GPA): scale of 4.0 (original values)
HS rank	High school class rank (HSrank): scale of 100 (original values)
Gender	Gender (Gen): male = 1; female = 2
Race	Race: white = 1; black = 2; other = 3 (Asian, Alaskan, Hispanic, Indian)
Student type (Stutyp)	Regular (control): No UTM credit for AP/credit-based college courses = 1
	AP: UTM credit for AP course = 2
	Credit-based: UTM credit for credit-based college course = 3
Dependent variables	
Persist1	Persistence after one year: no = 0; yes = 1
Degree5	Degree completion within five years or less: no = 0; yes = 1
GPA1st	Cumulative GPA after one year: scale of 4.0; original values
DegGPA	Degree cumulative GPA: scale of 4.0; original values

dependent variables. In addition, I performed two regression analyses for each research question for the purpose of comparing student types, resulting in four pairs of regression analyses (α-level = 0.05). I used the coefficient of determination to examine the proportion of variance explained by each variable within the eight regression models, and the Beta coefficients provide information on the relative effect of each independent variable within each model.

I included students who voluntarily withdrew from UTM between fall 1999 and fall 2006 and labeled them *nonpersisters*. I did not include involuntary dropouts (n=15) because persistence research needs to discriminate between voluntary and involuntary withdrawals (Astin, 1975; Bonham & Luckie, 1993; Grosset, 1993). Therefore, students who departed UTM while on academic probation or academic suspension were labeled *involuntary dropouts* and were not included in the study.

RESULTS

Descriptive Statistics: Representativeness of the Control Group

Tables 8.2 and 8.3 display the simple descriptive statistics. An examination of the data reveals some interesting comparisons.

- The control group (regular course students) is very similar to the general population.
- There are numerous and substantial differences between the control group (regular college course) and both the AP group and the credit-based college course group.

Any measurable differences between the control group and both the total sample and the total population can be explained by the higher values related to the AP, and the credit-based college course groups that are part of the total sample.

Persistence and Performance: Regression Analysis Results

With respect to persistence (tables 8.4 and 8.5), the achievement composite variable (ACHscale) was the only significant predictor, and there were no significant differences in first-year persistence or degree attainment between any of the student types (regular college course, AP, and credit-based college course) when preentry attributes were controlled.

The regression analysis results were very similar with respect to performance (tables 8.6 and 8.7) with the achievement composite variable again being the only significant predictor. There were no significant differences in first-year college GPAs or degree attainment in five years in any of the student types when preentry attributes were controlled.

While these associations are consistent through all the analyses carried out in this study, studies of this type are limited to identifying significant differences among groups. They cannot determine the cause of the differences, and they also do not consider the nature and context of learning experiences. Moreover, the number of AP/credit-based college courses taken by each student and the number of hours taken to complete a

TABLE 8.2 Descriptive statistics: Groups, sample, population (categorical variables)

Variable	Control regular N = 300	AP N = 181	Credit-based N = 305	Total sample N = 786	Total population N = 6,033
Female	172 (57.3)	122 (67.4)	191 (62.6)	485 (61.7)	3,393 (56.2)
Male	128 (42.7)	59 (32.6)	114 (37.4)	301 (38.3)	2,640 (43.8)
White	249 (83)	168 (92.8)	299 (98)	716 (91.1)	4,922 (81.6)
Black	46 (15.3)	11 (6)	3 (1)	60 (7.6)	991 (16.4)
Other	5 (1.7)	2 (1.2)	3 (1)	10 (1.3)	120 (2)
White female	143 (47.7)	110 (60.8)	186 (61)	439 (55.9)	2,701 (44.8)
White male	106 (35.2)	58 (19.3)	113 (37.5)	277 (35.2)	2,221 (36.8)
Black female	26 (5.4)	10 (5.5)	3 (1)	39 (4.9)	622 (10.3)
Black male	20 (6.6)	1 (3)	0 (0)	21 (2.7)	369 (6.1)
Persist first year	223 (74.3)	158 (87.3)	256 (83.9)	637 (81)	4,258 (70.6)
Degree in five years	28 (9.3)	28 (15.5)	46 (15.1)	102 (13)	767 (12.7)

Note: Values in parentheses represent the total percentage of the respective group or population; N is the number of subjects in a sample (or in the total population).

degree are additional factors—missing from this analysis—that might be expected to influence persistence and performance outcomes. It also may be important to look at AP and credit-based college course experiences and outcomes not only in general, as in this study, but to disaggregate dual credit experiences and outcomes to the level of specific disciplines. Finally, this study derived its data from a single institution, and therefore conclusions should be drawn with caution when applying the results to other settings.

TABLE 8.3   Means and standard deviations (continuous variables)

Variable	Control regular N = 300	AP N = 181	Credit-based N = 305	Total sample N = 786	Total population N = 6,033
Income	$58,766 ($35,012)	$73,816 ($44,631)	$66,131 ($46,861)	$65,089 ($42,513)	$45,954 ($48,414)
Mother's education (in years)	2.40 (.55)	2.53 (.52)	2.45 (.55)	2.45 (.55)	2.38 (.56)
Father's education (in years)	2.30 (.55)	2.47 (.55)	2.36 (.57)	2.36 (.56)	2.28 (.57)
ACT	21.49 (3.52)	27.4 (2.88)	23.85 (3.40)	23.58 (4.0)	21.53 (3.70)
High school GPA	3.25 (.49)	3.79 (.29)	3.62 (.31)	3.52 (.44)	3.26 (.52)
High school rank (percentile)	68.72 (19.95)	89.31 (12.34)	85.70 (11.77)	79.40 (18.25)	69.90 (21.07)
First-year GPA	2.77 (.65)	3.44 (.54)	3.16 (.58)	3.09 (.64)	2.84 (.66)
Degree GPA	2.50 (.94)	3.35 (.63)	3.08 (.72)	2.92 (.87)	2.57 (.94)

Note: Values in parentheses represent standard deviations; N is the number of subjects in a sample (or in the total population).

DISCUSSION

This study confirms findings from past dual credit research about the pre-college characteristics of AP and credit-based college course participants (Bailey & Karp, 2003; Chatman & Smith, 1998; Windham, 1997). The AP and credit-based college course sample groups had much higher mean values for nearly every independent and dependent variable when compared to the control group (regular course) and the total population. The differences were dramatic with the exception of parents' education and degree attainment.

Also of interest are comparisons of the descriptive statistics about first-year persistence, first-year GPA, and degree GPA. In each comparison, the

TABLE 8.4   Regression models: First-year persistence

Model 1	AP vs. credit-based			AP vs. regular		
(persist1)	B	S.E.	ß	B	S.E.	ß
Constant	.738 ***	.074		.790 ***	.072	
Gender	.012	.032	.015	.012	.032	.015
Race	.025	.045	.023	.025	.045	.023
SES scale	.020	.023	.034	.020	.023	.034
ACH scale	.069 **	.022	.151	.069 **	.022	.151
AP	.048	.051	.048	−.004	.047	−.004
Credit-based	.052	.039	.063			
Regular				−.052	.039	−.066

Notes: * p < 0.05; ** p < 0.01; *** p < 0.001.
For AP versus credit-based, R^2 =.030; for AP versus regular, R^2 =.030.

TABLE 8.5   Regression models: Degree attainment in five years

Model 1	AP vs. credit-based			AP vs. regular		
(persist1)	B	S.E.	ß	B	S.E.	ß
Constant	.064	.059		.053	.058	
Gender	.017	.026	.027	.017	.026	.027
Race	.023	.036	.026	.023	.036	.026
SES scale	−.020	.018	−.045	−.020	.018	−.045
ACH scale	.046 **	.018	.129	.046 **	.018	.129
AP	−.027	.040	−.035	-.016	.037	-.021
Credit-based	−.011	.031	−.017			
Regular				.011	.031	.018

Notes: * p < 0.05; ** p < 0.01; *** p < 0.001.
For AP versus credit-based, R^2 =.005; for AP versus regular, R^2 =.005.

might find a significant correlation between persistence and performance outcomes and high school abilities and performance, the correlation is typically less than 0.50 and usually accounts for only a relatively small percentage of the variance in students' persistence and performance college outcomes.

NOTES

1. I computed this composite using z-scores with the outliers removed to ensure normality and greater reliability for each composite variable scale. I verified Cronbach's alpha for each composite variable to ensure internal consistency of the composite variable. And I reviewed alpha coefficients for each composite variable scale to ensure the highest reliability and internal consistency was achieved for each composite variable scale.

REFERENCES

Adelman, C. (1999). *Answers in the tool box: Academic intensity, attendance patterns, and bachelor's degree attainment.* Washington, DC: U.S. Department of Education. http://ed.gov/pubs/Toolbox/toolbox.html

Adelman, C. (2006). *The toolbox revisited: Paths to degree completion from high school through college.* U.S. Department of Education. http://www.ed.gov/rschstat/research/pubs/toolboxrevisit/index.html

Andrews, H. A. (2000). Lessons learned from current state and national dual credit programs. *New Directions for Community Colleges, 111,* 31–39.

Andrews, H. A. (2001). *The dual credit phenomenon! Challenging secondary school students across 50 states.* Oklahoma: New Forums Press.

Astin, A. W. (1975). *Preventing students from dropping out.* San Francisco: Jossey-Bass.

Astin, A. W. (1982). *Minorities in American higher education.* San Francisco: Jossey-Bass.

Astin, A. W. (2001). *What matters in college? Four critical years revisited.* San Francisco: Jossey-Bass.

Attinasi, L. C., Jr. (1992). Rethinking the study of outcomes of college attendance. *Journal of College Student Development, 33,* 61–70.

Bailey, T., Hughes, K., & Karp, M. (2002). *What role can dual enrollment programs play in easing the transition between high school and postsecondary education?* Washington, DC: U.S. Department of Education, Office of Vocational and Adult Education.

Bailey, T., & Karp, M. (2003) *Promoting college access and success: A review of credit-based transition programs.* Washington, DC: U.S. Department of Education, Office of Adult and Vocational Education.

Barth, P. (2003). A common core curriculum for the new century. *The Education Trust—Thinking K–16, 7*(1), 3–25.

Bergeson, J. B. (1968). An unanswered question about the advanced placement program: Do examination questions predict grades? *Journal of Higher Education, 39*(2), 101–104.

Bonham, L., & Luckie, J. A. (1993). Community college retention: Differentiating among stopouts, dropouts, and opouts. *Community College Journal of Research and Practice, 17*, 543–554.

Braxton, J. M., Sullivan, A. V. S., & Johnson, R. M., Jr. (1997). Appraising Tinto's theory of college student departure. In J. C. Smart, (Ed.), *Higher education: Handbook of theory and research* (pp. 107–164). New York: Agathon Press.

Burham, P. S., & Hewitt, B. A. (1967). Study of advanced placement examination scores of the college entrance examination board. New Haven, CT: Yale University Press.

Cambra, R. E. (2000). *A survey of dual-enrollment practices in higher education in the United States* (Dual Credit Study Technical Report No. 3). Seattle, WA: Institute for Educational Inquiry.

Carnegie Foundation for the Advancement of Teaching. (n.d.) http:// classifications.carnegiefoundation.org/lookup_listings/view_institution.php? unit_id=221768&start_page=institution.php&clq={%22first_letter%22% 3A%22U%22}

Casserly, P. L. (1986). *Advanced placement revisited.* New York: College Entrance Examination Board. (ERIC Document Reproduction Service No. ED 278719)

Chatman, S., & Smith, K. (1998). *Dual credit preparation for further study in foreign languages. National Association of Secondary School Principals (NASSP) Bulletin, 82*(597), 99–107.

Chickering, A. W., & Schlossberg, N. K. (1995). *Getting the most out of college.* Boston: Allyn and Bacon.

Clark, R. W. (2001). *Dual-credit: A report of programs and policies that offer high school students college credits.* Seattle: The Pew Charitable Trusts, Institute for Educational Inquiry.

Cocking, D. J. (1990). Don't throw the baby out with the bath water. *Gifted Child Today, 13*(3), 13–15.

CollegeBoard.(n.d.). APcentral.http://www.collegeboard.com/student/testing/ ap/about.html

Delicath, T. A. (1999). *The influence of advanced college credit on college students' integration and goal attainment: A longitudinal study.* Unpublished doctoral dissertation, Saint Louis University, 1998.

Dodd, B. G., Fitzpatrick, S. J., De Ayala, R. J., & Jennings, J. A. (2002). *An investigation of the validity of AP grades of 3 and a comparison of AP and non-AP student groups* (College Board Research Report No. 2002-9). New York: College Entrance Examination Board.

Dupuis, J. (1999). California lawsuit notes unequal access to AP courses. *Rethinking Schools Online, 14*(1). http://www.rethinkingschools.org/archive/14_01/caap141.shtml

Education Commission of the States [ECS]. (2004). *Dual/concurrent enrollment.* http://ecs.org/html/IssueSection.asp?issueid=214&s=Quick+Facts

Education Commission of the States. (2006). *Statenote.* http://www.ecs.org/clearinghouse/67/87/6787.htm

Eimers, M. T., & Mullen, R. (2003). *Dual credit and Advanced Placement: Do they help prepare students for success in college?* Paper presented at the 43rd annual Association of Institutional Research (AIR) Conference, Tampa, FL.

Ethington, C. A. (1990). A psychological model of student persistence. *Research in Higher Education, 31*(3), 279–293.

Fincher-Ford, M. (1997). *High school students earning college credit: A guide to creating dual-credit programs.* Thousand Oaks, CA: Corwin Press.

Flores, C. (2002, February 22). Harvard U. raises standards for advanced-placement credit. *The Chronicle of Higher Education.*

Florida Department of Education. (2004). *Dual enrollment students are more likely to enroll in postsecondary education.* Fast Fact No. 79. http://www.fldoe.org/news/2004/2004_03_10/DualEnrollStudy.pdf

Gamoran, A. (1992). Is ability grouping equitable? *Educational Leadership, 50*(2), 11–17.

Geiser, S., & Santelices, V. (2004). *The role of advanced placement and honors courses in college admissions.* Berkley, CA: Center for Studies in Higher Education.

Grosset, J. M. (1993). A profile of community college stop-outs. *Community College Review, 20*(4), 51–58.

Gurule, J. M. (1996). *A study of high school to community college dual enrollment for underprepared/moderate student achievers.* Unpublished doctoral dissertation, Arizona State University.

Hansen, D., Gutman, M., & Smith, J. (2000). Scheduling AP classes in a 2×4 block schedule. *Phi Delta Kappan, 82*(3), 209–211.

Hoffman, N. (2003). College credit in high school: Increasing college attainment rates for underrepresented students. *Change, 35*(4), 43–48.

Hoffman, N. (2005, April). Add and subtract: Dual enrollment as a state strategy to increase postsecondary success for underrepresented students. *Jobs for the Future—Creating Strategies for Educational and Economic Opportunities.* http://www.jff.org/sites/default/files/Addsubtract.pdf

Hoffman, N., & Robbins, A. (2005, June). Head start on college: Dual enrollment strategies in New England 2004–2005. *Jobs for the Future—Creating
Strategies for Educational and Economic Opportunities.* http://www.jff.org/
sites/default/files/HeadStartOnCollege.pdf

Hurtado, S. (2000). The campus racial climate. In C. Turner, M. Garcia, A.
Nora, & L. I. Rendon (Eds.), *Racial and ethnic diversity in higher education*
(pp. 485–506). Needham Heights, MA: Simon & Schuster Custom.

International Baccalaureate Organization [IBO]. (n.d.). http://www.ibo.org/
facts/fastfacts/index.cfm

Johnstone, D. B., & Del Genio, B. (2001). *College-level learning in high school:
Purposes, policies, and practical implications.* Washington, DC: Association
of American Colleges and Universities.

Karp, M., Bailey, T. R., Hughes, K. L., & Fermin, B. J. (2004). *State dual enrollment policies: Addressing access and quality.* Washington, DC: U.S. Department of Education, Office of Adult and Vocational Education.

Klopfenstein, K., & Thomas, K. (2005). *The link between advanced placement
experience and college success: Fact or fiction?* Dallas: Texas Schools Project.
http://www.aeaweb.org/annual_mtg_papers/2005/0108_1015_0302.pdf

Lewin, T. (2002, February 22). Harvard to require top score to earn advanced
placement. *The New York Times.*

Lichten, W. (2000, June). Whither advanced placement? *Education Policy
Analysis Archives, 8* (29). http://epaa.asu.edu/epaa/v8n29.html

Lively, K. (1993, May 26). More states encourage advanced-placement courses
for college credit: Saving money is one goal. *The Chronicle of Higher Education, 39,* A21–A22.

Lord, M. (2000). The honors advantage AP and IB classes give applicants a leg
up. *U.S. News and World Report, 129*(10), 101.

Lord Fairfax Community College. (1995, September). 1995 Assessment report submitted to Virginia Community College System and State Council for Higher Education. (ERIC Document Reproduction Service No.
ED386243)

McMannon, T. J. (2000). *Dual credit: A review of the literature* (Dual Credit Study
Technical Report No. 1). Seattle, WA: Institute for Educational Inquiry.

Mendels, P. (1999, April 28). Advanced placement courses offered online. *The
New York Times* [Electronic version], 1–5. http://nytimes.com/library/
tech/99/04/cyber/education/28education.html

Morgan, R., & Crone, C. (1993). *Advanced placement examinees at the University of California: An examination of the freshman year courses and grades
of examinees in biology, calculus, and chemistry* (Statistical Report 93-210).
Princeton, NJ: Educational Testing Service.

Morgan, R., & Ramist, L. (1998). *Advanced placement students in college: An investigation of course grades at 21 colleges.* Princeton, NJ: Educational Testing Service.

National Alliance of Concurrent Enrollment Partnerships [NACEP]. (n.d.). http://www.nacep.org/pdfs/NACEP_Standards1.pdf

National Center for Education Statistics [NCES]. (2005a). *Dual enrollment of high school students at postsecondary institutions: 2002–03* (National Center for Education Statistics, Statistical Analysis Report 2005-008). Washington, DC: U.S. Department of Education, Office of Educational Research and Improvement.

National Center for Education Statistics [NCES]. (2005b). *Dual credit and exam-based courses in U.S. public high schools: 2002–03* (National Center for Education Statistics, Statistical Analysis Report 2005-009). Washington, DC: U.S. Department of Education, Office of Educational Research and Improvement.

National Commission on the High School Senior Year. (2001, January). *The lost opportunity of senior year: Finding a better way* [Preliminary report]. http://commissiononthesenioryear.org

Nelson, S. A. (1997, April). The dilemmas of dual-credit. *Texas Community College Teachers Association Messenger 28,* np. (ERIC Document Reproduction Service No. ED413976)

Nitzke, J. E. (2002). *A longitudinal study of dual credit enrollment of high school students as an accelerator for degree completion.* Unpublished doctoral dissertation, Iowa State University.

Pantages, T. J., & Creeden, C. F. (1978). Studies of college attrition: 1950–1975. *Review of Educational Research, 48*(1), 49–101.

Pascarella, E. T., Smart, J. C., & Ethington, C. A. (1986). Long-term persistence of two-year college students. *Research in Higher Education, 24*(1), 47–71.

Pascarella, E. T., & Terenzini, P. T. (1983, April). Predicting voluntary freshman year persistence/withdrawal behavior in a residential university: A path analytic validation of Tinto's model. *Journal of Educational Psychology, 75,* 215–226.

Pascarella, E. T., & Terenzini, P. T. (1991). *How college affects students: Findings and insights from twenty years of research.* San Francisco: Jossey-Bass.

Plucker, J. A., Chien, R. W., & Zaman, K. (2006). Enriching the high school curriculum through postsecondary credit-based transition programs. *Center for Evaluation and Education Policy: Education Policy Brief, 4*(2), 1–12.

Reisberg, L. (1998). Some professors question programs that allow high-school students to earn college credits. *The Chronicle of Higher Education, 44*(42), A39–A40.

Rothschild, E. (1999). Four decades of advanced placement program. *The History Teacher, 32*(2), 175–206.

Russo, F. (2000). Beyond advanced placement. *The Village Voice, 45*(15), 90–93.

Santoli, S. P. (2002). Is there an advanced placement advantage? *American Secondary Education, 30*(3), 23–35.

Schwartz, R. A., & Washington, D. M. (2002). Predicting academic performance and retention among African-American men. *NASPA Journal, 3*(4), 35–37.

Stanford University. (n.d.). Request for transfer credit evaluation. http://registrar .stanford.edu/pdf/xfer_credit_request.pdf

Tinto, V. (1987). *Leaving college: Rethinking the causes and cures of student attrition.* Chicago: University of Chicago Press.

Tinto, V. (1993). *Leaving college: Rethinking the causes and cures of student attrition* (2nd ed.). Chicago: University of Chicago Press.

Tinto, V. (2006). Research and practice of student retention: What next? *Junior College Student Retention, 8*(1), 1–19.

Treat, R. C. (2002). New investment to create 70 small high schools across the country: Foundation gives more than $40 million to enable students to graduate with high school diploma and associate's degree. Bill and Melinda Gates Foundation. http://gatesfoundation.org/Education/

Van de Water, S., & Rainwater, T. (2001). What is P–16 education? A primer for legislators; A practical introduction to the concept, language and policy issues of an integrated system of public education. Education Commission of the States. http://ecs.org/clearinghouse/24/28/2428.doc

Viadero, D. (2000). Study suggests fewer students receive AP credit. *Education Week, 19*(42), 5.

Western Interstate Commission for Higher Education [WICHE]. (2006). *Accelerated learning programs: Moving the needle on access and success* (Publication No. 2A358). http://wiche.edu/Policy/Accelerated_Learning/reprts.asp

Willingham, W., & Morris, M. (1986). Four years later: A longitudinal study of advanced placement students in college (Report No. 86-2). Princeton, NJ: College Entrance Examination Board. (ERIC Document Reproduction Service No. 280358)

Windham, P. (1996, August). What happens to community college dual enrollment students? Paper presented at the annual conference of the Southern Association for Community College Research, Panama City, FL. (ERIC Document Reproduction Service No. 398950)

Windham, P. (1997). High school and community college dual enrollment: Issues of rigor and transferability. *Journal of Applied Research in the Community College, 5*(2), 111–115. (ERIC Document Reproduction Service No. 413936)

PART FOUR

Policy Issues

CHAPTER 9

Advanced Placement Participation

Evaluating the Policies of States and Colleges

Kristin Klopfenstein and M. Kathleen Thomas

Since the turn of the century, university and public policies have extended the use and application of AP well beyond its original intent of giving academically advanced high school students the opportunity to place into sequent college courses or to obtain college credit for courses taken while in high school. AP experience, even in the absence of evidence of content mastery, is heavily valued in the college admissions process, and AP Program expansion is promoted nationwide as an education reform capable of simultaneously narrowing the achievement gap among the U.S. student population and increasing international competitiveness (Hess & Rotherham, 2007).

The implicit assumption behind the euphoria surrounding AP is that the benefits of rewarding and expanding AP-taking are greater than the associated costs. However, there has been little consideration of the magnitude of the benefits generated by AP, the adverse incentives of policies that disproportionately reward AP-taking, or the costs of AP relative to other reforms. In this chapter we discuss the policies that have spurred AP growth, the ambiguous results of research studying the benefits of AP, the unexamined costs of providing AP, and suggestions for policy in light of our current understanding of the benefits and costs.

POLICIES AND PRACTICES PROMOTING AP PARTICIPATION

In the admissions process, colleges widely implement policies that reward AP course participation without regard for AP exam-taking or scores. According to a 2000 survey of 962 four-year public and private colleges and universities, AP participation (exclusive of test-taking) factors directly or indirectly into five of the six most important factors in college admissions: high school GPA or class rank; SAT/ACT scores; pattern of high school coursework; AP, International Baccalaureate (IB), or dual credit coursework; AP coursework alone; and AP course grades (Breland, Maxey, Gernand, Cumming, & Trapani, 2002). A separate 2005 survey of 539 public and private four-year and two-year colleges and universities finds that 91 percent of postsecondary institutions take AP into account in the admissions process (Sathre & Blanco, 2006). Geiser and Santelices (2004) summarized well the unintended consequences of a strong emphasis on AP experience in university admissions: "It is now common for upper middle-class parents to evaluate and choose high schools based on the number of AP courses offered at those schools, thereby placing great pressure on schools to expand their AP offerings. According to a recent evaluation of AP and International Baccalaureate (IB) programs by the National Research Council, this pressure can lead schools to offer more advanced courses than they are able to support adequately with trained teachers and other resources" (p. 4). Later in the chapter we explore the impact of expanding AP with limited school resources.

Another example of the ways in which colleges and state policy makers promote AP course participation without regard to test performance is AP grade weighting. As of 2004, grade weighting was widespread at high schools across Texas, and it is reasonable to expect that schools in other states follow similar trends.[1] Typically, high schools award 10 to 25 percent extra weight for AP course grades when calculating student GPA. Colleges started weighting AP course grades before it was common practice at the high school level by recalculating applicants' GPA using transcript data (Geiser & Santelices, 2004). The incentives associated with grade weighting are complex due to the fact that class rank, which is determined exclusively by GPA, is highly valued in the college admissions process. This is particularly true in California, Florida, and Texas, where admission to public colleges and universities is guaranteed for the top X percent of each high school's graduating class. While theoretically valid because AP courses presumably require more effort to earn an A, grade weighting is sensitive to grade inflation because weights are not dependent on student scores on the AP exam; AP exam scores are not available until midsummer, well after seniors have graduated. Grade weighting also encourages students to take excessive numbers of AP courses as they compete for top class rankings.

An emerging policy trend is state-mandated AP course offerings. Increasing numbers of state governments are legislating that all high schools, regardless of size and resources, offer a minimum number of AP courses (see table 9.1). To comply with these mandates, hundreds of schools, many of them small, rural, or low income, are beginning new AP programs (Klopfenstein, 2004a). While these policies are well-intentioned, often driven by the desire to expand the AP Program to traditionally underrepresented student populations, they can have unintended consequences. In

TABLE 9.1   State-mandated AP course offerings

State	All high schools must offer AP	All districts must offer AP	All high schools must offer advanced classes, which may include AP	All districts must offer advanced classes, which may include AP
Arkansas	•			
Idaho			•	
Indiana	•			
Kentucky			•	
Mississippi[a]		•		
Ohio				•
Oregon				•
South Carolina[b]	•			
Vermont			•	
Virginia			•	
West Virginia[a]		•		

Source: Education Commission of the States (2009).
Notes: [a] Or offer IB.
   [b] Contingent on school size.

addition to the obvious consequences for course quality, state mandates to expand AP without regard to the unique financial and human resource needs of individual high schools may adversely affect non-AP students. Indeed, the harm to non-AP students may outweigh the benefits a new AP Program provides for participating students.

The push to expand AP participation is not limited to state legislatures. Another prominent stakeholder in the expansion of AP provision is the Education Commission of the States (ECS), a forty-year-old organization that provides state policy makers with education information, policy research, and analysis of education issues.[2] ECS recommends that each state adopt a comprehensive state AP policy. They suggest that states require that all high schools offer a minimum number of AP courses, give financial incentives to districts and schools to provide AP, tie AP course offerings to school accreditation, require students to take the AP exam before receiving course credit, and compel all public colleges and universities to award credit to students who earn a state-specified minimum AP exam score (ECS, 2006). In light of recent research and the potential for unintended consequences, these recommendations should be carefully examined before being implemented.

AP PARTICIPATION AND COLLEGE SUCCESS: CAUSE OR CORRELATION?

Implicit in policies that reward AP participation without any proof of content mastery is the notion that AP experience alone can increase the probability of success in college. While there is evidence of a correlation between AP experience and college success (because AP students tend to be capable and highly motivated), there is no evidence from methodologically rigorous studies that AP experience causes students to be successful in college. The distinction between cause and correlation is important when considering AP expansion as an education reform. If the relationship between AP experience and college success is not causal, then policies that broaden AP-taking will not improve rates of college success for nontraditional AP students.

There is a great deal of confusion about claims made by the College Board, its affiliated researchers, and others about the efficacy of the AP Program. While the College Board generally makes no explicit statements that AP experience is a cause of college success, their promotional literature readily leads readers to such a conclusion (e.g., College Board,

2003, 2005b). The most blatant example is a 2005 press release discussing the first annual Advanced Placement Report to the Nation, which stated that "many more students enter college each fall *than have first been prepared through successful completion of an AP course.* Gaps currently exist in each state between the percentage of students who entered college in fall 2004—56.8 percent—and the percentage of students who had mastered an AP course—13.2 percent. *'Closing these gaps is one solution for improving college graduation rates,'* [italics added] said [Gaston] Caperton [president of the College Board]" (College Board, 2005c).

Research favored by the College Board demonstrates a strong correlation between AP-taking and college outcomes. The most frequently cited studies include Morgan and Manackshana (2000) and Willingham and Morris (1986); recent research reaching the same conclusion includes Hargrove, Godin, and Dodd (2008) and Keng and Dodd (2008). The finding that AP experience is highly correlated with college success is unsurprising, but the policy relevance of such studies is limited. If students who succeed in the AP Program and in college do so because they come from families of high socioeconomic status, their success does not inform the likelihood of success among AP participants from very different socioeconomic backgrounds.

Research attempting to tease out the causal effect (net of student demographics) of AP experience on college outcomes is growing but is still in its early stages. Several articles examine the impact of AP after holding observable characteristics constant, such as other courses taken, prior academic achievement, high school quality, and family background (Dougherty, Mellor, & Jian, 2006b; Klopfenstein & Thomas, 2009; Geiser & Santelices, 2004). However, it is difficult for researchers with the best data to account for differences in unobservable characteristics, such as motivation and educational aspirations. Therefore, the causal implications of even the best studies remain dubious. The development of high-quality longitudinal statewide datasets and the application of appropriate statistical techniques will allow for better estimates of the causal impact of AP going forward.

The bulk of existing research on AP is primarily concerned with the association between AP experience and college outcomes, and this research focuses almost exclusively on the experience of students who take the AP exams. However, as discussed, there are compelling reasons for students to take AP courses without taking the exams. We devote the remainder of this paper to identifying the benefits and costs of a deliberate, even mandated, expansion of AP course offerings and to discussing the challenges associated with estimating the relative size of these costs and benefits.

ESTIMATING THE BENEFITS OF AP PARTICIPATION

In this section we discuss three theoretical benefits of AP participation: improved chance of admission to the college of one's choice; improved college success in terms of grades, persistence, and graduation; and decreased time to degree. While we acknowledge that there may be other benefits to the AP experience, they are likely to be difficult to quantify and at least partially incorporated into the measures we discuss. For example, if an AP course stimulates excitement about learning, that enthusiasm might lead to an increased probability of attending college, better college grades, and consequently shorter time to degree.

Increased Probability of College Admission

One benefit of AP participation is its effect on the probability of admission to college and, for many students, admission to a *particular* college. Assuming that higher education generally leads to more informed participants in democracy and to better public policy, the public benefit to AP occurs when it increases the likelihood of matriculation at *any* college. Getting into the first-choice college confers greater private than public benefit to the extent that the choice of college is driven by nonacademic or even sentimental concerns. However, if the rank order of college choices is based on academic fit, and, importantly, the student has correctly identified her best fit college, there may be a public as well as a private benefit to being accepted at a particular college.

Furthermore, Light and Strayer (2000) find that students of all ability levels are more likely to graduate if the quality of the university matches their skill level. If the right match leads to greater college success and higher graduation rates, then gaining admission to a particular college could have public as well as private benefits. For example, on average, college graduates earn higher salaries than those without college degrees, which would result in greater tax revenues. However, debate continues, particularly in discussions of the use of affirmative action in higher education admissions, over the hypothesis that students with ability levels below the average of the university to which they have been admitted have a below-average chance to succeed (Bowen & Bok, 1998).

The return to an investment, be it financial or educational, is the monetary or intrinsic value the investor gets in exchange for engaging in a behavior. Thus, the return to an improvement in the quality of the match between student and university could be a more positive learning experience for the student and increased wages on graduation. To calculate the public and private value of AP in terms of college admissions, the first step is to estimate the effect of AP experience on the likelihood that a student will attend any college. The public benefit of AP from increasing the likelihood of matriculation at *any* college may be substantial. The second step is to obtain estimates of the return to improving match quality between school and student and then the impact of AP experience on the quality of the match. Estimating the private return to attending a first-choice college is more involved, requiring the estimation of differences in utility and lifetime earnings potential from attending one college versus another. Given the rather strong assumption that high school students can and do correctly identify their best-fit college, and the uncertainty over whether match quality across purely academic dimensions affects the probability of college success, the public benefit of AP that derives from increasing the likelihood of admission to a particular college may be trivial. Because the returns to a high-quality match on nonacademic (e.g., social) dimensions may be substantial, the private benefit to AP may be much larger.

To our knowledge, there has been no research estimating models of the public or private returns to entering a first-choice college, let alone the impact of AP on improving match quality along a variety of dimensions. Based on theory alone, it seems reasonable to believe that the largest impact of AP experience is on the probability of acceptance to a first-choice college rather than to any college: traditionally, AP students are college-bound to begin with, and AP is viewed as a way to get a head start on college work. If the public returns for attending a first-choice institution are small even when the private returns are large, then the admissions effect may not justify spending public resources to promote AP participation.

Increased Probability of College Success

The best available research to date suggests that while AP experience may have a statistically significant positive impact on college outcomes for students who earn high scores on the AP exams, there is little such evidence for course participation alone or for students earning the lowest scores on the AP exam (Geiser & Santelices, 2004; Dougherty, Mellor, &

Jian, 2006a; Klopfenstein & Thomas, 2009).[3] In order to estimate the value of the benefits of AP in terms of college success, we focus on the magnitude of the AP effect for exam-takers, assuming (until more conclusive evidence exists to the contrary) that the positive effect of course-taking alone is zero. Given the increased use of AP as an education reform, which assumes some degree of causality between AP and future academic success, we discuss the magnitude of the effect of AP in terms of college success using only research that accounts for a number of important demographic and academic achievement variables.

The studies that find statistically significant AP effects on college grades estimate relatively small effects (Geiser & Santelices, 2004; Sadler & Tai, 2007). Geiser and Santelices (2004), using data from the University of California system, estimate that a one-point increase in AP exam grade is associated with an increase in the second-year college GPA of 9/100 of a grade point (e.g., from a 3.00 to a 3.09). Using a nationally representative sample, Sadler and Tai (2007) find that AP science students, regardless of whether they took the AP exam, earn a course grade just two points (out of 100) higher than similar peers when they retake the comparable science course in college. These represent upper-bound estimates of any true effect given that the unobservable characteristics of AP students (such as quality of prior academic training and motivation), and particularly AP exam-takers, tend to be highly correlated with achievement on college-level work.

The Geiser and Santelices (2004) finding may be a consequence of student selection because the analysis focuses exclusively on AP exam-takers, and this can make the direction of causality difficult to identify. Does the AP Program prepare students for academic success, or do the schools attended by AP exam-passers simply provide a higher-than-average quality college preparatory curriculum in general? Are the students who take AP exams made smarter by the experience, or were they encouraged to take AP because they were already good students? Some schools allow any interested student to enroll in AP classes regardless of their academic background, and others require application to the courses complete with letters of recommendation and parent contracts. Different selection criteria could lead to a positive estimate for the effect of AP exam scores on college grades if students who score higher are from schools that carefully screen AP applicants and if those with lower scores had weaker preparation at a school with open enrollment. In this case, differences in AP exam scores might be associated with higher college grades even when the AP experience itself has little or no causal impact.

The few studies that estimate the effect of AP experience on college success while controlling for what we consider to be a minimum of demographic and achievement indicators find little or no effect. While a plethora of College Board–affiliated reports find positive links between AP experience and college outcomes, they do not adequately account for the systematic differences between AP and non-AP students. Because schools cannot ethically administer the AP Program under experimental conditions, we may never know the causal impact of AP, but researchers can be clever about identifying meaningful sources of natural variation and applying appropriate statistical techniques. Dougherty, Mellor, and Jian (2006b) provide an accessible discussion of the conceptual and empirical challenges of estimating AP effects, and policy makers should pay careful attention to the interpretation of any finding before supporting public funding for AP over other interventions.

Decreased Time to Degree

Historically, AP benefits have accrued through tuition savings for students who earn college credit by passing the AP exams. If, in practice, AP students are systematically earning enough credit hours to shorten the time to graduation, then public investment in expanding AP-taking may be warranted. Given that the average length of time to degree for students who enroll continuously in four-year institutions is significantly longer than four years (NCES, 2003a), and tax dollars heavily subsidize the education of public university students, an emphasis on AP exams as a means to earn college credit and reduce time to degree is one possible way to save taxpayer money.[4]

While summing the monetary value of tuition dollars saved is perhaps the easiest calculation of an AP cost-benefit exercise, the estimation is complicated by the fact that there is no uniform standard by which colleges award credit for passing AP exams. Depending on the university, or indeed on the department within the university, students with the same AP exam score may earn college credit, may be placed into the next-level course in the subject area without credit, or may receive no special treatment at all. While receiving advanced placement frees students to take other courses, it does not diminish the total number of credit hours required to graduate and therefore would not justify public expense (in regard to decreasing time to graduation). In order to precisely estimate the tuition savings from AP exam-passers who earned college credit, data must be collected from all universities regarding their credit-by-examination policy for each AP exam. Klopfenstein (this volume) approximates the tuition savings in Texas under the generous assumption that all schools award credit for an AP exam score of 3.

There has been a move by some states (e.g., Florida and Virginia) to standardize the rewards for passing AP exam scores (ECS, 2006). Standardization would dramatically simplify the benefit calculation for tuition savings and would make it easier for students to optimize high school course-taking when they are unsure of which college they will attend. However, allowing academic departments discretion about if and when to award course credit for AP is justifiable educationally. Particularly at smaller universities, departments may not teach a particular subject the same way as the AP course that is designed to replicate a typical college offering. Departments that provide a unique introductory course experience should not be prevented from requiring that their students take the course on campus, regardless of students' AP scores. Rather than mandating course credit for one prespecified AP exam score, appropriate state-level higher education agencies should maintain Web-accessible databases of each public university's credit-by-examination policies.

ESTIMATING THE COSTS OF AP PROVISION

An increase in AP course offerings also increases the need for teacher professional development and college text books and lab equipment and inflates existing AP exam subsidies. However, the costs of offering an AP Program come disproportionately in the form of opportunity costs (the cost of what a school gives up in order to offer AP) rather than out-of-pocket costs. These implicit costs often affect the education experience of non-AP students. Although opportunity costs tend to be difficult to quantify, their impact is nonetheless real.

The Hidden Costs of AP Provision

Non-AP students can face substantial opportunity costs as a result of increasing the number of AP courses, and these costs are exacerbated in small schools. In order to expand AP course offerings with limited financial and staffing resources, schools must increase non-AP class sizes, divert the highest-quality teachers away from non-AP classes, and eliminate non-AP course offerings.

Larger Non-AP Class Sizes

Part of the advertised benefit of AP classes is that they allow students to learn college-level course material in a relatively intimate environment. Indeed, not only are AP classes smaller than the comparable introductory college course, they are smaller than the average high school course. While there are about seventeen students in the typical AP class, there are nearly twenty-four in the typical public secondary-school classroom (Milewski & Gillie, 2002; U.S. Department of Education, 2002). AP courses tend to be even smaller in small or rural high schools.

In order for a school with a fixed number of teachers to offer more small AP classes, class size in non-AP classes *must* increase. Although there has been much debate over the effect of class size in recent years, the emerging consensus among economists is that marginal changes in class size have little or no impact on student learning (Milesi & Gamoran, 2006; Hanushek, 1999). However, the existing research on class size is conducted almost exclusively during the elementary grades, and the appropriateness of extrapolating class size findings from elementary to high school is far from clear. Consequently, the impact of class size during the high school years is not well understood. Larger class sizes may adversely affect non-AP students in a variety of ways depending on the subject area. For example, science classes might offer fewer labs due to an insufficient number of lab stations or equipment, and composition classes might require fewer papers, and/or there may be fewer teacher comments on the papers that are assigned.

Estimating the cost of increased class sizes on non-AP students is problematic given the paucity of data on in-depth learning, the type of learning most likely to be affected by increases in class size. Standardized test scores, which are available in a growing number of states' administrative databases, are ill-suited for studying in-depth learning. An innovative study might examine the types of assignments frequently given, such as labs or essays, the frequency and quality of teacher feedback, and opportunities for revision across a range of high school course titles and class sizes. While the pedagogical methods of the teacher provide an inadequate measure of student learning, they may provide clues to the potential costs of AP course expansion on non-AP students.

Non-AP Classes Lose the Best Teachers

There is well-documented evidence that teacher sorting between schools is nonrandom, with the least experienced teachers disproportionately staffing schools that enroll at-risk students and the highest-quality teachers (in terms of certification status, degrees from prestigious universities, and experience) staffing schools that serve students from high-income, well-educated, predominantly white families (Clotfelter, Ladd, & Vigdor, 2006; Hanushek, Kain, & Rivkin, 2004). There is similar evidence that sorting also occurs within schools: instructional quality across tracks varies as teachers who are successful with general education students are promptly promoted to teach honors and AP classes (Clotfelter et al., 2006; Oakes, 1985). As AP course offerings grow, the highest-quality teachers are typically recruited to teach AP, leaving the least-experienced teachers with the non-AP students. Given that empirical evidence suggests that good teachers tend to be effective across student ability levels, schools that assign the most effective teachers to the best students must consider the practical and moral consequences of relegating the least qualified teachers to their struggling students (Hanushek, Kain, O'Brien, & Rivkin, 2005). Estimating the magnitude of the reduction in teacher quality for non-AP students requires student-level data with exact student-teacher matches. Unfortunately, there are only a couple of states that maintain such data, and political circumstances make it difficult for states to incorporate student-teacher matches into existing student-level databases.

Reductions in Non-AP Course Offerings

Programs and classes serving the needs of the local student population might need to be eliminated in order to expand AP offerings. If programs such as career and technical education, which are tailored to the needs of students with less interest or aptitude for academic work, are cut to make room for AP, the loss to non-AP students may very well exceed the gain to AP students. Rosenbaum (2004) finds that high schools already invest too little in students who will not attend a four-year college, and Klopfenstein and Thomas (2009) find that AP course-taking has no impact on first-year college outcomes because the students who typically enroll in AP will succeed in college with or without AP experience.

The Costs for Professional Development of Teachers

Appropriate supports for the AP teacher require a combination of out-of-pocket outlays and opportunity costs in terms of teacher time. For years the College Board has recommended only that AP teachers have three or more years of teaching experience, a bachelor's degree in a related field, and preferably an advanced degree and/or "significant mastery" of the subject matter. However, to address concerns about the dilution of AP course quality, the College Board recently issued a much more detailed set of standards for AP teachers (College Board, 2005a). It now explicitly recommends that all new AP teachers attend a one-day training session followed by a College Board–endorsed AP Summer Institute, which provides five days of subject-specific professional development. Similar workshops are encouraged for experienced AP teachers. AP training is required by law for teachers in Arkansas, Illinois, Mississippi, North Carolina, and Kentucky and is often subsidized in part by the states (ECS, 2007). Registration fees for one-day workshops range from $100 to several hundred dollars and realistically require a one-night stay to accommodate travel. Registration fees at Summer Institutes are typically $450 per teacher, with an additional $300 for five nights of housing for participants attending far from home.[5] Teachers are generally not reimbursed for their time to attend workshops, a hardship for teachers who must give up a session of summer school or other paid employment in order to spend a week at the Summer Institute.

The greatest professional development cost incurred by a school adhering to the College Board's recommendations is the release time and/ or supplemental pay for informal mentoring, networking, and collaborating as well as reading professional journals, participating in study groups, developing new pedagogies, and keeping abreast of the latest technology. The Southwest Regional Educational Laboratory provides an array of material about developing and supporting professional learning communities, teams of four to six teachers who work together to improve student learning based on school and classroom data, research and best practices, and reflective teaching (Hord, 1997). Such a model would be highly appropriate for AP teachers given that the teams need not consist of teachers from the same department.

One professional development opportunity not discussed in the College Board's recommendations but fully consistent with its ideals is auditing the relevant college-level course at a local college or university. This is a valuable exercise even if the university faculty member being audited is not exceptionally good. Teaching a college-level course is different than taking it, so even high school teachers with a bachelor's degree in their AP subject would benefit from spending time observing an introductory college classroom. AP teachers, new and experienced, may learn what not to do as well as what to do pedagogically, all while obtaining a deeper understanding of the material themselves. A teacher who audits a local college class will, over the duration of that course, spend forty hours in class time alone, which could be done after school hours to avoid the cost of a substitute. The cost of reimbursing an AP teacher for one week of time, as would be appropriate, would depend on local conditions as well as the teacher's level of experience.

An investment in professional development is an investment in "creating a culture of high standards for teachers"; investing in ongoing professional development professionalizes teaching and "will have a positive effect on non-AP teaching and overall student learning" (College Board, 2005a, p. 7). Student learning will improve not only because teachers have a better understanding of the content and appropriate pedagogy but because teachers are modeling learning as a way of life rather than something that occurs only during prespecified hours. Unfortunately, there is presently little systematic support, either intellectual or financial, for teachers wishing to pursue independently high-quality professional development. The opportunity costs of AP provision are already high and likely to be higher if schools and districts want to maintain quality programs that support the most important component of a successful AP classroom: the AP teacher.

Out-of-Pocket Costs of AP Provision

The books and equipment utilized in high schools can be significantly more expensive for AP courses than for traditional courses. Differences in textbook costs arise from two sources: differences in the costs of the books themselves and differences in frequency of replacement. High schools must purchase hardcover copies of texts for durability. High school texts are typically replaced every five to seven years, and, according to a random sample of one thousand teachers conducted by the National Education Association, 32 percent of teachers report using textbooks that are ten years old or older (Hunter, 2006). Such infrequent text replacement is problematic for many AP courses, particularly those in the physical, computer, and even the social sciences. Schools may tend to replace their AP texts more frequently than their other books and thus incur additional costs.

In addition to higher textbook costs, high schools face higher lab costs for AP science courses than for typical high school science courses. All AP science courses require a lab component. The greater cost of AP lab equipment is documented explicitly in the College Board's (2007a) course description for AP Biology: "administrators should be aware that an AP college-level laboratory is significantly more expensive to operate than a

Today, the expansion of the AP Program is being conducted with the belief that the benefits of AP experience are universal and large enough to justify supportive subsidies and/or legislation, but AP stakeholders likely overestimate the benefits and underestimate the associated costs. College admissions officials, state policy makers, and the Education Commission of the States are forming or encouraging policies that directly or indirectly support broad expansion of the AP Program, particularly in schools serving low-income students. These policies are well-intentioned, as they often involve increasing access to a high-quality curriculum for traditionally underserved minority and low-income students. But evidence suggests that resources might be better spent by improving academic preparation in the earlier grades rather than expanding AP in schools where a large fraction of students are performing below grade level (Dougherty et al., 2006a, 2006b; Dougherty & Mellor, this volume).

The College Board advertises, and the government funds, the AP Program as an intervention for traditionally underrepresented students to improve their chances of going to and succeeding in college. The College Board policy is that there should be no prerequisites for an AP class and that any motivated student should be allowed to enroll. To quote an AP promotional brochure, "AP isn't just for top students or those headed for college. AP offers something for everyone" (College Board, 2003, p. 4). However, the AP Program is designed to replicate college courses, not to remediate students who are not academically prepared for the rigors of college coursework. As the executive director of AVID (Advancement via Individual Determination), a program designed to coach high school students who would be first-generation college students, explains, encouraging students to take classes for which they do not have the necessary academic preparation is "to doom these students to failure or, at best, a superficial understanding instead of subject mastery" (Nelson, 2007, p. 73).

Even when the benefits of AP are believed to be substantial, administrators and policy makers should keep their eyes wide open to the hidden costs of implementing and maintaining a quality AP Program. Perhaps the most important and frequently overlooked cost of the AP Program is that of ongoing teacher development (which Paek and colleagues [this volume] show to be related to important student outcomes). States should provide greater financial and staffing support to high schools wishing to comply with the teacher standards recommended by the College Board (2005a). A formal mentoring system for new AP teachers should be coordinated by the district so that a high school's sole AP teacher can work with AP teachers across the district. Substitutes should be provided for new and experienced AP teachers to observe peer teachers, including classes at different high schools. Teachers should be compensated for time spent on professional development, be it mentoring or spending time at an AP Summer Institute.

Successfully expanding access to a meaningful AP experience necessitates a strengthening of the education pipeline, and intervention must begin early to prepare students for the rigors of an AP curriculum. One program that leads to a well-documented increase in AP-taking and college attendance, as well as other desirable outcomes, is AVID, which provides support for midperforming students who are typically the first in their families to attend college (Mehan, Villanueva, Hubbard, & Lintz, 1996; Guthrie & Guthrie, 2000; Watt, Powell, & Mendiola, 2004). AVID provides extensive individualized tutoring in study skills, note taking, essay writing, and test taking during an elective class period, and students are enrolled in a rigorous college preparatory curriculum the rest of the day (Cunningham, 2003; Mehan et al., 1996). If the goal of policy makers is to improve access to college for a broad range of students, investment in a program like AVID may provide a higher return on investment than AP-related mandates or subsidies.

Policy makers and administrators need to recognize all of the costs incurred in creating a high-quality AP program and compare the net benefits of AP to that of other interventions. When considering AP-related legislation, policy makers should avoid rigid, unfunded mandates that require districts and high schools to provide AP in ways that can lead to unintended consequences.

NOTES

1. Based on survey data Klopfenstein (2004b) gathered on the grade-weighting practices of more than seven hundred Texas public high schools during the 2003–2004 academic year.
2. See http://www.ecs.org for more information regarding the mission and history of the Education Commission of the States.
3. College outcomes examined in the studies cited here include college GPA, retention to the sophomore year, grades in introductory college science classes, and college graduation rates.

4. State appropriations account for 35.6 percent of current fund revenue for public degree-granting institutions in 2000–2001, the most recent year for which data are available (NCES, 2003b).
5. Costs are average for the College Board's Southwest Region for summer 2007 (Jensen, personal communication, Sept. 5, 2007).
6. New York received the next largest grant of $1.4 million. The third-largest grant was considerably smaller: Washington received $273,975.
7. We thank Cliff Adelman for this analogy.

REFERENCES

American Recovery and Reinvestment Act. (2009). http://www.ed.gov/policy/gen/leg/recovery/guidance/uses.doc

Bowen, W. G., & Bok, D. (1998). *The shape of the river*. Princeton, NJ: Princeton University Press.

Breland, H., Maxey, J., Gernand, R., Cumming, T., & Trapani, C. (2002). *Trends in college admission*. http://airweb.org/trends.html

Clotfelter, C. T., Ladd, H. F., & Vigdor, J. L. (2006). Teacher-student matching and the assessment of teacher effectiveness. *Journal of Human Resources, 41*(4), 778–820.

College Board. (2003). *Get with the program*. New York.

College Board. (2005a). *2005 AP teacher standards*. http://apcentral.collegeboard.com/apc/public/repository/ap05_teacherstandards_46509.pdf

College Board. (2005b). *The Advanced Placement Program at [insert school name]* [Presentation]. New York.

College Board. (2005c). Advanced Placement proves gateway to success [Press release]. http://www.collegeboard.com/press/releases/41022.html

College Board. (2007a). *Advanced Placement Biology course description, May 2008, May 2009*. http://apcentral.collegeboard.com/apc/public/repository/ap07_bio_coursedesc.pdf

Cunningham, A. (2003). *Investing early: Intervention programs in selected U.S. states*. Montreal: Canada Millennium Scholarship Foundation.

Dougherty, C., Mellor, L., & Jian, S. (2006a). *The relationship between Advanced Placement and college graduation*. Austin, TX: National Center for Educational Accountability.

Dougherty, C., Mellor, L., & Jian, S. (2006b). *Orange juice or orange drink? Ensuring that "advanced courses" live up to their labels*. Austin, TX: National Center for Educational Accountability.

Education Commission of the States [ECS]. (2006). *Advanced Placement*. http://www.ecs.org/clearinghouse/67/44/6744.htm

Education Commission of the States [ECS]. (2007). *Advanced Placement: State programs and funding for teacher training.* http://mb2.ecs.org/reports/Report.aspx?id=1002

Education Commission of the States [ECS]. (2009). *Advanced Placement: State mandates AP course offerings.* http://mb2.ecs.org/reports/Report.aspx?id=996

Geiser, S., & Santelices, V. (2004). *The role of Advanced Placement and honors courses in college admissions.* Berkeley, CA: Center for Studies in Higher Education.

Guthrie, L. F., & Guthrie, G. P. (2000). *Longitudinal research on AVID 1999–2000: Final report.* http://www.avidonline.org

Hanushek, E. (1999). The evidence on class size. In S. E. Mayer & P. E. Peterson (Eds.), *Earning and learning: How schools matter* (pp. 131–168). Washington, DC: Brookings Institution Press.

Hanushek, E., Kain, J. F., O'Brien, D., & Rivkin, S. G. (2005). The market for teacher quality (NBER Working Paper 11154). National Bureau of Economic Research. http://www.nber.org

Hanushek, E., Kain, J. F., & Rivkin, S. G. (2004). Why public schools lose teachers. *Journal of Human Resources, 39*(2), 326–354.

Hargrove, L., Godin, D., & Dodd, B. (2008). *College outcomes comparisons by AP and non-AP high school experiences* (College Board Research Report 2008-3). New York: College Board.

Hess, F. M., & Rotherham, A. J. (2007). *Can NCLB survive the competitiveness competition?* Education Outlook (Vol. 2). Washington, DC: American Enterprise Institute.

Hord, S. (1997). *Professional learning communities: Communities of continuous inquiry and improvement.* Austin, TX: Southwest Educational Development Laboratory.

Hunter, K. (2006). A textbook case. *T H E [Technological Horizons in Education] Journal, 3*(15), 48–49.

Keng, L., & Dodd, B. (2008). A comparison of college performances of AP and non-AP student groups in 10 subject areas (College Board Research Report No. 2008-7). New York: College Board.

Klopfenstein, K. (2004a). The Advanced Placement expansion of the 1990s: How did traditionally underserved students fare? *Education Policy Analysis Archives, 12*(68).

Klopfenstein, K. (2004b). Texas public high school counselor survey. Unpublished data.

Klopfenstein, K., & Thomas, M. K. (2009). The link between Advanced Placement experience and early college success. *Southern Economic Journal, 75*(3), 873–891.

Light, A., & Strayer, W. (2000). Determinants of college completion: School quality or student ability? *Journal of Human Resources, 35*(2), 299–332.

Mehan, H., Villanueva, I., Hubbard, L., & Lintz, A. (1996). *Constructing school success: The consequences of untracking low-achieving students.* New York: Cambridge University Press.

Milesi, C., & Gamoran, A. (2006). Effects of class size and instruction on kindergarten achievement. *Educational Evaluation and Policy Analysis, 28*(4), 287–313.

Milewski, G. B., & Gillie, J. M. (2002). *What are the characteristics of AP teachers? An examination of survey research.* New York: College Board.

Morgan, R., & Manackshana, B. (2000). *AP students in college: An investigation of their course-taking patterns and college majors.* Princeton, NJ: Educational Testing Service.

National Center for Education Statistics [NCES]. (2003a). *The condition of education 2003* (NCES 2003-067). Washington, DC: U.S. Government Printing Office.

National Center for Education Statistics [NCES]. (2003b). Current-fund revenue of public degree-granting institutions, by source of funds: Selected years, 1980–81 through 2000–01. http://nces.ed.gov/programs/digest/d06/tables/dt06_336.asp

National Center for Education Statistics [NCES]. (2007). *The condition of education 2007* (NCES 2007-064). Washington, DC: U.S. Government Printing Office.

Nelson, J. (2007). Avidly seeking success. *Educational Leadership, 64*(7), 72–74.

No Child Left Behind Act. (2001). http://www.ed.gov/policy/elsec/leg/esea02/index.html

Oakes, J. J. (1985). *Keeping track: How schools structure inequality.* New Haven, CT: Yale University Press.

Rosenbaum, J. (2004). *Beyond college for all: Career paths for the forgotten half.* New York: Russell Sage Foundation.

Roza, M. (2009). Breaking down school budgets. *Education Next, 9(3),* 29–33.

Sadler, P. M., & Tai, R. H. (2007). Advanced Placement exam scores as a predictor of performance in introductory college biology, chemistry, and physics courses. *Science Education, 16*(2), 1–19.

Sathre, C. O., & Blanco, C. D. (2006). Policies and practices at postsecondary institutions. In Western Interstate Commission for Higher Education, *Accelerated learning options: Moving the needle on access and success* (pp. 25–36). Boulder, CO.

Texas Education Agency. (2006). Despite rapid expansion of AP Program, too few minority students in college-prep classes [Press release]. http://www.tea.state.tx.us/press/apnationrelease.pdf

U.S. Department of Education. (2009). Advanced Placement test fee program. http://www.ed.gov/programs/apfee/index.html

Watt, K. M., Powell, C. A., & Mendiola, I. D. (2004). Implications of one comprehensive school reform model for secondary school students underrepresented in higher education. *Journal of Education for Students Placed at Risk, 9*(3), 241–259.

Willingham, W. W., & Morris, M. (1986). Four years later: A longitudinal study of Advanced Placement students in college. New York: College Board.

CHAPTER 10

Does the Advanced Placement Program Save Taxpayers Money?

The Effect of AP Participation on Time to College Graduation

Kristin Klopfenstein

The Advanced Placement Program has grown dramatically in recent years, and AP expansion is frequently touted as an education reform that couples high expectations with strong accountability in the form of standardized end-of-course exams (Klopfenstein, 2004b). Consequently, public subsidies for the program are rapidly expanding at the local, state, and federal levels and include funding for AP teacher training, exam fee subsidies, and performance incentives for teachers and students who do well on AP exams.

Advanced Placement Incentive Program Grants from the U.S. Department of Education have been available since the late 1990s and were expanded under the No Child Left Behind Act (2001). Section 1702, the Access to High Standards Act, provides competitive grants for the expansion of AP in schools with high concentrations of low-income students with the intention of reducing racial achievement gaps. Local funding has also become a substantial and growing source for AP subsidies. Dallas-based AP Strategies was one of the first organizations to facilitate the pairing of philanthropists with local school districts for the purpose of funding AP. AP Strategies has matched more than sixty corporate and individual donors with over one hundred Texas school districts and is a model for similar activity in other states (AP Strategies, 2008). The decentralized nature of local programs makes it difficult to estimate the total amount of money spent in support of AP each year, but with organizations like AP Strategies leading the way, the amount is growing rapidly.

Subsidies of the AP Program are typically justified on the basis of the belief that AP courses are college preparatory (NCLB, 2001, section 1702). College prep courses couple the opportunity to learn rigorous material with the scaffolding necessary to build the skills and habits of mind necessary for success in college, including communication skills, reading for comprehension, organizational habits, and study skills. However, by design, AP courses *are* college courses. College-level courses generally assume that these skills—in particular reading, organizational, and study skills—are already in place. Thus, AP courses are not preparation for college any more than throwing a child in the deep end of a pool is preparation for swimming (Klopfenstein & Thomas, 2009). The subtle distinction between AP courses as college preparatory versus college level is important from a public policy standpoint because it changes the metric by which the success of the program should be measured.

While the impact of the AP Program could be studied through a variety of analytical lenses, I take an economic approach by weighing the costs of AP subsidies against the benefits. More specifically, if AP experience shortens the time it takes the average student to earn a degree, then taxpayers save money at publicly funded universities. To calculate the size of the benefit, I estimate the impact of AP experience on how long it takes students to earn the baccalaureate degree using survival analysis, a statistical method that exploits longitudinal data that are collected over time on the same students.[1] Then I compare these estimated benefits to the costs of AP subsidies over the same time period. Such cost-benefit analyses can provide a reality check for policies driven by anecdotes and good intentions. I also estimate the benefits of dual credit courses, another form of accelerated learning, and discuss reasons why the costs of the two programs differ.[2] I study time to degree in part because of claims from the College Board (2008) that "AP helps students graduate on time and realize significant savings on college." While shortened time to degree is frequently invoked as justification for AP expansion and subsidies, until now there have been no rigorously designed research studies testing the claim.

I examine the progress toward graduation for five years for 28,702 public university students using the Texas Schools Microdata Panel (TSMP). The data provide no evidence that AP courses cause students to graduate more quickly than students who have not taken AP courses. Passing AP exams increases the likelihood of graduating in three years for a small number of students, those attending high schools that offer a wide array of AP courses and who have the support necessary to pass multiple AP exams. Passing AP exams does not increase the likelihood of graduating in four years for the typical student or in five years for those who have not graduated in four years. However, the costs of AP exam fee subsidies, a subset of all subsidies directed toward the AP Program during the years of the study, are substantial.

The findings are consistent with the notion that most AP students would do well in college even without AP experience and that they use the increased flexibility provided by passing one or two AP exams to explore multiple areas of interest in college. In contrast, high school students who enroll in dual credit courses at local public postsecondary institutions are more likely to earn their baccalaureate degrees in three, four, or five years than students who do not take dual credit courses. The findings suggest the possibility that public funding currently spent on the AP Program would be better utilized in support of dual credit programs.

CONCEPTUAL FRAMEWORK FOR THE COST-BENEFIT ANALYSIS

The College Board (2005) claims that "students who take AP courses and exams are much more likely than their peers to complete a bachelor's degree in four years or less" (p. 2). While this is certainly true, the statement implies that AP courses and exams *cause* students to graduate more quickly. The logic is reasonable: the vast majority of public universities award course credit for passing AP exam scores, and consequently students have fewer courses to complete while at college. AP experience might also help students identify their interests sooner and reduce the number of times they change majors, thereby reducing time to degree. In reality, however, it is quite possible that the type of students who are attracted to and take AP would have graduated in the same amount of time even without AP experience because they tend to be highly motivated and goal oriented by nature (Bailey & Karp, 2003).

We do not know from existing research whether AP experience causes students to graduate quicker (the causal effect) or whether it is simply associated with other student characteristics that cause students to graduate quicker (the selection effect) (Klopfenstein & Thomas, 2009; Dougherty, Mellor, & Jian, 2006; Bailey & Karp, 2003). In the absence of evidence of a causal link between AP experience and college success, the efficiency and equity of AP subsidies are called into question. For example, if students who take AP are uniquely capable and motivated and would do well in college even in the absence of AP experience, then it is inefficient for the public to subsidize AP. If the students who take AP are disproportionately nonrural and middle class, it is inequitable as well because these groups already have broad access to the AP Program (Klopfenstein, 2004b).

Few studies have used a rigorous methodology to study the relationship between AP and time to degree specifically. Adelman (1999) models the effect of advanced coursework, including AP, on the likelihood of graduating within eleven years of completing high school, but Adelman's study was not designed to study AP specifically. Rather, AP was one component of many in an index defined as "academic intensity." Adelman used statistical techniques, ordinary least squares and logistic regression, that ignore the time-dependent aspects of college completion. As I will discuss later, neither independent variables nor their effects are allowed to vary over time even though theory and prior research suggest that in reality both do (DesJardins, Ahlburg, & McCall, 2002). While the College Board self-publishes findings linking AP exam-taking to time to degree, its results are simple correlations that fail to adequately account for the substantial differences between AP and non-AP students (e.g., Camara, 2003).

While it is not clear that taking less time to graduate is better across all dimensions than taking more time, there are private costs to students and their families and public costs to taxpayers of prolonged time to degree. Privately, more time in school translates to foregone wage income and, for many, greater debt. Students who would proceed to professional schools delay advanced study and the accumulation of on-the-job training that is only possible in the field. Publicly, extended time to degree increases the need for Pell Grants, federally subsidized Stafford Loans, and other aid and decreases income and sales tax revenue. For students whose families can afford to finance a leisurely college experience, exploring multiple fields of study in the spirit of liberal education may make them well-rounded and build their character. However, given unprecedented increases in the costs of attending college, it is impractical for many students to take longer than absolutely necessary to earn the baccalaureate degree.

AP experience is likely to affect time to degree in two ways. First, students who earn sufficient points on an AP exam are awarded college credit by many institutions. In fact, some students earn enough credits from AP exams to enter the university as sophomores by credit hours. As seniors in 1998, 6 percent of 23,565 students tested in Texas in their last two years of high school had earned scores of 3 or higher on five or more AP exams (TSMP, 1997–1998). If these students enter colleges that grant credit for their particular AP exams, they will have earned one full semester of credit hours before they attend their first university lecture.

A second way AP experience may influence time to degree is by helping students identify their interests early and change majors fewer times. In a survey of the parents of 1992 and 1993 baccalaureate degree recipients who took longer than four years to graduate, the number-one reason parents identified for their child's extended time to degree was changing majors (Sanford & Rivera, 1994). Students surveyed in California confirm that changing majors is a primary reason for taking longer than four years to graduate (CSPEC, 1988). With students taking more and more AP classes and exams, it may be the case that the AP Program is helping students identify their interests while in high school rather than during the more costly college years. College courses, and the AP courses that emulate them, offer a different perspective on many fields than students see during their standard K–12 schooling, and it can take time for students to reconcile their naive understandings with the realities of advanced study. Therefore, getting early college-level experience might help students avoid the costly major changes that occur after students begin program-specific upper-level coursework.

Dual credit programs provide an alternative to the AP Program for students wishing to earn college credit while in high school. Historically, students traveled to the local community college to take dual credit courses, and credits from the courses applied concurrently toward both a postsecondary degree and toward the high school degree. For this reason, dual credit courses are often called concurrent enrollment classes. Today, dual credit courses are sometimes offered at the high school and taught by either college faculty or high school teachers with advanced degrees, or the courses are broadcast from the community college via interactive television.[3] Unlike AP courses, which are supposed to follow the College Board's AP course descriptions, dual credit courses are no more standardized than any first-year college courses.

When given a choice between AP and dual credit courses, a choice most commonly available to students in suburban schools, students find dual credit courses relatively more attractive for two reasons. First, unlike the AP Program, where students must pass the AP exam to be eligible for college credit, students who earn a grade of C or better in a dual credit course are eligible for college credit without additional testing. Second, community college credit is fairly uniformly portable, while AP credit policies vary substantially across (and even within) universities. Despite concerns about consistency and quality, dual credit programs play a unique and important role in the United States because they typically serve students at small or rural schools where it is not feasible to offer a quality AP Program. For the remainder of this chapter, I refer to the AP Program and dual credit programs as *accelerated learning* opportunities.

The Cost of a Fifth Year

Although public institutions of higher education are primarily funded by tuition revenues and state appropriations, perceptions that the average time to degree was lengthening fueled a 1993 amendment to the federal Higher Education Act of 1965 requiring institutions to publicly report their graduation rates (Sanford & Rivera, 1994). In advance of the federal legislation, the California legislature requested that the University of California and California State University systems survey students in order to identify the primary reasons students do or do not graduate in four years (CSPEC, 1988). Both reports found that among 1987 graduates, three of the most commonly cited reasons were taking extra courses "out of interest," changing majors, and working while in school.

The California reports determined that the public cost of extended time to degree depended on the reason a student took longer than eight semesters to finish (CSPEC, 1988). If students take a reduced course load each semester in order to fulfill employment or family demands, there is no additional cost to the state because the university is funded based on student credit hours attempted, and these students do not enroll in extra credit hours. However, there is a public cost to the additional semesters of study for students who enroll in a full course load each semester but fail to graduate in four years because they (1) explore a variety of courses that are not directly related to the degree requirements, (2) are unable to enroll in the specific courses they need to complete their degree, (3) change major, or (4) retake courses due to low or failing grades. In all cases, however, there are private costs to additional years of study that include the opportunity cost of foregone income from full-time employment as well as tuition and fees.

In Texas, the policy arena for the current study, appropriations are allocated using a mixed formula that combines credit hours attempted and enrollment, so there are costs to taxpayers of extended time to degree regardless of whether students are taking a full course load (Legislative Budget Board, 2007). The potential savings to taxpayers of decreasing the time to graduation is substantial. The National Center for Education Statistics' Integrated Postsecondary Education Data System (IPEDS) data allow for the calculation of a crude measure of the average per-student cost of an additional year of study at a four-year public university. Using the sample of thirty-four four-year public universities in Texas in 2000, the average taxpayer savings from graduating one in-state student in four years instead of five was nearly $4,500, or $2,250 per semester (IPEDS, 2008).[4]

The Public Return to Accelerated Learning Subsidies

Rough estimates of the expected public return to AP exam and dual credit program subsidies are provided in equations 1 and 2.

(1) Expected public return to an AP exam subsidy

$$= \sum_{\substack{subsidy \\ recipients}} \text{Prob(pass exam)} \cdot (\text{change in \# semesters to degree} \mid \text{pass exam}) \cdot (\text{public cost of 1 semester})$$

(2) Expected public return to dual credit funding

$$= \sum_{\substack{subsidy \\ recipients}} \text{Prob(pass class)} \cdot (\text{change in \# semesters to degree} \mid \text{pass class}) \cdot (\text{public cost of 1 semester})$$

The equations indicate that for each subsidy recipient, the expected return is the probability of shortening time to degree (in fractions of a semester) times the dollar amount in public savings from the shortened time to degree. The savings are then summed across all subsidy recipients. The equations assume that there are no benefits to accelerated learning other than shortened time to degree.[5] To calculate the private return, simply replace the "public cost of 1 semester" with "private cost of 1 semester."

Depending on the funding formula, shortening the time to degree by a fraction of a semester may not benefit taxpayers because semesters are not divisible. If the funding formula depends on enrollment only, then the change in the number of semesters in the above formula must be rounded down to the nearest integer, and if the accelerated learning experience shortens time to degree by less than one semester, then tax-payers do not save. If the funding formula depends on credit hours taken in addition to enrollment, and accelerated learning allows a student to take a lighter course load, then taxpayers do save. However, students re-ceiving financial aid must be enrolled full time (twelve hours or more), which limits their ability to decrease the number of credit hours taken.[6]

DATA

I estimate the effect of AP course experience on time to college graduation by tracking a cohort of Texas students for ten postsecondary semesters us-ing the Texas Schools Microdata Panel (TSMP). Students in the sample graduated from Texas public high schools in spring 1997 and matricu-lated directly at one of twenty-nine four-year Texas public universities.[7] This cohort of traditional college students provides a relatively straight-forward foundation for gaining an initial understanding of the influence of AP on time to degree. We do not observe student behavior for the full ten semesters (i.e., their data is censored) when students graduate, trans-fer to another university, or stop-out for more than two semesters.[8] Of the 32,922 students in the original sample, 4,220 are missing information on the college attended, major, credit hours, and/or GPA and are dropped from the sample. Thus, the final sample in the first semester of college consists of 28,702 students.

Overall, 24 percent of freshmen at Texas public universities graduate four years later compared to 36 to 39 percent nationally (IPEDS, 2008; Bradburn, Berger, Li, Peter, & Rooney, 2003; Knapp, Kelly-Reid, Ginder, & Miller, 2008).[9] Partly due to the inclusion of private universities in many of the national statistics, four-year graduation rates are lower at Texas four-year public institutions than those nationally. Four-year gradua-tion rates are also underestimated in the Texas data for groups with large rates of out-of-state or private transfer students.[10] Not only do Texas on-time graduation rates tend to be lower than those reported in national datasets, disparities in the on-time graduation rates between stayers and transfers, men and women, and whites and nonwhites tend to be larger. Students attending only one public institution graduate on time 53 per-cent of the time in Texas, more than double the rate of all students. The closest available nationally representative comparison reflects a 58 per-cent on-time graduation rate for students from public and private univer-sities combined. Because private schools post higher on-time graduation rates than public schools, the national rate for public schools alone is closer to Texas's 53 percent (Bradburn et al., 2003). Thus, stayers are 40 percent more likely than all students to graduate in four years nationally compared to 121 percent more likely in Texas.

Nationally, women at public institutions are 42 percent more likely to graduate in four years than are men (Knapp et al., 2008), while the comparable difference between men and women in Texas public institutions is 69 percent. Nationally, 41 percent of white students graduated on time versus 29 percent in Texas; 27 percent of black students graduated on time versus 14 percent in Texas; 30 percent of Hispanic students graduated on time versus 14 percent in Texas; and 43 percent of Asian students graduated on time versus 31 percent in Texas (Bradburn et al., 2003). While the levels are at times starkly different, partly due to the inclusion of private universities in the B&B data, the ordinal rankings of graduation rates by sex and race are the same nationally as in Texas.

Accelerated learning, such as that provided by the AP and dual credit programs, facilitates timely (four-year) baccalaureate degree completion by allowing students to start earning college credits while in high school. In order to account for differences in time to degree that can be explained by student characteristics other than accelerated learning experience, I incorporate variables in the statistical analyses that are measured once during high school or college and others that are measured each semester during college. The former, which for the purposes of the analysis are invariant with respect to time, include enrollment at a rural high school, gender, race, special education experience, English proficiency, family income while in high school, class rank, high school GPA, SAT or ACT score, admission with an undeclared major, and the number of times a student changes major. The time-varying variables include cumulative college GPA and whether the student works for pay. Changes away from the undeclared major are not included in the total number of major changes because being undeclared necessitates one change in major. The variables used to explore whether AP experience shortens time to degree are (1) whether a student took an AP course, (2) whether a student passed an AP exam with a score of 3 or higher, and (3) whether a student enrolled in a dual credit course. While the vast majority of students who take the AP exam have taken the relevant AP course, many students take the course but do not take the exam. Thus, students who passed an AP exam are, for all intents and purposes, a subset of students in the AP course-taking sample. However, the AP and dual credit samples are largely unique. The number of AP exam-passers is approximately equal to the number of dual credit course-takers, and the groups overlap little; just 14 percent of AP exam-passers also took a dual credit course and vice versa. Table 10.1 presents descriptive statistics and sources for each of these variables.

While there are students who change majors up to six times, frequent major changes are rare. A majority of students (52 percent) carry the same major until censored by graduation, transfer, or dropping out, and 97 percent of students change majors never, once, or twice.[11] There is no evidence that accelerated learning students, be they AP or dual credit students, are more or less likely than other students to change their major. However, students with college-level course experience from either AP or dual credit programs are slightly less likely to enter with an undeclared major (the simple correlation between accelerated learning experience and entering undeclared is -0.10). If undeclared majors are significantly less likely to graduate in four years than other students, as theory would predict, then AP and dual credit experience may indirectly decrease time to degree by facilitating early identification of the major with which a student will ultimately graduate.[12]

Figure 10.1 shows hazard functions of the probability that a student will graduate in each semester given that he or she did not graduate in a prior semester. The plots are presented separately for students who had no accelerated learning experience, students with AP course experience, students with dual credit course experience, and students who passed an AP exam. As intuition would predict, students with accelerated learning experience generally have higher probabilities of graduation than those without such experience.[13] AP exam-passers are more likely than other groups to graduate each semester, followed closely by dual credit course-takers. Students who took AP courses are no different from students without accelerated learning experience in semesters six and seven, but they are more likely to graduate in semesters eight, nine, and ten. The smaller gap between AP course-taking and students with no accelerated learning experience is consistent with the fact that taking AP courses alone does not generate college credit while the other two options can and often do.

The curves in figure 10.1 are "unconditional" in that they demonstrate the differences in time to degree between accelerated learning groups when no other differences between the groups (e.g., SAT scores or family income) are accounted for. Thus, differences between the groups could be due to the causal *or* the selection effects previously discussed. Students who participate in accelerated learning (especially those who did so in the

TABLE 10.1 Descriptive statistics

Variable	N	Fraction of sample or mean[a]	Standard deviation	Minimum	Maximum	Description	Source[c]
Enduring variables							
Demographic							
Female	28702	0.55	—	0	1	Female	PEIMS
Asian	28702	0.07	—	0	1	Asian	PEIMS
Black	28702	0.10	—	0	1	Black	PEIMS
Hispanic	28702	0.18	—	0	1	Hispanic	PEIMS
White	28702	0.65	—	0	1	White	PEIMS
Free or reduced-price lunch	28702	0.21	—	0	1	Qualified for free or reduced-price lunch in any year between 1991 and 1997	PEIMS
Special education	28702	0.02	—	0	1	Special education student in any year between 1991 and 1997	PEIMS
Limited English proficient	28702	0.03	—	0	1	Limited English proficient in any year between 1991 and 1997	PEIMS
Low income	28702	0.14	—	0	1	Parent income less than $15,000	FAFSA
Middle income	28702	0.20	—	0	1	Parent income between $15,000 and $52,500	FAFSA
High income	28702	0.10	—	0	1	Parent income above $52,500	FAFSA
Income missing	28702	0.01	—	0	1	Parent income not reported because student not a dependent	FAFSA
No apply	28702	0.55	—	0	1	Student did not apply for aid	FAFSA
Rural	28702	0.29	—	0	1	Student attended a rural Texas public high school	GIS

(continued)

TABLE 10.1 Descriptive statistics (*continued*)

Variable	N	Fraction of sample or mean[a]	Standard deviation	Minimum	Maximum	Description	Source[c]
Academic							
SAT equivalent	28702	1001	192	400	1600	SAT score or, if no SAT, ACT equivalent composite score	CB/ACT
In top 25% in class rank	28702	0.51	—	0	1	=1 if in top 25% of high school graduating class	CB/ACT
HS GPA: A	28702	0.53	—	0	1	=1 if report high school GPA is an A	CB/ACT
HS GPA: High B	28702	0.33	—	0	1	=1 if report high school GPA is a B to a B+	CB/ACT
Dual credit	28702	0.15	—	0	1	=1 if enrolled in college courses for dual credit while in high school	PEIMS
AP any dummy	28702	0.43	—	0	1	=1 if took any AP courses	PEIMS
AP any	12189	2.23	1.51	0.5	10	total AP credits taken (given take an AP course)	PEIMS
AP exam 3 dummy	28702	0.14	—	0	1	=1 if passed any AP exams with score of 3 or higher in senior year	CB
AP exam 3	4130	1.76	1.12	1	9	AP exams in which earned a 3 or higher in senior year (given take an AP exam)	CB
Undeclared major	28702	0.25	—	0	1	Undeclared, liberal arts, or general studies major in first semester	THECB
Number major changes	13782	1.38	0.63	1	6	Number of times changed major from anything other than undeclared	THE CB
Censored due to stopout or transfer	28702	0.33	—	0	1	Not enrolled for more than two consecutive semesters or transfer to another Texas public four-year	THECB
Graduate	28702	0.46	—	0	1	Graduate in ten semesters or fewer	THECB

Variable	N	Mean	SD	Min	Max	Description	Source
Graduate, given do not stopout or transfer	19121	0.70	—	0	1	Graduate in ten semesters or fewer, given do not stopout or transfer	THECB
Time to degree (in semesters), given graduate	13444	8.80	1.0	4	10	Time to degree for graduates	THECB
Time-varying variables[b]							
Cumulative college GPA	28702	2.51	0.97	0	4	College GPA on a four-point scale	THECB
Working	28702	0.50	—	0	1	Earned income in a social security covered sector	TWC

Notes: [a] For dummy variables, the mean represents the proportion of the sample reporting a 1.
[b] For time-varying variables, the reported mean reflects the value in semester 1 (fall 1997).
[c] Guide to source abbreviations: PEIMS, Texas's Public Education Information Management System; FAFSA, Free Application for Federal Student Aid; GIS, author's calculations using Geographic Information System; CB, College Board; ACT, ACT, Inc.; THECB, Texas Higher Education Coordinating Board; TWC, Texas Workforce Commission.

mid-1990s, when this sample was taken) tend to be high achieving and highly motivated and to attend schools that are relatively well-funded, employ high-quality teachers, and serve few minority and low-income students (Klopfenstein, 2004a, 2004b). Consequently, the AP and dual credit students depicted in figure 10.1 may have graduated sooner than others even in the absence of accelerated learning experience.

ANALYSIS AND RESULTS

All analyses are conducted using survival analysis to estimate whether, on average, students who engage in accelerated learning options while enrolled at Texas public high schools graduate with a baccalaureate degree more quickly, holding other observable characteristics constant, from Texas public universities than students who do not. Survival analysis is a statistical method suitable for the study of longitudinal data where information is repeatedly collected on the same individuals over time. Short of an experimental design, longitudinal data provides the best available information on programmatic effectiveness. An experimental design would be preferable because it would solve the selection problem; rather than students electing to participate based on their individual and school

FIGURE 10.1 Unconditional probability of graduation by accelerated learning experience

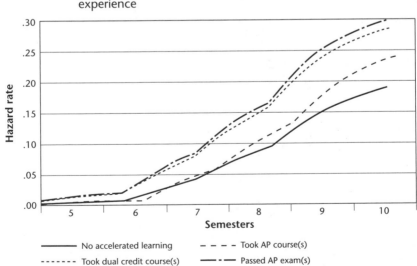

attributes, students would be randomly placed in accelerated learning programs and their subsequent performance compared to a randomly chosen control group of students who were not given the same opportunity. However, as in many educational settings, such an experiment is practically impossible and would be unethical for a variety of reasons.

Given that a longitudinal design is the best available analytic method, survival analysis is appropriate for studying time to degree because it allows for the inclusion of time-constant or time-varying variables and time-constant or time-varying effects. While some variables in the data are inherently constant (e.g., gender), others are variable across time (e.g., cumulative GPA). Moreover, the effect of variables may be constant or vary over time. While most models assume a constant effect over time, there are cases where it is reasonable to expect an effect to vary. For example, working is a time-varying variable since a student may work during some semesters but not others. In addition, working may have a larger adverse effect on time to degree for freshmen than for upperclassmen because freshmen often have more difficulty managing their time. Thus, it is important to capture the dynamic nature of working by observing repeatedly whether students are actually working and by allowing the impact of working on time to degree to differ over the years.

Even when a variable itself is time-invariant, like race or gender, there can be intuitive reasons to allow for flexibility in its effect. For example, black or Hispanic students often face great challenges in the early college years as they adjust (or fail to adjust) to a new environment without the immediate support of culturally similar family and friends (Tinto, 1993). Once the student has adjusted, the impact of race on time to degree might be markedly diminished. Constraining the effect of race to be constant over time would produce incorrect estimates if the true effect varies from one year to the next.

Survival analysis can also account for unobserved differences (heterogeneity) between students. An explicit treatment for unobserved heterogeneity is potentially important when studying time to degree because of sample attrition as students drop out, transfer, or graduate. Students exit the sample nonrandomly, so the average observable and unobservable characteristics of students who remain in the sample change (DesJardins, McCall, Ahlburg, & Moye, 2002). For example, students who drop out after their freshman year are likely different in both observable and unobservable (to the researcher) ways from students who do not drop out. As more students drop out over time, the sample of stayers becomes less and less similar to the original full sample. Traditional methods of statistical analysis can provide misleading results in such a case.

I estimate a variety of statistical models with different assumptions to check the robustness of the models (Blossfeld, Golsch, & Rohwer, 2007). Readers interested in the technical details of the analysis should consult Klopfenstein (2008). All models account for the unobserved heterogeneity that comes from nonrandom exit of the sample discussed above. I provide results in table 10.2 for the Cox proportional hazard model (Cox, 1972) and a Weibull model under the proportional hazard assumption. In both models I allow the accelerated learning variables, along with several control variables, to have time-varying effects. Because no students graduate in year one, and just eight students graduate in year two, only the estimates for years three through five are displayed. The findings are robust across a wide variety of specifications and modeling assumptions. Estimates on the control variables, which account for observable differences between students that might confound the effect of accelerated learning on time to degree, are reassuring in that they behave as theory, and/or previous research would predict and are essentially unaffected by changes in the modeling assumptions.[14]

The estimated hazard ratios in table 10.2 indicate a positive effect on the probability of graduating in each year (given that a student has not graduated prior to that time) if they are greater than 1.0, and the percentage larger than 1.0 indicates the magnitude of the effect. For example, if the coefficient on passing an AP exam is 1.08 in year four, as is the case for the Cox model in table 10.2, the interpretation is that "among students who did not graduate prior to year four, an AP exam-passer is eight percent more likely to graduate in year four than is a student who has not passed an AP exam." If the hazard ratio were 0.80, this would indicate that the probability of graduating in year four for AP exam-passers is 80 percent of that of a similar nonpasser. The estimates on continuous variables are similarly interpreted. An estimated hazard ratio of 2.73 on college cumulative GPA indicates that a student with a one-point-higher GPA than an otherwise similar student has a 173 percent higher probability of graduation in year four (assuming he or she did not graduate prior to year four).

The results in table 10.2 clearly indicate that the effects of gender, race, working, college GPA, and accelerated learning experience differ over the college years and that estimating a model that does not allow for change

TABLE 10.2 Time-varying hazard-ratio estimates, Cox and Weibull models

	Year 3		Year 4		Year 5	
	Cox[a]	Weibull[b]	Cox[a]	Weibull[b]	Cox[a]	Weibull[b]
Female	1.56***	1.76***	1.37***	1.46***	1.16***	1.18***
	(0.19)	(0.28)	(0.04)	(0.14)	(0.03)	(0.04)
Asian	1.65***	1.97**	1.12**	1.28***	0.98	0.81***
	(0.29)	(0.58)	(0.06)	(0.10)	(0.05)	(0.04)
Black	0.54	0.72	1.02	1.26***	1.11**	0.80**
	(0.21)	(0.24)	(0.06)	(0.11)	(0.06)	(0.08)
Hispanic	0.83	0.90	0.97	1.01	0.98	0.67***
	(0.18)	(0.20)	(0.04)	(0.12)	(0.04)	(0.05)
Working	0.94	1.14	0.95*	1.12***	0.97	0.79***
	(0.11)	(0.09)	(0.03)	(0.03)	(0.02)	(0.02)
Cumulative GPA	4.73***	17.03***	2.73***	5.65***	2.26***	1.59***
	(0.58)	(1.62)	(0.07)	(0.43)	(0.05)	(0.16)
Took AP course(s)	1.06	1.17	1.04	1.10***	1.00	0.99
	(0.13)	(0.13)	(0.03)	(0.04)	(0.03)	(0.04)
Passed AP exam(s)	1.71***	1.47**	1.08**	0.98	0.91***	1.01
	(0.22)	(0.25)	(0.04)	(0.07)	(0.03)	(0.04)
Took dual credit	2.89***	3.19***	1.27***	1.34***	1.16***	1.19***
	(0.33)	(0.52)	(0.04)	(0.03)	(0.04)	(0.03)

Notes: [a] Gamma shared frailty on university. Standard errors in parentheses.
[b] Unshared inverse-gaussian frailty. Robust standard errors in parentheses.
* $p \leq .10$, ** $p \leq .05$, *** $p \leq .01$

over time would obscure meaningful information. The differential effect of race over time provides one possible explanation for why black students, despite a decreased likelihood of graduation in three years, are equally as likely as white students to graduate in year four. The positive female and Asian effects are largest in the early years, although the possible causal forces are less intuitive. The GPA effect is also largest in the early years, although it maintains the largest magnitude of any variable across all five years. A one-grade-point increase in GPA (e.g., from a 2.5 to a 3.5) more than quadruples the likelihood of graduating in year three and almost triples the likelihood of graduating in year four.

The value of incorporating time-varying coefficients becomes particularly apparent when examining the effect of the accelerated learning variables. Consider first the Cox regression results in table 10.2. While taking an AP class has no statistically significant impact in any single year, passing one or more AP exams increases the likelihood of graduating in year three by 71 percent. The practical significance of this result is limited, however, given that a very small fraction of students graduate in three years (350 out of 14,854 graduates in this sample). The effect of AP exam-passing on the probability of graduation decreases to 8 percent in year four and is completely dissipated, and even negative, by year five. Interestingly, the effect of taking one or more dual credit classes is nearly triple the probability of graduating in year three relative to students who did not take such courses. The dual credit effect is 3.5 times the size of the AP exam effect in year four and, unlike the AP exam effect, remains positive and significant in year five.[15]

There is a possibility, however, that accelerated learning may impact time to degree indirectly by helping students identify their field of interest prior to entering college. Among all students in the sample, 25 percent enter with an undeclared major, compared to 22 percent of dual credit students and 13 percent of AP exam-passers. AP exam-passers and dual credit students also change majors with half the frequency of all students (0.7 times over the college career versus 1.4 times). The Cox and Weibull models estimate that students who enter college undeclared are 50 percent less likely to graduate in a given semester, and each time a student changes major, the probability of graduation in a given semester reduces by 7 percent (results not shown). Future research might model these outcomes directly to better understand the role of accelerated learning in the timing and choice of college major and the magnitude of the effects.

Figure 10.2 displays predicted hazard functions for a typical student, meaning one with the average characteristics of the sample but with different accelerated learning experiences.[16] Figure 10.2 can be thought of as a version of figure 10.1 that accounts for the observable differences between students who participate in accelerated learning and those who do not. Students are much more likely to graduate in the spring (even-numbered semesters) than in the fall (odd-numbered semesters), so the predicted hazards peak at eight semesters, dip at nine semesters, and

FIGURE 10.2 Predicted probability of graduation in each semester for the average student

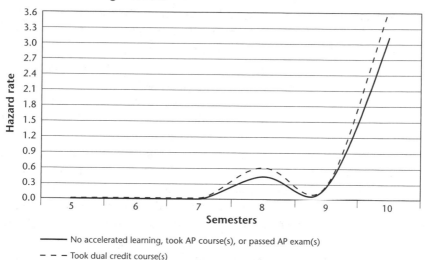

——— No accelerated learning, took AP course(s), or passed AP exam(s)

− − − Took dual credit course(s)

spike for the final observation in the tenth semester. The solid line reflects the predicted probability of graduation in any given semester after accounting for all the student characteristics previously discussed for students with no accelerated learning experience, students with AP course experience, and students who pass an AP exam. Only the dual credit course-takers depart from the baseline group, those who have no accelerated learning experience. The interpretation of this graph is that AP course-takers and exam-passers would have, on average, graduated in approximately the same length of time if they had not had any AP experience. The practical implication of this result is that pressing students into AP classes who are unlikely to take and pass the AP exam provides no benefit in terms of shortening time to a college degree. Even though the results in table 10.2 show that AP exam-passing increases the probability of graduating in year three by almost 50 percent and dual credit courses by over 200 percent, the baseline probability of graduating in three years is so low that even tripling that probability does not create a discernible difference for the average student.

Figure 10.2 indicates that dual credit course-taking might have a causal impact on time to degree for the typical student (that is, a student with average characteristics on the control variables) in eight and ten semesters, but there is no similar evidence for AP course-taking or AP exam-passing. The differences in graduation rates between AP students and those without accelerated learning in figure 10.1 disappear in figure 10.2 because they are driven entirely by preexisting differences between AP and non-AP students. Differences between dual credit and other students are not definitively causal because we do not have an experimental design. Students select into accelerated learning programs based on characteristics that are unobservable to the researcher, like work ethic and curiosity, in addition to those that are observable, like SAT score, and only observable characteristics can be accounted for in the models. It is possible, even after controlling for observable characteristics that students in accelerated learning programs graduate sooner than other students due to the unobserved differences between groups of students.

Although it is not possible with the available data to determine to what extent the observed positive effect of dual credit courses in figure 10.2 is driven by the program itself, we can reasonably rule out causal effects for the AP Program when, after accounting for observed differences in program participants, the hazard curves for AP students (course-takers or exam-passers) and students without accelerated learning experience merge like they do in figure 10.2. The identification of a causal mechanism is important for scalability: if the impact of accelerated learning is specific to the type of students who tend to participate in the program rather than to the program itself, similar benefits will not be observed when the program is expanded to other types of students.

CONDUCTING THE COST-BENEFIT ANALYSIS

While public money is also used for AP teacher training and incentive payments, by far the largest percentage of AP Program subsidies is dedicated to exam fees. In 1997, when students in the sample studied here were seniors in high school, more than $1.5 million was spent on AP test fee subsidies in Texas alone (see table 10.3). By 2004 this number had increased to $4.3 million. These subsidies go directly to the College Board and its subcontractor, the Educational Testing Service.

Calculating the expected return to AP subsidies is more involved than calculating the cost of the subsidies. For students who have not yet taken an AP course or gone to college, the expected benefit of AP subsidies can be calculated using equation 1. However, the TSMP contains actual outcomes for the 1997 cohort of Texas public high school graduates, and I

TABLE 10.3 Estimated expenditures on AP test fee subsidies in Texas by year

Year	Number of AP test-takers at Texas public high schools	Number of AP tests taken by Texas public high school students		Cost of state subsidy for all students[b] ($)	Cost of additional subsidy for low-income students[c] ($)	Total expenditure on test fee subsidies ($)
		Not low income	Low income[a]			
1997	27,682	37,669	9,630	1,418,970	144,450	1,563,420
1998	32,331	42,815	12,901	1,671,480	193,515	1,864,995
1999	37,705	49,282	17,440	2,001,660	313,920	2,315,580
2000	46,399	60,650	23,774	2,532,720	427,932	2,960,652
2001	53,227	69,690	29,867	2,986,718	537,609	3,524,328
2002	54,070	69,621	32,763	3,071,516	589,731	3,661,247
2003	57,531	73,036	37,625	3,319,817	677,243	3,997,059
2004	61,270	75,327	42,371	3,530,950	762,685	4,293,635

Notes: [a] Due to data limitations, starting in 2001 the percentage of exams taken by low-income students is extrapolated based on patterns in previous years and is assumed to increase at a conservative 2.0 points per year.
[b] Texas has provided a $30 subsidy for AP exam fees since 1997 for all students who take the appropriate AP course or have a principal's recommendation.
[c] Texas subsidized low-income student AP exam fees at $15 per test in 1997 and 1998 and at $18 per test thereafter.

calculate the benefit to AP exam-taking by assuming that, consistent with the findings in table 10.2, AP experience has a causal impact on graduation for all students who graduated in three years (six semesters or fewer) and passed one or more AP exams. Calculated this way, the estimated benefit represents a ceiling on the true benefit to AP subsidies, because some of these students would have graduated early even in the absence of AP exams. Clearly, AP or dual credit experience is not necessary for early college graduation: there were 105 students in the same cohort who had no such experience and graduated in six semesters or fewer.

In this sample, there were ninety-eight students graduating in three years or fewer who had passed an AP exam and thirty-six who had both passed an AP exam and taken a dual credit course.[17] Suppose, for the sake of argument, that half of the thirty-six students with both passing AP exams and dual credit experience were able to graduate early due to AP and half due to dual credit. Thus, there were 116 students for whom AP was a potential causal factor leading to early graduation. Recalling that the public savings from a one-semester shortening of time to degree for an in-state student during this time period was $2,250, and assuming that students would have graduated in eight semesters without AP exams, I calculate the public benefit of AP in terms of shorter time to degree as

$$(3) \quad \sum_{i=1}^{6} 2250 \, N_i i$$

where

$i=$ (8 – semester in which graduated | semester graduated ≤ 6)

$N_i =$ number of students graduating i semesters early

In other words, calculate the savings for all the students graduating one semester early, add to this the savings for all the students graduating two semesters early, add to this the savings for all the students graduating three semesters early, and so on through the students graduating six semesters early. For the high school class of 1997, the gross public savings from AP exam fee subsidies using equation 3 is $550,125, but recall that this is an upper bound on the true benefit to AP subsidies because some of these students would have graduated early even in the absence of AP exams.[18] The process outlined here shows that in the best-case scenario AP subsidies cost Texas taxpayers at least $1.5 million and returned at most $500,000 in tuition savings.

Ideally, I would conduct a similar cost-benefit analysis for the dual credit program. However, since that program is administered without the involvement of private third parties, the costs are less easily identifiable. There are reasons to believe that the costs associated with dual credit are quite different than those associated with AP, not only because dual credit is implemented within the existing public education infrastructure but also because the programs have quite different formats and serve different student populations. Different demographics among students participating in dual credit programs can affect both the cost and benefit sides of the equation in ways that are difficult to measure or predict.

A critical difference between the AP Program and dual credit programs, according to AP proponents, is the standardization provided by the AP exams that ensure consistency and high quality that cannot be ensured for students passing dual credit courses. The fact that dual credit students progress through college at a faster rate than even AP exam-passers, once differences in student demographics are accounted for, indicates that this problem may not be as large as many fear. At least part of the reason dual credit students progress more quickly through college is demographic. Relative to AP exam-passers, dual credit students are more rural, have lower income (as measured by qualification for free or reduced-price lunch while in secondary school, filing a Free Application for Federal Student Aid (FAFSA) form, and working in the first semester of college), have lower academic achievement (as measured by SAT scores, class rank, high school and first-semester college GPAs), and are more likely to be black or Hispanic (table 10.4). While both AP and dual credit students are highly

TABLE 10.4   Selected descriptive statistics of AP exam-passers and dual credit enrollees

	AP exam-passers	Dual credit course-takers
SAT equivalent	1214.824	1048.049
Top 25% in class rank	76.08	65.08
HS GPA: A	80.10	67.23
HS GPA: High B	15.23	25.03
HS GPA: Low B	1.82	4.26
HS GPA: High C	0.27	0.84
First-semester college GPA	3.03	2.71
Free or reduced-price lunch	10.77	13.05
Working first semester	43.87	48.02
No apply for financial aid	67.19	59.28
Asian	14.29	4.72
Black	2.13	3.78
Hispanic	8.91	12.26
White	74.67	79.23
Female	52.81	59.54
Rural	17.70	43.38
Undeclared major	13.34	22.13
Number of times changed major	0.70	0.71
N	4130	4175

Source: Texas Schools Microdata Panel (1991–2002).

motivated, schools with large AP programs tend to be well financed and have a culture of college-going. It may be more socially and financially acceptable for AP students to engage in intellectual exploration while in college, and they may, as a group, view college as a rite of passage and opportunity for personal growth more than as a means to an end. Thus, AP experience allows for more freedom while in college but does not, on average, shorten time to degree. In contrast, dual credit students as a group appear to have a more pragmatic view of college. They are less likely to have the cultural and/or financial means to treat the college years as a time for personal growth, and by and large they are motivated to limit debt and enter the job market as soon as possible.

DISCUSSION AND CONCLUSIONS

I utilize survival and cost-benefit models to obtain a more accurate and complete picture of the costs and benefits of AP subsidies than was previously available. I find that AP course-taking alone has no impact on time to degree after accounting for differences in several observable characteristics between AP and non-AP students. Passing an AP exam increases the likelihood that a student will graduate in three years and has no effect thereafter. This suggests that the students for whom AP exams have an impact are those who pass enough AP exams to obtain advanced (sophomore) standing when they enter college—a very small group of students who have access to a wide array of quality AP courses in high school and the resources, financial and academic, to successfully prepare for multiple exams each May. Dual credit experience not only increases the likelihood of graduation in three years, it also has large positive effects on the likelihood of graduation in four and five years, conditional on not having already graduated.

While some might view the minimization of time to degree as inconsistent with the mission of liberal education, the reality is that students and their families often accumulate substantial sums of debt to finance college. Moreover, students incur a considerable opportunity cost in terms of foregone wage income for every day they are not in the labor force. On the public side, in addition to the direct expenses the university incurs for a student in their fifth or later year, the government loses revenue from payroll and consumption taxes. Thus, from a financial standpoint, it is in the students' and the public's best interests to promote programs and policies that facilitate timely degree completion.

Based on the evidence presented here, subsidies to the AP Program are not justified on the grounds that AP experience shortens time to degree. I am also skeptical that any AP effects on time to degree will be observed in cohorts of high school students graduating after 1997. The mid- and late-1990s were the early years of the expansion of AP to traditionally underserved populations (Klopfenstein, 2004b). Up to this time, the students who took AP were among the most well-prepared of all high school students. Cohorts entering college after 1997 are likely to include more first-generation college students whose struggles in college are neither well understood nor adequately addressed by most colleges (Tinto, 1993). If the vast majority of the AP exam-passer effect on time to degree is driven by selection, it is unlikely that AP experience will shorten time to degree for future cohorts. If the policy objective is to provide incentives for students to graduate in a more timely fashion, manipulation of the tuition structure—or, as Adelman (2006) suggests, limits on no-penalty withdrawals and no-credit repeats—are likely to be more effective than AP subsidies.

These findings must be viewed in the context of equity as well as the efficiency and cost concerns raised here. There are two types of AP subsidies: those targeted to low-income students and the schools that serve them and those for which income is not an eligibility requirement. AP subsidies for low-income students are designed to improve equity in accelerated learning opportunities. However, the efficacy of AP subsidies in this regard is questionable because of the dismal performance of low-income students on AP exams, in large part owing to the fundamental failings of schools that serve large proportions of black, Hispanic, and/or low-income students (see Dougherty & Mellor, this volume; College Board, 2007). While some proponents suggest that an AP Program generates high expectations that trickle down to the lower grades, there is no evidence that such a top-down strategy works, particularly in schools where many students are performing below grade level. Thus, AP subsidies for low-income students fail to improve educational equity and can, ironically, divert resources from proven programs that would benefit disadvantaged students.

AP subsidies without income eligibility requirements go largely to students at schools that offer a number of AP courses, and these schools tend to serve students who are not low income (Klopfenstein, 2004b). In theory, such subsidies would generate a public return by facilitating timely baccalaureate degree completion. In practice, AP students earn baccalaureate degrees in about the same amount of time as students without AP experience. Thus, taxpayer money spent on AP subsidies generates zero public return, although it potentially generates some private return to students through the admissions benefit (see Klopfenstein & Thomas, this volume).

On the metric examined here, time to college degree, dual credit programs perform as well or better than AP programs, but the cost burden for the two programs differs. The cost of AP programs falls largely on the school district and state through the K–12 curriculum and state-funded incentive programs that finance teacher training and performance incentives. The federal government also finances significant test fee subsidies. Dual credit programs utilize existing postsecondary infrastructure and therefore require less funding for new program development. Moreover, students bear these costs through tuition payments, as is the case in Texas, which can then be reimbursed by the school district or the state (Michelau, 2006). With AP exam fee subsidies, taxpayer money is transferred directly to private entities. With dual credit subsidies, taxpayer dollars remain not just within Texas but within the public education system.

This work is a first attempt to identify the impact of AP experience on time to baccalaureate degree. Future research should examine the impact of AP for a broader demographic, including transfer students. Transfers have dramatically lower on-time graduation rates, especially in Texas, and AP credits may play a role in mitigating the credit losses inherent in transfers between four-year institutions. Future studies might also consider whether AP and dual credit effects differ for a variety of college majors. Finally, as new data become available, future studies should examine whether the impact of AP on college graduation is different for students who passed AP exams in the new century, after the 1990s expansion, than that for earlier and less racially and economically diverse cohorts.

NOTES

My thanks go to Stephen DesJardins for substantive help with the research design. I thank Kelly Callaway and Debbie Gonzales from Advanced Academics/Gifted Education at the Texas Education Agency for providing information on AP exam subsidies. I am grateful to Fran Huckaby, Gerhard Sonnert, Cliff Adelman, Robert Tai, Kathleen Thomas, Chrys Dougherty, and Tim Diette for editorial advice. I also thank Laura Mason for research assistance. All errors remain my own.

1. Survival analysis has its roots in epidemiological studies that consider the impact of factors, such as a therapeutic intervention, on the length of time until an event occurs, such as heart attack or death.

2. The International Baccalaureate is another accelerated learning option, but there were not enough high schools offering the program in Texas in the late 1990s for it to be included in the analysis.

3. Information based on survey data Klopfenstein (2004c) gathered about dual credit course offerings at more than seven hundred Texas public high schools in 2003–2004.

4. This is calculated as annual funding for instruction, academic support, and student services minus in-state tuition and fees per full-time equivalent student. This excludes funding for day-to-day operations that are not directly influenced by the marginal student/year, such as institutional support ("expenditures for general administrative services, executive direction and planning, legal and fiscal operations, and public relations and development" (IPEDS, 2008), debt servicing, research, utilities, and grounds maintenance. Scholarships are also excluded under the assumption that recipients are eligible for eight semesters only.

5. Given the relatively short time horizon and for simplicity, future values are not discounted; discounting would decrease the value of future benefits.

6. While students in their final semester can prorate their financial aid based on a lower number of credit hours, doing so requires both the knowledge that this is possible and coordination with the university's financial aid office.

7. The vast majority of students who graduate from college matriculate within one year of graduating from high school. In the 2000–2001 Baccalaureate and Beyond Longitudinal Study (B&B), 83 percent of first-time bachelor's degree recipients in 2000 attended college less than one year after graduating from high school (Bradburn, Berger, Li, Peter, & Rooney, 2003). Only students who matriculate directly following high school graduation are considered here because students who take time off between high school and college have much higher dropout rates and lower graduation rates (Ahlburg, McCall, & Na, 2002).

8. By censoring departing students at the time of exit, I prevent circumstances faced by transfer students from confounding estimates of the effect of AP on time to degree. The possibility of confounding effects is driven by the fact that students who initially attend two-year schools and transfer to four-year colleges, as well as students who transfer between four-year colleges, have significantly longer average time to degree (NCES, 2003).

9. B&B surveyed four-year degree recipients in 2000, and IPEDS provides data from four-year degree recipients in 2004 (Knapp et al., 2008; Bradburn et. al., 2003). B&B statistics reported here are from Bradburn et al. (2003), which combines public and private institutions. IPEDS statistics are from Knapp et al. (2008), which separates private and public institutions. Both sources include stop-outs in their calculations.

10. The TSMP sample used here includes stop-outs and in-state transfers, but students who transferred to out-of-state or private universities cannot be identified separately from stop-outs. Thus, these transfers appear in the denominator but not the numerator, and, consequently, four-year graduation rates are underestimated for groups with large rates of out-of-state or private transfer. The magnitude of this sampling error is mitigated in part by the fact that transferring decreases the likelihood of on-time graduation.

11. This figure includes students who enter undeclared and subsequently declare a subject-specific major. This approach differs from the regression analyses where I give undeclared majors one "free" major change, which is analytically appropriate given the inclusion of the undeclared dummy variable in all regression models.

12. Morgan and Maneckshena (2000) provide some exploratory analysis of the link between AP experience and choice of college major.

13. The null hypothesis for the equality of the survivor functions can be rejected in each case with greater than 99 percent confidence using both log rank and Wilcoxon test statistics.

14. For a discussion of the theoretical predictions for the control variables, see DesJardins Ahlburg, and McCall (1999). Estimates for the control variables across all models are available in Klopfenstein (2008).

15. Hypothesis tests confirm that the AP exam coefficients are different from the dual credit coefficients at better than 1 percent.

16. Predictions are calculated based on estimates generated from the full Weibull model in table 10.2.

17. Among students who only had dual credit experience, ninety-eight graduated in six semesters or fewer.

18. If subsidized students go to a private college or out of state, they do not appear in this sample. However, there is no public benefit from subsidies to these students unless they graduate early and gain employment in Texas sooner than they might have without passing AP exams. The scant evidence of a causal effect of AP exams on early graduation coupled with the question of whether out-of-state students return to work in Texas after graduation yields a trivial expected return for this group.

REFERENCES

Adelman, C. (1999). *Answers in the tool box: Academic intensity, attendance patterns, and bachelor's degree attainment.* Washington, DC: U.S. Department of Education, Office of Educational Research and Improvement.

Adelman, C. (2006). *The toolbox revisited: Paths to degree completion from high school through college.* Washington, DC: U.S. Department of Education.

Ahlburg, D. A., McCall, B. P., & Na, I. (2002). Time to drop out from college: A hazard model of college dropout with endogenous waiting [Working paper]. University of Minnesota Industrial Relations Center. http://www.legacy-irc.csom.umn.edu/RePEC/hrr/papers/0102.pdf

AP Strategies. (2008). Incentive programs. http://www.apstrategies.org/ip/

Bailey, T., & Karp, M. M. (2003). *Promoting college access and success: A review of credit-based transition programs.* Washington, DC: U.S. Department of Education, Office of Vocational and Adult Education.

Blossfeld, H., Golsch, K., & Rohwer, G. (2007). *Event history analysis with Stata.* Mahwah, NJ: Erlbaum.

Bradburn, E. M., Berger, R., Li, X., Peter, K., & Rooney, K. (2003). *A descriptive summary of 1999–2000 bachelor's degree recipients one year later, with an analysis of time to degree* (NCES 2003-165). Washington, DC: U.S. Department of Education, National Center for Education Statistics.

California State Postsecondary Education Commission [CSPEC]. (1988). *Time to degree in California public universities: Factors contributing to the length of time undergraduates take to earn their bachelor's degree* (Report 88-12). http://www.cpec.ca.gov/CompleteReports/1988Reports/88-12.pdf

Camara, W. J. (2003). *College persistence, graduation and remediation* (College Board Research Note 19). New York: College Board.

College Board. (2005). *The value of AP courses and exams.* http://www.collegeboard.com

College Board. (2007). AP: Exam grades, summary reports: 2007. http://www.collegeboard.com/student/testing/ap/exgrd_sum/2007.html

College Board. (2008). AP central. http://apcentral.collegeboard.com/apc/Controller.jpf

Cox, D. R. (1972). Regression models and life tables. *Journal of the Royal Statistical Society, Series B (Methodological), 34*(2), 187–220.

DesJardins, S. L., Ahlburg, D. A., & McCall, B. P. (1999). An event history model of student departure. *Economics of Education Review, 18*(3),375–390.

DesJardins, S. L., McCall, B. P., Ahlburg, D. A., & Moye, M. J. (2002). Adding a timing light to the "tool box." *Research in Higher Education, 43*(1), 83–114.

Dougherty, C., Mellor, L., & Jian, S. (2006). Orange juice or orange drink?

Ensuring that "advanced courses" live up to their labels (NCEA Policy Brief No. 1). Austin, TX: National Center for Educational Accountability.

Integrated Postsecondary Education Data System [IPEDS]. (2008). Peer analysis system. http://nces.ed.gov/ipedspas

Klopfenstein, K. (2004a). Advanced Placement: Do minorities have equal opportunity? *Economics of Education Review, 23*(2), 115–131.

Klopfenstein, K. (2004b). The Advanced Placement expansion of the 1990s: How did traditionally underserved students fare? *Education Policy Analysis Archives, 12*(68). http://epaa.asu.edu/epaa/v12n68/

Klopfenstein, K. (2004c). Texas public high school counselor survey. Unpublished data.

Klopfenstein, K. (2008). The effect of AP participation on time to college graduation: Technical report. http://www.utdallas.edu/research/tsp-erc/publications .html

Klopfenstein, K., & Thomas, M. K. (2009). The link between Advanced Placement experience and early college success. *Southern Economic Journal, 75*(3), 873–891.

Knapp, L. G., Kelly-Reid, J. E., Ginder, S. A., & Miller, E. (2008). *Enrollment in postsecondary institutions, fall 2006; graduation rates, 2000 & 2003 cohorts; and financial statistics, fiscal year 2006* (NCES 2008-172). Washington, DC: U.S. Department of Education, National Center for Education Statistics.

Legislative Budget Board, State of Texas. (2007). Financing higher education in Texas: Legislative primer (3rd ed.). http://www.lbb.state.tx.us/Higher_ Education/HigherEd_FinancingPrimer_0107.pdf

Michelau, D. K. (2006). The state policy landscape. In Western Interstate Commission for Higher Education (Ed.), *Accelerated learning options: Moving the needle on access and success* (pp. 7–23). Boulder, CO.

Morgan, R., & Maneckshana, B. (2000). AP students in college: An investigation of their course-taking patterns and college majors (ETS Report No. SR-2000-09). Princeton, NJ: Educational Testing Service.

National Center for Education Statistics [NCES]. (2003). *The condition of education 2003* (NCES 2003-067). Washington, DC: U.S. Government Printing Office.

No Child Left Behind Act [NCLB]. (2001). http://www.ed.gov/policy/elsec/ leg/esea02/index.html

Sanford, T. R., & Rivera, N. (1994). Parents' perceptions of students' time to degree. AIR 1994 annual forum paper. (ERIC document ED373639)

Texas Schools Microdata Panel [TSMP]. (1991–2002). Texas schools project. University of Texas at Dallas. Unpublished data.

Tinto, V. (1993). *Leaving college: Rethinking the causes and cures of student attrition* (2nd ed.). Chicago: University of Chicago Press.

CHAPTER 11

Preparing Students for Advanced Placement

It's a PreK–12 Issue

Chrys Dougherty and Lynn T. Mellor

A growing number of educators and policy makers have adopted the goal of preparing all high school students for college and other postsecondary learning opportunities (NGA Center for Best Practices et al., 2008).[1] In support of this goal, reports by ACT and the American Diploma Project emphasize that readiness for college and readiness for workplace training increasingly require similar skills, especially for careers that pay above minimum wages (ACT, 2006b; Achieve, 2004). A content-rich preK–12 curriculum is also important for preparing students for citizenship and for closing achievement gaps between advantaged and disadvantaged students (Campaign for Fiscal Equity, 2003; Hirsch, 2007).

Policy makers and education leaders have embraced the Advanced Placement Program as a tool to strengthen the high school curriculum and prepare students for college (U.S. Department of Education, 2006). The popularity of AP among some policy leaders reflects their belief that the traditional high school curriculum has often failed to provide intellectually challenging courses with well-specified curricular content and end-of-course exams to verify that students have mastered that content— and that AP courses and exams can provide the missing rigor to the high school curriculum (U.S. Department of Education, 2001).

In order to promote educational equity and college readiness of minority and disadvantaged students, policy makers and funders have sought to expand the AP program in schools serving those students (U.S. Department of Education, 2008; National Math and Science Initiative, 2009). We view this policy as having both short- and long-term goals. The short-run goal is to improve the educational experience of the better-prepared disadvantaged students—often with the goal of increasing participation of academically stronger disadvantaged students in science, engineering, and mathematics fields. Conceptually, one might think of this as a focus on the "talented tenth" of disadvantaged students (DuBois, 1903).[2] The longer term goal is to use the AP Program to promote the readiness of the great majority of disadvantaged students for college and skilled careers. The difference between these two goals parallels the distinction that Hess and Rotherham (2007) make between the "competitiveness" agenda of focusing on top students and the "equity" agenda of bringing up all students, including those in the bottom half of the achievement distribution.

The short-term goal can be addressed by identifying disadvantaged students who are already reasonably well-prepared and enrolling them in AP courses. However, the long-term goal—enabling a much broader group of disadvantaged students to succeed in college-level courses while they are still in high school—requires an emphasis on preparing students ahead of time (Dougherty & Mellor, 2009). Thus, the problem of college readiness is a key issue for AP: since properly taught AP courses are college-level courses, a student should be college ready in the relevant subject on day one of an AP course in order to be adequately prepared for that course. Facile slogans that "Advanced Placement is for everyone" do not relieve educators of the responsibility to prepare students in the earlier grades so that they can do the college-level work required by an AP course that is true to the College Board's course description.[3]

Our own research on the relationship between eighth-grade academic preparation, high school AP participation and exam success, and college graduation yielded four results that bear directly on the importance of preparing students for AP (Dougherty, Mellor, & Jian, 2006a). First, it matters greatly whether students take and pass AP exams. There is little evidence that simply increasing the number of students taking AP courses will have an impact on college graduation rates if students do not demonstrate mastery on the exams. Second, low-income and minority students have low AP exam passing rates. Third, this pattern fits with other evidence we found that many students receive credit for high school courses with little indication that they have mastered the content implied by the course titles (Dougherty, Mellor, & Jian, 2006b). Finally, academic preparation prior to high school, as measured by eighth-grade test scores, is strongly predictive of whether students will take and pass any AP exam in a mathematics, science, English, or social studies subject.

It Matters Greatly Whether Students Can Pass AP Exams

Our analysis of the relationship between AP and college graduation used data from Texas, as that state's data system made it possible to follow students from grade 8 in 1994 through five years of college by 2003. We found that simple comparisons of AP students with non-AP students show that even students who take AP courses but fail AP exams do better in college than do students who do not take AP courses (Dougherty et al., 2006a). However, these comparisons can be extremely misleading. They might simply show that whatever personal characteristics cause students to choose to enroll in AP courses—such as motivation and family support—also help students succeed in college. They should not be interpreted as demonstrating that the AP courses themselves prepared the students better for college, especially in the absence of evidence that the students actually learned the AP course content.

This cautious interpretation was supported by the fact that when we ran the analysis at the school level, the relationship between AP participation and college graduation disappeared for most groups of students who did not pass AP exams.[4] In particular, once we controlled for students' demographic characteristics and academic preparation in eighth grade, schools with higher percentages of students taking AP courses but not passing AP exams did not have higher percentages of students graduating from college. Only the percentage of the school's student body taking and passing AP exams predicted the future college graduation rate of the school's students (Dougherty et al., 2006a).[5] We were also cautious about interpreting this relationship. Because success on AP exams is related to students' overall levels of academic preparation in high school, we were careful not to conclude that the relationship between AP exam passing rates and college graduation rates by itself demonstrates an "AP effect." Instead, we may be observing an overall effect of better student academic preparation. That is, high schools and school districts that do a better job of preparing students for college produce more students who take and pass AP exams and also produce more students who later graduate from college.

Our conclusion is that the percentage of the student body that takes and passes academic AP exams can be a useful indicator of the strength of a school's or district's academic program.[6] More can be learned about the value-added of high schools if one disaggregates students by their level of academic preparation leaving eighth grade. However, the percentage of the student body *taking* AP courses and exams appears to be related to college graduation only through the relationship of that statistic to the percentage of the students *taking and passing* AP exams. There is no evidence of an independent effect of AP course-taking on college graduation for students who fail the AP exam.

Low-Income and Minority Students Have Low AP Exam Passing Rates

Table 11.1 shows AP exam passing rates measured as a percentage of students earning high school credit for AP courses and as a percentage of the entire student population, including students who do not participate in the AP program. AP course completers are defined as students who completed at least one AP course in one of the four academic subject areas of English, mathematics, science, and social studies. AP exam-passers are students who passed at least one AP exam in one of these subject areas. These results are for a cohort of Texas students because the availability of

TABLE 11.1   AP exam passing rates

	Students passing AP exams	
	As percentage of AP course completers	As percentage of all graduates
African American	11.2	1.9
Hispanic	14.3	2.8
White	35.1	12.3
Other	50.9	28.9
Low income	13.0	2.2
Non–low income	35.4	13.1
All students	29.8	8.5

Note: These percentages are taken from a cohort of 1998 Texas students who graduated from high school in 2002.
Source: NCEA (2005).

the necessary longitudinal student data in that state made the analysis possible. As is evident from the table, the percentage of low-income, African American, and Hispanic students in 2002 who passed one or more exams was low measured either as a percentage of those students completing one or more AP courses or as a percentage of the graduating student population from each of those groups. This information indicates that we have a long way to go to prepare the low-income and minority student population to succeed in the AP Program.

To increase the percentage of low-income, African American, and Hispanic students succeeding in the AP Program, policy makers and funders have established incentive programs to encourage more students to take AP courses and pass the exams. A large incentive program of this type was established in the Dallas public schools in the late 1990s and later extended to other school districts in Texas (Advanced Placement Strategies, 2008).

Table 11.2 reflects results from the early years of the Texas AP incentive programs. The table shows the percentage of Texas low-income high school graduates taking and passing at least one academic AP exam in 1998, when the incentive programs were new, and in 2002 after these programs had increased AP course and exam participation. We show AP passing rates as a percentage of the entire low-income student population in order to gauge increases in the percentage of this population who are able to master the skills measured on at least one academic AP exam. We disaggregated magnet from nonmagnet schools because magnet schools tend to recruit the strongest students. Although the percentage increases in these passing rates are large, those increases are from a very low base.

TABLE 11.2 Change in population AP exam passing rates for low-income students, 1998–2002

		Percentage of low-income high school graduates passing AP exams		
		1998	2002	% change 1998–2002
Schools in AP incentive programs	Magnet	3.96	6.03	52%
	Nonmagnet	0.99	2.93	196%
Schools not in AP incentive programs	Magnet	1.01	2.08	106%
	Nonmagnet	1.00	1.61	61%

Thus the low-income students who are able to take and pass AP exams still made up a very elite group in 2002. Only magnet schools with AP incentive programs registered population exam passing rates above 3 percent in 2002 for low-income students. We expect that if updated percentages such as these were published nationally, they would still be low.[7]

Course Completion Information Can Be Misleading

Several studies have noted the relationship between academic course-taking in high school and college readiness and success (Adelman, 1999; ACT, 2006c, 2007a). As a result, as of 2007 thirteen states had established a college preparatory course curriculum as the default academic program for graduating students (Gandal, Cohen, & Kraman, 2007). In addition, twenty-four states had State Scholars programs that encourage high school students to complete such a curriculum (State Scholars Institute, 2007).

However, as the student population taking these courses expands to include many less-well-prepared students, teachers and school systems appear to have adapted by adjusting the course content to the academic level of the students—without creating the systems needed to bring the students up to the level implied by the course titles. Algebra II, for example, may not be algebra II when the students spend most of the year catching up on algebra I or even pre-algebra. This may account for the evidence that a large percentage of students, particularly disadvantaged students, are receiving credit for college preparatory courses without mastering the content implied by the course titles (Dougherty et al., 2006b). We refer to this as the "orange juice or orange drink" problem, using the metaphor that giving course credit to students who have learned little of the course content is like selling orange drink mislabeled as orange juice. Like the erroneous drink labels, the course titles on the students' transcripts may bear little relationship to what those students have actually learned.

Table 11.3 provides evidence that course labels often do not convey what the students have learned. The majority of low-income, African American, and Hispanic students who completed the basic college preparatory curriculum in Texas needed remediation when they got to college.[8] Again, the examples in table 11.3 are taken from Texas because Texas is one of the few states that can match student-level preK–12 and higher education data longitudinally. Texas made a college preparatory curriculum the default curriculum for students entering grade nine in the 2004–2005 school year (TEA, 2006).

TABLE 11.3   Percent of Texas students who graduated from high school in
2000 and completed state-recommended college preparatory
course sequence who still needed remediation in college

African American	61%
Hispanic	59%
White	27%
Low income	63%
Not low income	33%

Source: J. Dilling, Texas Higher Education Coordinating Board (e-mail to L. Mellor, March 3, 2005).

End-of-course (EOC) exams are needed to inform student, parents, educators, and policy makers about whether students who receive credit for college preparatory courses have mastered content consistent with the course titles.[9] In addition, states and school districts should routinely match student records longitudinally and examine whether students completing courses with the right titles are in fact college-ready as measured by their success on college readiness exams and by their ability to succeed in college.

Academic Preparation in the Early Grades Is Critical for AP Readiness

Simply putting more students into college preparatory high school courses is unlikely to have the desired impact on college readiness rates if students are not academically well prepared for those courses (Dougherty & Mellor, 2009). Prior preparation is especially important for enabling students to master AP course content and pass AP exams, since AP exams require the ability to do college-level work while still in high school.

A focus on the goal of college readiness for the majority of disadvantaged students requires early intervention, ideally in preschool and elementary school, to place those students on a path to college readiness. Using the metaphor of an academic growth ramp that extends from early childhood to eventual readiness for college, many advantaged students are on this ramp from the beginning. Most disadvantaged students are on a much lower ramp from an early age. For example, one study by Hart and Risley (1995) found that as early as age three, children whose parents were professionals had about double the vocabulary size of children of parents on public assistance—an average of 1,100 versus 525 words. Gaps between advantaged and disadvantaged students tend to widen over time (Rathbun, West, & Hausken, 2004).

Because of the differences in prior preparation between economically advantaged and disadvantaged students, effective interventions for disadvantaged students that start as late as middle or high school tend to be quite drastic. For example, the KIPP Academies, which generally start in fifth grade, rely on a 60-percent increase in learning time and often retain students in fifth grade in order to give them additional time to catch up (Mathews, 2007). Jaime Escalante's celebrated program to prepare students for the AP Calculus exam put students into summer school, early morning, and Saturday classes to catch them up. But neither KIPP nor Escalante's program has provided an example of bringing a majority, or even a very large minority, of the disadvantaged students in an entire community up to college or AP readiness (Mathews, 1989, 2007, 2009).[10]

Figure 11.1 illustrates the importance of students' eighth-grade academic preparation for their ability to take and pass AP exams in high school. The chart disaggregates the state's low-income students into four groups based on their level of academic proficiency in reading and

FIGURE 11.1   AP results disaggregated by 8th grade TAAS performance in 1999: Low income students

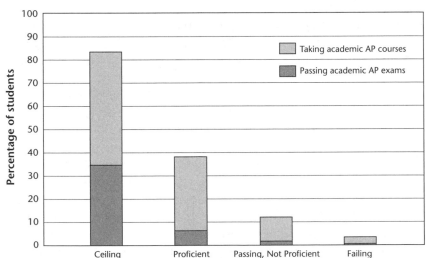

mathematics leaving eighth grade in 1999. For each group the chart shows the percentage of students taking at least one AP course and taking and passing at least one AP exam in any of the four academic subject areas. The *ceiling* group had scored at the top of the state test in both subjects; this was the only group with as many as a third of their students passing academic AP exams. Less than 7 percent of students in the next higher *proficient* group passed an AP exam in any academic subject, and the corresponding statistic was around 1 percent for students who met the state's passing standard on both tests but missed proficiency on at least one of them.[11]

CONCLUSION

Using AP to improve the academic experience of the relatively better prepared disadvantaged students poses many challenges. Yet those challenges pale in comparison with those associated with making courses at the AP level *academically accessible* to the vast majority of disadvantaged students. Here the issue is one of prior academic preparation more than anything else.

To assist with the process of preparing students, educators in states and school systems must improve curriculum, assessment, and data systems so that parents and educators can tell whether elementary, middle, and high school students are on the academic readiness ramp to AP courses and college. End-of-course exams are needed to make sure that high school course transcripts convey accurate information. Interventions need to start early and be part of a seamless preK–12 effort to get students ready. The strategy of focusing on one level at a time—high school reform, preschool expansion, etc.—needs to be replaced with an effort that recognizes the academic connection among the different levels (National Center for Educational Achievement, 2010). And education and community leaders must commit to the steps necessary to prepare disadvantaged students to handle the work in challenging high school courses, including AP courses that require students to do college-level work while still in high school.

NOTES

The authors would like to acknowledge the assistance of Shuling Jian in conducting this research and of Janey Chaplin in preparing this article.

1. *All students* means everyone in the general student population without major cognitive deficits. Although many students do not plan to attend college when they leave high school, almost three-quarters of high school graduates enroll in college within two years (ACT, 2006a). In addition, students' future opportunities should not be constrained by their own level of foresight as teenagers or by the preconceptions about them held by adults.

2. The "tenth" number is not too far off given recent measures showing college readiness rates below 10 percent for minority students (ACT, 2008).

3. And just as nonselective colleges admit many students who are not college ready, so many high schools admit less-well-prepared students into AP courses in the hopes that those students will work hard and catch up. Thus, making adequate preparation of students for AP courses a priority does not imply that less-than-ready students should be excluded from the courses. Research has not resolved the issue of how unready students should be before it is best to counsel them into taking a preparatory course first.

4. Our research on AP exam performance focused on schools' *population academic AP exam* passing rates. We defined this rate as the percentage of an entire student cohort in a school taking and passing at least one AP exam in at least one of the four academic subject areas of English, mathematics, science, and social studies. We used *population* passing rates as opposed to *exam-taker* passing rates because the percentage of AP exam-takers passing exams can be raised artificially by restricting AP exam participation to the best-prepared students. The College Board's Excellence and Equity statistic is an example of a population AP exam passing rate (College Board, 2005). We used population AP exam passing rates *in the four academic subject areas* in order to develop a measure that did not include AP Spanish exams taken by native Spanish speakers. The large percentage of Hispanic students taking and passing these exams is likely to distort the picture on college readiness of those students.

5. To understand why a relationship that appears strongly in student-level data can disappear at the school level, consider a hypothetical high school that sorts its best-performing 20 percent of students into Room A, while the remaining students remain in Room B. Under those circumstances, Room A students are likely to outperform Room B students on every outcome indicator, even if Room A itself has no effect on those outcomes and even after the analysis controls for measured variables such as student demographics and prior achievement. That is because Room A students are likely to also excel in unmeasured characteristics such as

student motivation. (This problem of selection bias is why researchers prefer studies based on random assignment of students, an approach often not available in educational settings.) If Room A is just a place to put the stronger students but itself has no effect on them, any apparent Room A effect is likely to disappear when the predictor is the percentage of students that the school chooses to place in Room A. Students who take AP courses but do not pass AP exams are subject to this vanishing Room A effect. Aggregation to the school level to reduce the impact of selection bias is also used in Allensworth, Correa, and Ponisciak (2008).

6. Clearly, the fact that some high schools offer many rigorous courses in addition to AP means that AP exam passing rates should not be the *only* indicator. It is important to (1) develop multiple indicators for evaluating the strength of school programs and (2) distinguish stronger from weaker indicators in the hopes that multiple strong indicators can be developed.

7. For example, the authors backed-out population-wide AP exam passing rates for African American students from the College Board (2007) and obtained a statistic of 3.6 percent for African American students. The Hispanic statistic was higher but in all appearances strongly influenced by native Hispanic Spanish speakers passing the AP Spanish-language exam.

8. The low AP exam passing rates in the left-hand column of table 11.1 for students earning credit for AP courses is further evidence of this problem. Additional evidence is provided by comparisons of students' ACT scores with their self-reported course-taking patterns (ACT, 2007a). For example, in 2007 only 15 percent of ACT test-takers who completed or were enrolled in mathematics courses through algebra II, but took no courses beyond that level, reached the College Readiness Benchmark on the ACT Mathematics exam (ACT, 2007b). However, the skills students need to master in order to reach the benchmark are those that should normally be taught in pre-algebra, algebra I, and geometry classes (ACT, 2006a).

9. As of spring 2007, fourteen states—Arkansas, California, Georgia, Indiana, Maryland, Massachusetts, Mississippi, North Carolina, New York, Oklahoma, South Carolina, Tennessee, Utah, and Virginia—had EOC exams in one or more high school subjects. In addition, in fall 2007 ACT introduced its QualityCore program with EOC exams and formative assessment item pools in eight high school courses. As of spring 2009, twelve core high school courses were covered by this program (ACT, 2009).

10. One need simply compare the numbers of students who have succeeded in each of these programs with the total number of students in the high school (in the case of Escalante's program) or in the immediately surrounding school district (in the case of KIPP schools).

11. The proficiency level referred to in figure 11.1 was an academic achieve-
    ment target identified in 1998 by NCEA's predecessor organization, Just
    for the Kids (JFTK), based on the belief that the state's passing standard
    was too low to drive school improvement around strong teaching and
    learning. This level consisted of a Texas Learning Index (TLI) score of 85
    or higher (versus 70 or higher for passing) on the Texas Assessment of Ac-
    ademic Skills (TAAS) test. A TLI of 85 was one standard deviation above
    the passing score of 70 in 1994, the year the TLI scale was established.

REFERENCES

ACT, Inc. (2006a). *Ready to succeed: All students prepared for college and work.*
    http://www.act.org/path/policy/pdf/ready_to_succeed.pdf

ACT, Inc. (2006b). *Ready for college and ready for work: Same or different?* http://
    www.act.org/path/policy/pdf/ReadinessBrief.pdf

ACT, Inc. (2006c). *Crisis at the core.* http://www.act.org/path/policy/pdf/crisis
    _report.pdf

ACT, Inc. (2007a). *Rigor at risk.* http://www.act.org/path/policy/pdf/rigor_report
    .pdf

ACT, Inc. (2007b). *National and state scores for 2007: Course rigor effects on col-
    lege readiness.* http://www.act.org/news/data/07/rigor.html

ACT, Inc. (2008). *ACT High school profile: Section III, college readiness and the
    impact of course rigor.* http://www.act.org/news/data/08/pdf/three.pdf

ACT, Inc. (2009). *What is QualityCore?* http://www.act.org/qualitycore/quality
    core.html

Achieve, Inc. (2004). *Ready or not: Creating a high school diploma that counts.*
    http://www.achieve.org/files/ADPreport_7.pdf

Adelman, C. (1999). *Answers in the tool box: Academic intensity, attendance pat-
    terns, and bachelor's degree attainment.* Washington, DC: U.S. Department
    of Education.

Advanced Placement Strategies. (2008). *Incentive programs.* http://www.ap-
    strategies.org/ip/

Allensworth, E., Correa, M., & Ponisciak, S. (2008). *From high school to the fu-
    ture: ACT preparation—too much, too late.* http://ccsr.uchicago.edu/content/
    publications.php?pub_id=124

Campaign for Fiscal Equity. (2003). *Today's students tomorrow's citizens: Prepar-
    ing students for civic engagement.* http://www.cfequity.org/civengreport.pdf

College Board. (2005). *Advanced Placement report to the nation.* http://www
    .collegeboard.com/prod_downloads/about/news_info/ap/2005/ap-re-
    port-nation.pdf

College Board. (2006). *Excellence and equity.* New York: College Board.(2007). *Advanced Placement report to the nation.* http://www.collegeboard.com/ prod_downloads/about/news_info/ap/2007/2007_ap-report-nation.pdf

College Board. (2008). *Advanced Placement report to the nation.* http://professionals .collegeboard.com/profdownload/ap-report-to-the-nation-2008.pdf

Dougherty, C., Mellor, L., & Jian, S. (2006a). *The relationship between Advanced Placement and college graduation.* www.just4kids.org/en/research_policy/ college_career_readiness/

Dougherty, C., Mellor, L., & Jian, S. (2006b). *Orange juice or orange drink? Ensuring that "advanced courses" live up to their labels.* www.just4kids.org/en/ research_policy/college_career_readiness/

Dougherty, C., & Mellor, L. (2009). *Preparation matters.* National Center for Educational Achievement. http://www.nc4ea.org/files/preparation_matters -04-01-09.pdf

Dougherty, C., & Rutherford, J. (2010). *Six guiding principles for school improvement efforts.* Austin, TX: National Center for Educational Achievement.

DuBois, W. E. B. (1903). *The talented tenth.* http://www.teachingamericanhistory .org/library/index.asp?document=174

Gandal, M., Cohen, M., & Kraman, J. (2007). Is a default curriculum in high school a good strategy for promoting the humanities? In C. Finn & D. Ravitch (Eds.), *Beyond the basics: Achieving a liberal education for all children* (pp. 63-77). Washington, DC: Thomas B. Fordham Institute.

Hart, B., & Risley, T. R. (1995). *Meaningful differences in everyday experience of young American children.* Baltimore: Paul H. Brookes.

Hess, R., & Rotherham, A. (2007). *Can NCLB survive the competitiveness competition?* http://www.aei.org/publications/filter.all,pubID.26339/pub_detail.asp

Hirsch, E. D. (2007). *Narrowing the two achievement gaps.* http://coreknowledge .org/CK/about/articles/NarrowingGaps.htm

Mathews, J. (1989). *Escalante: The best teacher in America.* New York: Henry Holt.

Mathews, J. (2007, April 24). Looking at KIPP, coolly and carefully. *The Washington Post.* http://www.washingtonpost.com/wp-dyn/content/article/2007/ 04/24/AR2007042400558.html

Mathews, J. (2009). *Work hard. Be nice.* Chapel Hill, NC: Algonquin Books.

National Center for Educational Achievement. (2005). Unpublished analysis of Texas Advanced Placement passing rates of 1998 eigth graders graduating from high school in 2002.

National Governors Association Center for Best Practices, National Conference of State Legislatures, National Association of State Boards of

Education, & Council of Chief State School Officers. (2008). *Accelerating the agenda: Actions to improve America's high schools.* Washington, DC: National Governors Association.

National Math and Science Initiative. (2009). *NMSI boosts minority student participation in AP classes.* http://www.nationalmathandscience.org/index.php/blog/nmsi-boosts-minority-student-participation-in-ap-classes.html

Rathbun, A., West, J., & Hausken, E. G. (2004) *From kindergarten through third grade: Children's Beginning School Experiences.* National Center for Education Statistics. http://nces.ed.gov/pubs2004/2004007.pdf

State Scholars Institute. (2007). *State scholars initiative.* http://www.wiche.edu/statescholars/states/index.aspx

Texas Education Agency. (2006). *2006 Comprehensive annual report on Texas public schools.* www.tea.state.tx.us/research/pdfs2006_comp_annual.pdf

U.S. Department of Education. (2001). No Child Left Behind Act of 2001. Sec. 1701: Access to High Standards Act. http://www.ed.gov/policy/elsec/leg/esea02/pg14.html#sec1702

U.S. Department of Education. (2006). *Expanding the Advanced Placement incentive program.* http://www.ed.gov/about/inits/ed/competitiveness/expanding-apip.html

U.S. Department of Education. (2008). *Advanced Placement incentive program grants.* http://www.ed.gov/programs/apincent/index.html

CHAPTER 12

Whither Advanced Placement—Now?

William Lichten

In 2000 Richard Riley, the U.S. secretary of education, and Gaston Caperton, the president of the College Board, announced their recommendation to offer ten Advanced Placement classes in every high school in the United States in spite of the College Board's own research findings that predicted a high rate of failure for schools with a history of low PSAT scores. In fact, rather than raising achievement in inner-city schools, this surge appears to have catalyzed a series of failures. The program's implementation put AP courses in schools with unprepared students and teachers. This chapter suggests some lessons to be learned: schools and school districts should report AP scores openly; students need to be ready for AP before they enroll; and most minority and disadvantaged students are better served by other means than AP.

BAD OMENS IN THE INNER CITY AND THE AP SURGE

"In the 1995–96 school year, 29 students took an Advanced Placement American History course at Andrew Jackson High School and took [the] American History AP Exam to qualify for college credits. No one passed" (Pfankuch, 1997). Similar reports of failure in nonselective, inner-city schools have come out of Detroit (Lichten & Wainer, 2000), Washington, DC, and New York City (Mathews, 2000). But strangely, rather than slow the proliferation of AP courses in light of these outcomes, the AP program continued to grow and expand. It is not a lack of intellectual capacity among inner-city school students that is the question here. The talent of youth attending these schools is not the issue, but the lack of resources is. Both the students and their teachers lack the preparation for success from these resource-starved educational environments. With the joint announcement of Secretary Richard W. Riley and College Board President Gaston Caperton, the goal for every U.S. high school was to offer at least ten advanced courses by the year 2010, a surge into high schools of new college-level courses and exams. (College Board, 2000; "College Board Launches Drive," 2000). This policy did not account for schools with high poverty concentrations, high dropout rates, and historically low PSAT, SAT, or ACT scores. Indeed, rather than being prepared for college, many times graduates from struggling high schools have the need for remedial courses on arrival at college. A simple question apparently left unasked is how high schools that have graduates in need of remedial college coursework can be expected to teach students to succeed on AP exams designed to determine if students may bypass introductory college courses for advanced college courses. The error in reasoning is palpable. These indices did not augur well for the success of the AP Program in these schools.

Yet, despite these incongruities (Lichten, 2000), the College Board (2008, 2009) moved ahead with a recruitment pitch that claimed that "AP isn't just for top students or those headed for college. AP offers something for everyone."

AP IN PHILADELPHIA—A CASE STUDY

I now turn to the outcome of Riley and Caperton's grand announcement in the Philadelphia Public Schools (see figure 12.1). A total of 179 AP classes were taught in forty-one schools in 2006, about 45 percent of Riley and Caperton's goal of ten classes in each school in ten years, only slightly less than the progress expected toward their growth target. Thus, the Philadelphia public schools were doing their part toward reaching the enrollment number goal. No goal for quality of learning, as evidenced by examination scores, was announced.

A few schools (e.g., Central, Girls', and Masterman) did as well as the rest of the nation in AP scores. These high schools have long traditions of academic excellence, selective admission, and SAT and presurge AP exam scores at the national average or higher. However, schools with a history of low SAT scores performed poorly on the AP exams. Many of these high

FIGURE 12.1   Philadelphia public high schools in 2006.

Each point represents one high school. Forty-one high schools are arranged by their average 2006 SAT-V scores and by the percentage of the 2006 senior class that took at least one AP test and scored at least a 3. The red line is the expected percentage in each school of AP exams to have a score of 3 or more, based on the average SAT-V scores.

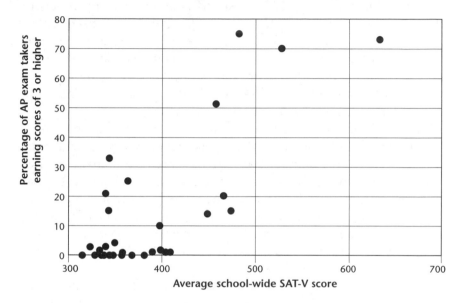

Sources: "Report Card on the Schools" (2007); Ewing et al. (2006).

schools did not have a single AP exam score as high as 3, the lowest score claimed as passing by the College Board.

For the schools without competitive admissions, the surge was nearly a total failure. Of the thirty-two high schools reporting average SAT-V scores between 313 and 408, only five reported AP exam passing rates of 10 percent or higher. The highest passing rate reported for any of these schools was 33 percent, which still indicates that two-thirds of the students received failing scores of 1 or 2 on their exams.

This pattern of AP failure is by no means peculiar to Philadelphia but is widespread throughout the nation in "non-exam" urban schools where students do not have to undergo a competitive admissions process. It is also true in nonurban high schools that have low average SAT or PSAT scores (Lichten, 2000; Lichten & Wainer, 2000; Ewing, Camara, & Millsap, 2006; deVise, 2007).

SOME QUESTIONS ABOUT THE OUTCOMES OF THE AP SURGE

Why is the performance on AP tests so poor in so many inner-city schools? Could it be racial (Herrnstein & Murray, 1994; Jensen, 1969)? Yet Renaissance High School in Detroit, with an almost 100 percent black student body, had AP math scores far above the national average and comparable to other top-performing schools in Michigan (Lichten & Wainer, 2000). This and other examples reported in major national newspapers refute this notion of a racial divide (e.g., deVise, 2007).

Is it that urban teachers and administrators are less competent? Yet, a comparison of urban-suburban performance shows no evidence for this hypothesis (Lichten & Wainer, 2000). On the contrary, perhaps AP teachers in nonselective urban schools were being asked to achieve unrealistic goals in preparing students with very low PSAT scores to do college-level work. Figure 12.2 casts light on this matter. In figure 12.2 the estimated percentage of students earning 3 or higher and 4 or higher is graphed across varying levels of performance on the PSAT exam for African American students. About a quarter of this group earns scores of 3 or higher, with a smaller percentage obtaining a more realistic passing score of 4 or higher. These successful students typically attend suburban or competitive-admissions urban high schools, where students are granted admission because they exhibit both academic talent and preparation and where teachers typically have more experience with high-achieving students. By the very nature of the process, students with lower PSAT scores have only the option of attending non-exam schools. Figure 12.2 shows that students with PSAT scores lower than roughly 90 have small estimated passing rates with scores of 3 or higher and practically no chance of scoring 4 or higher. The evidence from College Board and other research (Ewing et al., 2006; Lichten & Wainer, 2000) supports the conclusion that PSAT and SAT performance strongly predict aggregated scores on the AP exams. Furthermore, figure 12.1 shows that the nearly total washout for AP scores among non-exam inner-city schools, the very targets of the surge that Riley and Caperton proposed. In their joint statement (College Board, 2000), it is clear that Riley and Caperton were aware of the importance of adequate prerequisites. Yet, it appears from the schedule they proposed (one AP course added each year) that they put the AP courses cart before the prerequisites horse.[1]

FIGURE 12.2   Estimated percentage of students scoring 3 or higher and 4 or higher on the Advanced Placement English Literature exam

Probability of passing (squares for an AP score of 3 or higher; circles for 4 or higher) the AP English Literature exam as determined by PSAT scores. The "AV" arrow is for the national average PSAT score of students taking the AP English Literature exam (mean = 116, standard deviation = 17.7, 2006); "A-A" for the author's estimated average PSAT score for African Americans who take this examination.

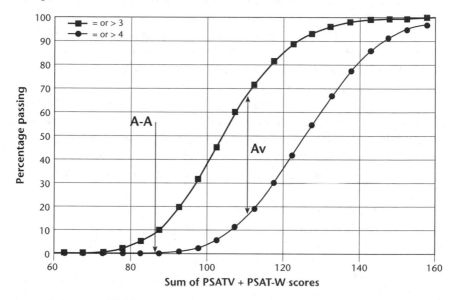

Source: Ewing et al. (2006).

It appears that bold top-down reinventions of education from the outside often have unrealistic and unattainable goals and fail to attend to the complexities of educational reform. Instead, effective school reforms are more likely to come from the inside (Tyack & Cuban, 1995).

LOOKING BACKWARD TO SEE FORWARD: PROPHETIC WARNINGS AND THE SHAPE OF FUTURE AP POLICIES

In 1937 Carl Brigham, the inventor of the SAT, foresaw the potential dangers of establishing a new testing agency. "What worried him most, because of his long experience with the incaution of testers . . . was that any organization that owned the rights to a particular test would inevitably become more interested in promoting it than in honestly researching its effectiveness" (Lemann, 1999). According to psychologist Donald T. Campbell (1976), "The more any quantitative social indicator is used for social decision making, the more subject it will be to corruption pressures and the more apt it will be to distort and corrupt the social processes it is intended to monitor" (49). Although Campbell addressed a multitude of human activities, he often found examples of his law in education. Walberg (1998) puts matters in a historical perspective: "The principle of 'conflict of interest' is hardly news. Aristotle warned his fellow citizens to consider the source, and the ancient Romans asked who would benefit from the proposed conclusions and decisions. What is new is the pervasiveness of what we will call 'the Diogenes factor' in program evaluation. According to ancient Athenian lore, Diogenes searched, with a lighted lantern, through daytime Athens for honesty. Though fabrication may be rare in educational evaluation, we can easily find selective evidence and misleading comparisons, which favor funded programs. These lead to overestimates of program effectiveness."

One might imagine that if Brigham were alive today, he might well advise the College Board to reconsider its policies in light of its own research findings. The unfortunate history of the AP surge into inner-city schools highlights some general points to keep in mind in any discussion of the future of the Advanced Placement Program. Because of the widespread use of AP in the nation's schools, and because much of the financing of the program comes out of public funds, *the American people have the right to know the truth about AP*.

Beginning with the College Board's qualification scale, the policy lists an AP exam score of 3 as passing or "qualified" for college-level credit. About three-quarters of all AP exams score 3 or higher; however, data indicates that only about half of these truly qualify for college credit, suggesting that to warrant granting college-level credit, scores should be 4 or higher (Lichten, 2007). (See figure 12.2.) To cite a precedent, the "recentering" of the College Board's SAT scale (Dorans, 2002) restored realism to a confused public discourse.

In regard to the reporting of AP exams scores, especially for schools in urban areas, the College Board has refused to release test score results on a school-by-school or school district basis. Success stories of schools and students abound, and not much is being said about the failures. But it is from the failures that we learn the most about how we may make change and improvements. Only through the efforts of newspaper reporters has the truth about AP scores in urban schools been revealed, as was the case for the data presented in figure 12.1. Reporters from the *Philadelphia Inquirer,* rather than the College Board, gathered this information about AP exam passing rates and reported the results to the public.

Given the commitment of public funds to subsidize the AP exams, it seems only prudent that the College Board should be obliged to give complete information about aggregate AP exam performance for schools and school districts. This can be done without violating the privacy of individual students. For example, the No Child Left Behind Act requires disclosure of test scores except where the number of persons in a disaggregated group is so small that student privacy would be violated.

Open and candid reporting and interpreting of school district and school average scores are needed. The current head of the AP Program, Trevor Packer, has begun a cautious move toward this goal (T. Packer, personal communications, 2007). From the beginning, the AP Program has preselected the most qualified students to participate (Lichten & Wainer, 2000). As the number of students taking AP courses expanded, it was predictable that AP exam performance would decline (Lichten, 2000). Indeed, the percentage of passing examinations has been steadily falling since 1986 (Lichten, 2000, 2007). (This is the case regardless of whether a 3 or 4 is taken to be passing.)

The most positive outcome of the surge may be to focus the attention of educators and policy makers on the importance of prerequisites for success. The College Board has paid lip service to adequate qualification and preparation for AP courses, but this policy has seldom been translated into action. An expansive effort to audit high school curricula for courses to be listed as Advanced Placement ended in 2008 with more a thud than a bang. The effort, funded in part by the National Science Foundation, more or less declared the problem of weak curriculum as having been solved with the curriculum audits. The argument made by the College Board was that high schools fielding weak courses intended for AP exam preparation were remediated and the weaknesses corrected. However, little information was provided about how lack of AP teaching experience and weak content background were handled by the AP review effort.

Finally, it must be realized that tests and grades do not always serve well minority and impoverished students. The long history of the black-white test score gap (Jencks & Phillips, 1998) indicates that AP and other programs based on standardized testing are less likely to reach the disadvantaged than are moves that directly address educational inequalities, such as affirmative action and achievement of diversity.

The AP Program of the College Board is now half a century old and has grown to be highly successful, with more than two million AP exams administered each year, an annual budget running into hundreds of millions of dollars, and plaudits bestowed by parents and public officials from the White House on down. Yet there has been a lack of critical evaluation in light of the massive scale of this program. In recent years, the National Research Council (2002) has also pointed out weaknesses in the science curriculum of AP courses taught by high schools, noting the lack of standards and the shockingly lower exam passing rates. In several papers (Lichten, 2000, 2007; Lichten & Wainer, 2000) I have pointed out the deterioration of the quality of AP students' examinations as the program expanded its base by accepting less-qualified applicants. The program's recent attempt to expand into nonexam urban high schools can best be characterized as a disaster, which realizes the prescient predictions of Carl Brigham half a century ago and should serve as a signal to the College Board for the need to reform the AP Program.

POSTSCRIPT: AP, INTELLIGENCE, AND MEASURABILITY IN EDUCATION

This book has performed a valuable function in taking a dispassionate look at one of America's most successful educational programs, Advanced Placement. But I should like to add a few words to put the discussion in a broader context.

A dominant feature of American culture is the exaggerated respect awarded to measurability. In psychology its personification has been intelligence as measured by IQ. In education it has resulted in a national preoccupation with grades and test scores.

In this P.S. I choose two examples of wartime leaders, Colin Powell and McGeorge Bundy, whose successes and failures hinged not only on their intellectual ability but also on other factors.

Consider Colin Powell, the first African American leader of the Joint Chiefs of Staff, whose single-minded leadership led, in just a few days, to a stunning victory in the Persian Gulf War. In all likelihood, if he had wanted it, he could have been the nation's president. Yet, as Powell put it, he graduated from college "with an average that barely crept above a C. The only way it did creep above a C was four straight years of A in ROTC, which, thank goodness, counted on your academic record . . . I have not done particularly well in college . . . I discovered that I was . . . not pretty good in physics, calculus, geology, history, languages or any of the other [courses]" (Means, 1992).

Powell biographer Means (1992) says, "Powell gets credit for understanding what one high ranking Pentagon official—someone who has worked closely with him—calls 'the simple things' that no academic course in government can teach. 'He understands how executive, political and military power are wielded in Washington'" (p. 78). "'I've often said in the jobs I've had, spare me geniuses,' Powell's mentor Frank Carlucci (Sect. of Defense) adds. 'Judgement doesn't always accompany genius'" (p. 79).

Powell's greatest failure was his speech before the United Nations in 2003 which he charged that Iraq had weapons of mass destruction (en .wikipedia, 2009). The discredited evidence that he presented necessarily involved scientific matters, which, by his own admission, were not among his strong points.

McGeorge Bundy, however, had a mixture of successes and failures and was the mirror image of Colin Powell. His academic brilliance was blinding. He was a star at Groton, the first Yale student to get perfect scores in all three College Board entrance examinations, and dean of Harvard University at a young age and went on to serve as national security adviser to two presidents and later become head of the Ford Foundation. "You can't beat brains," said President Kennedy of Bundy (Halberstam, 1992, p. 44). Bundy's greatest failure was his role in promoting the escalation of the war in Vietnam (Goldstein, 2008; Halberstam, 1992). President Johnson pronounced the epitaph to this "best and brightest" man: "a smart kid, that's all" (Halberstam, 1992, p. 625).

What do these two biographies have to do with Advanced Placement? I conclude that academic brilliance or dullness, as shown by these two biographies, is not the be-all or end-all of life success. Wisdom and judgment are as indispensable as the more easily measured indices of academic ability.

NOTES

I am indebted to Eric Schaps, president of the Developmental Studies Center; Trevor Packer, College Board vice president and director of the AP Program; and Shirley Archie, an English teacher in Germantown High School, Philadelphia, for their helpful communications.

1. One must read the actual statement (College Board, 2000) to appreciate the atmosphere in which the proposal for the surge was made. For example, Riley said: "About the surest and fastest way to create an angry, 19-year-old, illiterate dropout is to give that young person a watered-down curriculum. Low expectations say to youngsters that they are not smart enough to learn anything more" (p. 20). Was he seriously proposing AP as a solution to the dropout problem?

REFERENCES

Campbell, D. T. (1976). *The corrupting effect of quantitative indicators* (Occasional Paper Series No. 8). Hanover, NH: Dartmouth College.

College Board. (2000). *Dispelling the culture of mediocrity: Expanding Advanced Placement.* New York: College Board. (ERIC Document Reproduction Service No. ED445106).

College Board. (2007). *Review process.* http://apcentral.collegeboard.com/apc/public/courses/teachers_corner/51268.html

College Board. (2008a). *Get with the Program.* Retrieved February 6, 2010 from http://professionals.collegeboard.com/profdownload/ap-get-with-the-program-08.pdf

College Board. (2008b). *Avanza con el Programma.* Retrieved February 6, 2010 from http://professionals.collegeboard.com/profdownload/ap-get-with-the-program-spanish-08.pdf

College Board launches drive for AP availability. (2000, April 12). *Education Week.*

deVise, D. (2007, June 27). Blacks in Fairfax, Montgomery outdo U.S. peers in AP. *The Washington Post,* A1.

Dorans, N. J. (2002). The recentering of SAT scales and its effects on score distributions and score interpretations (Report No. 2002-11). New York: College Board.

En. Wikipedia, (2009). http://en.wikipedia.org/wiki/Colin_Powell#Secretary_of_State

Ewing, M., Camara, W. J., & Millsap, R. E. (2006). *The relationship between PSAT/NMSQT scores and AP examination grades: A follow-up study* (Report No. 2006-1). New York: College Board.

Goldstein, G. M. (2008). *Lessons in disaster: McGeorge Bundy and the path to war in Vietnam.* New York: New York Times/Holt.

Halberstam, D. (1992) *The best and the brightest.* New York: Ballantine.

Herrnstein, R. J., & Murray, C. (1994). *The bell curve: Intelligence and class structure in American life.* New York: Free Press.

Jencks, C., & Phillips. M. (1998). *The black-white test score gap.* Washington, DC: Brookings Institute.

Jensen, A. R. (1969). How much can we boost IQ and scholastic achievement? *Harvard Educational Review, 59*(1), 1–123.

Lemann, N. (1999). *The big test: The secret history of the American meritocracy.* New York: Farrar, Straus, & Giroux.

Lichten, W. (2000). *Whither Advanced Placement?* Educating Policy Analysis Archives. http://www.epaa.asu.edu/v8n29.html

Lichten, W. (2007, January 16). Equity and excellence in the College Board Advanced Placement Program. *Teachers College Record.* http://www .tcrecord.org

Lichten, W., & Wainer, H. (2000). The aptitude-achievement function: An aid for allocating educational resources, with an Advanced Placement example. *Educational Psychology Review, 12(*2), 201–228.

Mathews, J. (2000, July 18). D.C. students pushed to take AP courses: Classes are beneficial, educators say. *The Washington Post,* B1.

Means, H. (1992). *Colin Powell: Soldier/Statesman, statesman/soldier.* New York: Donald J. Fine.

National Research Council. (2002). *Learning and understanding: Improving advanced study of mathematics and science in US high schools.* Committee on Programs for Advanced Study of Mathematics and Science in American High Schools. J. P. Gollub, M. W. Bertenthal, J. B. Labov, & P. C. Curtis Jr. (Eds.). Center for Education. Division of Behavioral and Social Sciences and Education. Washington, DC: National Academies Press.

Pfankuch, T. (1997, June 23). Students losing full advantage of advanced placement. *The Jacksonville (FL) Times-Union.*

Report card on the schools. (2007, March 25). *The Philadelphia Inquirer.*

Tyack, D., & Cuban, L. (1995). *Tinkering toward utopia. A century of public school reform.* Cambridge, MA: Harvard University Press.

Walberg, H. J. (1998, April 8). The Diogenes factor. *Education Week.*

CHAPTER 13

Advanced High School Coursework and College Admission Decisions

Philip M. Sadler

Earning high grades in high school raises students' chances of being admitted to the college of their choice, often with the bonus of substantial financial aid. Successfully completing advanced coursework in high school is an additional factor indicating that a student can be a high achiever in college, thereby upping the chances of admission to elite colleges and universities. These two quantifiable factors, along with standardized test scores, are weighed by college admissions officers using a range of techniques that have evolved as rules of thumb unsupported by research studies. In this chapter I use an analytical approach to examine ways to integrate high school grades and advanced coursework into a single, useful measure.

High school transcripts sent to each college to which a student applies provide a detailed report of which classes were taken and the grade earned in each. Often a student's high school grade point average (HSGPA) has been precalculated on the transcript. The HSGPA is also used to determine a student's rank-in-class (RIC) as a percentile (e.g., top 20 percent of the graduating class), giving additional comparative meaning to the HSGPA. Students with the highest RIC receive high school graduation honors (e.g., valedictorian), which can impact access to college financial aid (Herr, 1991a; Hout, 2005) and guarantees automatic acceptance at many state universities (e.g., Texas, Maine). There is no uniformity in how high schools calculate HSGPA (Cognard, 1996; Dillon, 1986; Jones, 1975; NRC, 2002, p. 40). Some leave out nonacademic course grades in their calculation (e.g., physical education), although research in this area shows no increase in the accuracy of prediction of college performance with this exclusion (Goldman & Sexton, 1974).

Many high schools add in bonus points for advanced coursework (Hawkins & Clinedinst, 2006), thereby increasing the course grade for each advanced course. This process can dramatically raise a student's HSGPA or RIC. The justification for this is that advanced coursework is thought to attract only the top students and that the normal range in grading does not reflect the extraordinary effort that students put into their honors, Advanced Placement , or International Baccalaureate (IB) courses in high school (Attewell, 2001; Capasso, 1995).[1] Moreover, students reason that they could earn higher grades by selecting less rigorous courses, and thus improving their HSGPA, if there was no adjustment for advanced courses. AP exam scores are not incorporated into HSGPA; half of students take their AP courses in their senior year, and exam scores are not reported until the summer after graduation.[2]

With the expansion of AP and other programs, often as a part of state mandates (e.g., Florida, Louisiana, Utah, South Carolina) or federal programs, an increasing number of high schools offer advanced courses (Adelman, 1999; Schneider, Kirst, & Hess, 2003). Parents and students are highly supportive of these program offerings (Klopfenstein, 2004; NRC, 2002, p. 52; Thompson & Joshua-Shearer, 2002). As a result, the AP program has expanded in the last five decades to involve 1,200,000 students taking 2,100,000 AP exams in over thirty-two different subjects (Camara, Dorans, Morgan, & Myford, 2000; Rothschild, 1999; CEEB, 2005a; Hershey, 1990). In 2006 61.6 percent of college freshmen reported that they had taken at least one AP course, and 14.9 percent took five or more AP courses (Hurtado & Pryor, 2007). With half of AP exams taken before the senior year in high school (CEEB, 2006), exam scores are often forwarded to colleges when students apply for admission, but colleges are unsure how to use them in the admissions process. A National Research Council (2002) study predicts that "it is anticipated that [AP and IB] examination scores may play a greater role in the admission process in the future" (p. 57). The way in which AP courses are treated in the calculation of HSGPA and the resulting RIC and graduation honors has an increasingly large impact on the colleges to which student apply and are accepted.

For the purpose of clarity here, we will assume that high school grades are based on the familiar 4-point scale (i.e., A=4, B=3, C=2, D=1, F=0), although in reality most schools use pluses and minuses and some use a 100-point scale. Honors, AP, or IB courses often are graded using a scale that is one point higher (A=5, B=4, C=3, D=2, F=1) or that simply adds a bonus point to the scale used for regular courses. Of course, all sorts of anomalies exist, where, for instance, an A+ garners a 4.3 (or 5.3 on a 5-point scale), remedial courses are dropped, a lighter course load is accounted for, or repeating courses do not affect HSGPA (Downs, 2000; Vickers, 2000).

Given the variation in the formulas used by highs schools to calculate HSGPA, most colleges and universities recompute this measure from provided transcripts, giving special status to advanced courses (Hawkins & Clinedinst, 2006). We must keep in mind that any such recalculation will not have an effect on a student's RIC, which has been predetermined. Others accept each high school's calculation assuming special provision has been made for advanced coursework (Cognard, 1996; Dillon, 1986; Jones, 1975; NRC, 2002). We see an opportunity to reconcile high school course rigor, grade earned, and AP exam scores in a way that is useful for the college admission process.

PRIOR RESEARCH

Research on predictors of college success is of great interest to those responsible for college admission, professionals who hope to build a cohort of entering freshmen who succeed in their college coursework and graduate on schedule. The grades students earn in high school are generally considered the best predictor of future college performance (Noble & Sawyer, 2004). And high schools that offer more rigorous courses graduate students who are more successful in college (Bassiri & Schultz, 2003; Lang, 1997). Taking advanced coursework in high school is viewed as a way for students to better prepare themselves for the demands of college courses (Venezia & Kirst, 2005). And so while standardized test scores (i.e., SAT and ACT) exhibit some gender bias in favor of males (Bridgeman & Lewis, 1996; Bridgeman & Wendler, 1991; Gallager & Kaufman, 2005; Wainer & Steinberg, 1992), admissions officers can counter that bias with HSGPA, which generally favors female students. In surveys of college admissions officers, weighted HSGPA is favored over unweighted measures;

college admissions officers prefer when the high school uses bonus points for advanced courses to create a weighted GPA; unweighted HSGPA does not employ bonus points (Seyfert, 1981; Talley & Mohr, 1993). Students from schools who use unweighted HSGPA to calculate RIC (Downs, 2000)—or when compared to those with higher, weighted HSGPA—may be at a disadvantage in the college admissions process (Lockhart, 1990; Rutledge, 1991).

Students who enroll in AP courses generally have higher college grades (Burton & Ramist, 2001; Chamberlain, Pugh, & Shellhammer 1978; Morgan & Ramist, 1998). Weighted HSGPA has been found to predict first-year college GPA in particular more accurately than unweighted HSGPA (Bridgeman, McCamley-Jenkins, & Ervin 2000; Dillon, 1986). The fact that many student background variables are related to high school course-taking patterns clouds the issue of whether it is the AP courses themselves or some other student attribute that contributes more to college success. For example, advanced coursework is more commonly offered in more affluent communities, whose students generally perform better in college (Geiser & Santelices, 2004; Klopfenstein & Thomas, 2005; Ruch, 1968). Compared with enrollment in AP courses, the scores students earn on AP exams are an even stronger predictor of college grades (Dodd, Fitzpatrick, & Jennings, 2002; Geiser & Santelices, 2004) and offer an opportunity for their integration into the college admissions process.

It is helpful to keep in mind that while standardized test scores are, by nature, designed to distribute student scores into a normal distribution, high school grades have slowly been creeping up (CIRP, 2005; Kirst & Bracco, 2004). This grade inflation results in a ceiling effect whereby the distribution in HSGPA is more concentrated at the high end, making its use for discriminating between students for admission more problematic (Ziomek & Svec, 1997; Woodruff & Ziomek, 2004). A weighted HSGPA has the potential to widen the distribution in this key measure of students' high school performance and thereby make it easier to identify the highest-performing students.

METHODS

The analysis presented in this chapter is drawn from the Factors Influencing College Science Success (FICSS) study described earlier in this book (chapters 3 and 7). FICSS surveyed college students in their introductory biology, chemistry, and physics courses. These students had a range of high school experiences in the sciences. Some had taken no high school course in the particular science field. Others had taken regular, honors, and/or AP courses. Of those who enrolled in AP courses in the particular science, many took the AP exam. A range of exam scores, from 1 to 5, were reported, with an AP exam score of 3, 4, or 5 considered "passing." Presumably, many of these students could have received course credit for their AP performance but instead took their college's introductory course. Reasons given ranged from individuals wanting to increase their mastery of basic concepts to following the advice of older students or faculty advisers to their AP scores not meeting a more rigorous standard for course credit at the college they attend.

FICSS researchers administered the survey to students in their college science courses, and, after the term was over, the professors supplied the grade each student earned. With students providing answers to questions concerning their high school course-taking, grades earned, and AP exam performance, our team could then develop models that examined the relationship of the rigor of student courses taken, the grades earned, and any AP exam performance. We took great care in constructing the survey to use best practices to ensure high student accuracy (Bradburn, Rips, & Shevel, 1987; Groves, 1989; Niemi & Smith, 2003; Pace, Barahona, & Kaplan, 1985). Our reliability testing showed a high level of student consistency. With the inclusion of other data the admissions officers consider in their deliberation (e.g., community socioeconomic status, race/ethnicity, grades in other courses, and standardized test scores), we were able to construct models that related course grades to course rigor, and to AP exam scores while accounting for variables that admissions officer consider separately (figure 13.1). We used the college course grade as

FIGURE 13.1 High school course background of student in introductory college science

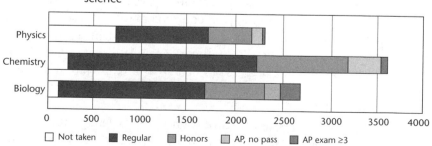

the metric to compare the effects of differences in students' course-taking patterns and their performance in high school science.

Our sample is generated from a random sample of all U.S. four-year colleges and universities stratified by enrollment. Our analysis employs 113 introductory biology, chemistry, and physics courses in which enrollment was greater than ten students. Only 5 percent of students attending a college biology class had not taken a biology course in high school. Of the students in college chemistry, 6 percent had not taken a high school chemistry course. College physics students were far more likely not to have had high school physics preparation, with 32 percent lacking a high school course. Our analysis uses only students who had taken a relevant high school science course and received a grade in it, 88 percent of our sample. Because professors can differ in terms of grading stringency, we accounted for institution by including dummy variables for the institutions in our regression models. Those who took an AP course are a small fraction of those enrolled in introductory college science in that field, with those who passed the AP exam with a score of 3 or higher being a comparatively even smaller group.

RESULTS

From student data concerning high school coursework, we find that most students appear to have performed quite well in their high school biology chemistry, or physics courses (figure 13.2). The majority in each level of the course received an A, with 70 percent of those who passed the AP exam with a score of 3 or higher earning this grade. However, it becomes clear that the AP exam measures something quite different from what the course grade measures, because many students who pass the AP exam earn grades lower than an A. This is supported by the fact that the correlation between the grade in an AP subject and the AP exam score is not particularly strong for each subject: biology, 0.314; chemistry, 0.351; and physics 0.423. Taken together, AP course grades only account for 11 percent of the variance in AP exam scores. Many students earning high course grades do not perform well on the AP exam (Hershey, 1990). Some suggest this is evidence of a decrease in quality as the program has grown (Lichten, 2000). Others argue that the quality of AP courses varies considerably (Honowar, 2005).[3]

It is instructive to view the level of high school science course taken and the high school course grade received together as predictors of the

FIGURE 13.2 Distribution of grades in last high school course taken in science subject

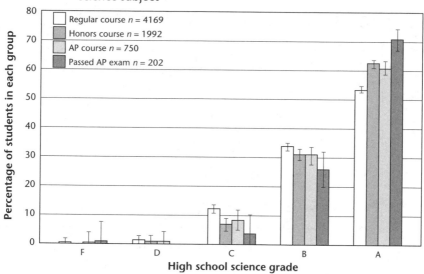

earned college grade in biology, chemistry, or physics (as well as passing the AP exam). Figure 13.3 shows that both high school grade and course rigor predict college grade (using a 100-point scale where an A=95, B=85, etc.). Students who take more rigorous high school courses do better in college science by about 2.4 points, on average, for each level of rigor. This is the average difference in introductory college science grade between successive lines in figure 13.3 (i.e., raising the *regular course* line up by 5 points would align it with the *honors course* data). Students who earn higher grades in high school science courses also earn higher grades in college by about 5 points for each letter grade, the average difference of the slope of the lines in figure 13.3. Using the common metric of college course grade in introductory science, one can estimate the difference in value in letter grade units of earning the same grade in high school courses of different levels of rigor. Each level of rigor increases the value of the letter grade earned by 2.4/5, or approximately half of a letter grade. Hence, an A earned in honors is worth more than in a regular class, an A in AP is worth more than in honors, and passing the AP exam is worth more than an A in an AP course.

FIGURE 13.3   Mean introductory college science course grade by grade earned in each high school course

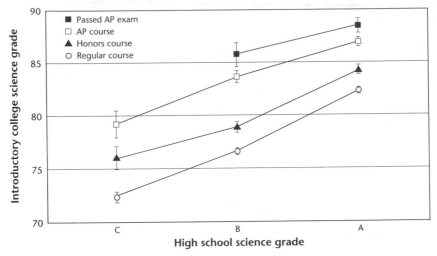

Note: Categories with fewer than fifty students are not plotted.

Formalizing this calculation for college admissions purposes requires accounting for factors that may be considered separately in the admissions process. This is necessary because we wish to remove the effects of these other important factors from a student's enrollment and performance in advanced coursework. These factors are commonly SAT scores (or equivalent ACT scores), race/ethnic group, level of community affluence (from zip code data), and type of high school (public, private, magnet, homeschooled). Since our analysis uses college science grades, the level of high school mathematics course completed (e.g., precalculus, calculus, AP Calculus) is another relevant predictor (see Sadler & Sonnert, this volume) that admissions officers examine for students interested in science, engineering, mathematics, or premedicine. We also include the college year of participants and the university in our model to account for student maturity and for grading stringency, both of which can impact college science grades.

The model in table 13.1 reports the significance of each of the variables along with the number of degrees of freedom. This model accounts for 0.326 of the overall variance in the college science grade of students.

TABLE 13.1   Variables and their significance in model relating high school course rigor and grade to college grade in biology, chemistry, or physics

Variable	Degrees of freedom	Sums of squares	F-ratio	Probability
Constant	1	42416707	484464	≤ 0.0001
College professor	112	97782	9.97	≤ 0.0001
Year in college	3	595	2.26	0.0784
Race/Ethnicity	4	4328	12.35	≤ 0.0001
Mean education level of community	1	1072	12.25	0.0005
High school type	8	2265	3.23	0.0011
SAT/ACT Math score	1	15756	179.96	≤ 0.0001
SAT/ACT Verbal score	1	4084	46.65	≤ 0.0001
Highest level of math in high school	2	9080	51.85	≤ 0.0001
Science course level in high school	3	11621	44.24	≤ 0.0001
High school letter grade value	1	30537	348.78	≤ 0.0001
Error	6324	553691		
Total	6460	821657		
Variance explained (r^2)		0.326		

Note: 7,006 total cases, of which 545 subjects are not included due to missing data

Employing a dummy variable for each of the 113 college classrooms accounted for differences in grading stringency by professor. The year in which students took their college course was not significant. Student background variables were all significant: race/ethnicity, the mean educational level of the adults in the students' home zip code, and the type of high school attended. Standardized test scores and the highest level of math course taken (below precalculus, precalculus, non-AP calculus, AP Calculus) also were all significant.

The two variables of most interest, science course level in high school in the same subject that a student took in college and the letter grade earned in this course, are both significant. The values and standard errors of these coefficients are shown in table 13.2. We use the regular science course as a baseline and calculate the difference in college performance of students taking more rigorous courses. Those who take an honors course earned a college grade 1.28 points higher than those who took a regular course. Those who took an AP course but did not take or pass the AP exam in the subject earned a college grade 3.21 higher than those who took a regular course. Students who passed the AP exam with a score of 3 or higher earned a grade 6.48 points higher. For each difference in letter grade (e.g., B to A, C to B), students earned, on average, college grades 3.41 points higher.

The calculation of these coefficients allows for the empirically based generation of bonus points associated with each science course level by dividing the difference due to course level by the high school letter grade value (table 13.2). Regular courses, acting as a baseline, receive no bonus points. Honors courses should receive 0.38(±0.08) bonus points on the 4-point letter grade scale. Those who take an AP course and either do not take the exam or earn a score less than 3 are entitled to 0.94(±.11) bonus points. Those students who pass their AP exam should be credited with 1.90(±0.18) bonus points. For ease of calculation, values of 0.5 points can be used for honors courses, 1 point for AP courses, and 2 points for those who pass the AP exam.

TABLE 13.2 Increase in college science performance associated with high school: Science course level, passing the AP exam, and with one letter grade increase

Science course level	Difference from regular course	SE	Cell count	Bonus points	SE
Regular course	0.00	0.24	3757	0.00	0.00
Honors course	1.28	0.26	1887	0.38	0.08
AP course	3.21	0.35	579	0.94	0.11
AP exam ≤3	6.48	0.50	238	1.90	0.18
High school letter grade value	3.41	0.18			

SUMMARY

The award of bonus points for students taking honors or AP coursework in high school is found to be supported. Students who take these courses earn higher grades in their college science courses when accounting for background variables that covary with advanced course-taking. These covariates are usually considered separately in the college admissions process. To customize the model to the admissions process, in the study we excluded other measures collected from our model, since they are typically unavailable in consideration for college admission (e.g., parental education, family income).[4] We also aggregate results from biology, chemistry, and physics for simplicity in application of our findings. The use of bonus points in letter grade units (0.5 for honors, 1 for AP, and 2 for AP exam-passers) accounts for advanced coursework in the calculation of a weighted HSGPA for use in college admissions. This weighted measure can also be used by high schools for calculation of RIC and attendant graduation honors. The use of bonus points deals with the problem of students potentially earning lower course grades when taking AP and honors courses in high school.

We believe that our findings should be applied with care. Schools in lower socioeconomic status communities, rural schools, and small high schools may not offer advanced coursework with the same frequency as those in wealthier communities, thus withholding from their students the opportunity to earn bonus points in a weighted HSGPA. Hence, community socioeconomic status should be accounted for separately in the admissions process. Otherwise, the use of bonus points to produce a weighted HSGPA will contribute to a "two-tiered educational system" (Dupuis, 1999, p. 1) in which students from higher socioeconomic statuses will enjoy greater advantage. Colleges that accept students who are less-well-prepared academically should offer support programs and adopt retention strategies designed to help compensate for these differences (Marable, 1999).

This chapter takes an analytical approach to combine two key college admission variables into one. High school course grades and the level of high school science courses taken can be integrated to produce a HSGPA that accounts for both using bonus points. The study's findings validate a system often used by high school and colleges but previously lacking validation in any supporting research study. For students who have taken and passed an AP exam, this additional result can also be accommodated.

Furthermore, the methodology we use could further be employed to integrate other predictive admission variables into a single measure (e.g., SAT or ACT standardized exam scores). This study only applies to science coursework. Generalizing to advanced coursework in other subjects would require the finding of similar results concerning the use of bonus points in some future study.

NOTES

The author would like to acknowledge those who helped make this research possible: Janice M. Earle, Finbarr C. Sloane, and Larry E. Suter of the National Science Foundation; James H. Wandersee, Joel J. Mintzes, Lillian C. McDermott, Eric Mazur, Dudley R. Herschbach, Brian Alters, and Jason Wiles of the FICCS Advisory Board, for their guidance; and Nancy Cianchetta, Susan Matthews, Dan Record, and Tim Reed of our High School Advisory Board, for their time and wisdom. This research has been aided by our research team: Michael Filisky, Gerhard Sonnert, Hal Coyle, Cynthia Crockett, Bruce Ward, Judith Peritz, Annette Trenga, Freeman Deutsch, Zahra Hazari, Jaimie Miller, John Loehr, Adam Maltese, and Marc Schwartz. Matthew H. Schneps, Nancy Finkelstein, Alex Griswold, Tobias McElheny, Yael Bowman, and Alexia Prichard of our Science Media Group constructed our dissemination Web site (www. ficss.org). We also appreciate advice and interest from several colleagues in the field: Michael Neuschatz of the American Institute of Physics; William Lichten of Yale University; Kristen Huff and Trevor Packer of the College Entrance Examination Board; Charles Alcock, Irwin Shapiro, William Fitzsimmons, Marlyn McGrath Lewis, and Georgene Herschbach of Harvard University; Rory Browne of Boston College; and Kristen Klopfenstein of Texas Christian University.

This work has been carried out under a grant from the Interagency Educational Research Initiative (NSF-REC 0115649). Any opinions, findings, and conclusions or recommendations expressed in this material are those of the author and do not necessarily reflect the views of the National Science Foundation, the U.S. Department of Education, or the National Institutes of Health.

This chapter draws on research published in Sadler (2007) and Sadler and Tai (2007).

1. In some schools, an honors course is a prerequisite for enrollment in an Advanced Placement course; in others it is the highest-level course offered (Herr, 1991a; Herr, 1991b). The IB program is offered in only 564 North American schools, too small a fraction for our study to examine.

2. An estimated 30 to 40 percent of students in AP courses nationally do not take the associated AP exam (NRC, 2002, p. 18).

3. The College Entrance Examination Board (2007) responded by implementing an audit of high school AP offerings aimed to "help colleges and universities better interpret secondary school courses marked AP on students' transcripts" (p. 3).
4. The model we use differs from that described in Sadler and Sonnert (this volume), although we draw from the same dataset.

REFERENCES

Adelman, C. (1999). *Answers in the toolbox: academic intensity, attendance patterns, and bachelor's degree attainment.* Washington, DC: U.S. Department of Education, Office of Educational Research and Improvement.

Attewell, P. (2001). The winner-take-all high school: Organizational adaptations to educational stratification. *Sociology of Education, 74*(4), 267–295.

Bassiri, D., & Schulz, E. (2003). *Constructing a universal scale of high school course difficulty* (ACT Research Report 2003-4). Iowa City, IA: ACT.

Bradburn, N., Rips, N., & Shevell, S. (1987). Answering autobiographical questions: The impact of memory and inference on surveys. *Science, 236*(4798), 157–161.

Bridgeman, B., & Lewis, C. (1996). Gender differences in college mathematics grades and SAT-M scores: A reanalysis of Wainer and Steinberg. *Journal of Educational Measurement, 33*(3), 257–270.

Bridgeman, B., McCamley-Jenkins, L., & Ervin, N. (2000). *Prediction of freshman grade-point average from the revised and recentered SAT I: Reasoning test* (Research Report No. 2000-1). New York. College Entrance Examination Board.

Bridgeman, B., & Wendler, C. (1991). Gender differences in predictors of college mathematics performance and in college mathematics course grades. *Journal of Educational Psychology, 83*(2), 275–284.

Burton, N., & Ramist, L. (2001). *Predicting long-term success in undergraduate school: A review of predictive validity studies.* Princeton, NJ: Educational Testing Service.

Camara, W., Dorans, N., Morgan, R., & Myford, C. (2000). Advanced placement: access not exclusion. *Education Policy Analysis Archives, 8*(40). http://epaa.asu.edu/epaa/v8n40.html

Capasso, J. C. (1995). Grade weighting: Solution to disparity, or creator of despair? *NASSP Bulletin, 79*(568), 100–103.

Chamberlain, P., Pugh, R., & Shellhammer, J. (1978). Does advanced placement continue through the undergraduate years? *College and University, 53*(2), 195–200.

Cognard, A. (1996). *The case for weighting grades and waiving classes for gifted and talented high school students.* Storrs: National Research Center on the Gifted and Talented, University of Connecticut.

College Entrance Examination Board [CEEB]. (2005a). *2005–2006 AP fact sheet.* New York: College Board.

College Entrance Examination Board [CEEB]. (2005b). *Student grade distributions.* New York: College Board.

College Entrance Examination Board [CEEB]. (2006). *Advanced Placement report to the nation 2006.* http://www.collegeboard.com/prod_downloads/about/news_info/ap/2006/2006_ap-report-nation.pdf

College Entrance Examination Board [CEEB]. (2007). *AP course audit manual.* New York: College Board.

Cooperative Institutional Research Program [CIRP]. (2005). *The American freshman: National norms for fall 2004.* Los Angeles: Author.

Dillon, D. (1986, Fall). The advanced placement factor. *Journal of College Admission, 113,* 14–17.

Dodd, B., Fitzpatrick, R., & Jennings, J. (2002). *An investigation of the validity of AP grades of 3 and a comparison of AP and non-AP student groups.* New York: College Board.

Dorans, N. (1999). *Correspondence between ACT and SAT I scores* (College Board Research Report 99-1). New York: College Entrance Examination Board.

Downs, G. C. (2000). *Weighted grades: A conundrum for secondary schools* (Occasional Paper No. 35). Orono: University of Maine, Center for Research and Evaluation.

Dupuis, J. (1999). California lawsuit notes unequal access to AP courses. *Rethinking Schools Online, 14*(1). http://www.rethinkingschools.org

Gallager, A., & Kaufman, J. (2005). *Gender differences in mathematics: An integrative psychological approach.* Cambridge: Cambridge University Press.

Geiser, S., & Santelices, V. (2004). *The role of Advanced Placement and honors courses in college admissions.* Center for Studies in Higher Education. http://repositories.cdlib.org/cshe/CSHE-4-04/

Geiser, S., & Santelices, V. (2006). The role of Advanced Placement and honors courses in college admissions. In P. C. Gandara, G. Orfield, & C. L. Horn (Eds.), *Expanding opportunity in higher education: leveraging promise* (pp. 75–103). Albany: State University of New York Press.

Goldman, R. D., & Sexton, D. W. (1974). Archival experiments with college admissions policies. *American Educational Research Journal, 11*(2), 195–201.

Groves, R. (1989). *Survey errors and survey costs.* New York: Wiley & Sons.

Hawkins, D., & Clinedinst, M. (2006). *State of college admission 2006.* Alexandria, VA: National Association for College Admission Counseling.

Herr, N. (1991a). Perspectives and policies regarding advanced placement and honors coursework. *College and University, 62*(2), 47–54.

Herr, N. (1991b). The influence of program format on the professional development of science teachers: A within-subjects analysis of the perceptions of teachers who have taught AP and honors science to comparable student populations. *Science Education, 75*(6), 619–621.

Hershey, S. (1990, Summer). College admission practices and the advanced placement program. *Journal of College Admission, 128,* 8–11.

Honowar, V. (2005). To maintain rigor, College Board to audit all AP courses. *Education Week, 24*(3), 8–10.

Hout, M. (2005). *Berkeley's comprehensive review method for making freshmen admission decisions: An assessment.* http://www.berkeley.edu/news/media/releases/2005/05/16_houtreport.pdf

Hurtado, S., & Pryor, J. (2007). *The American freshman: National norms for fall 2006.* Los Angeles: Cooperative Institutional Research Program.

Jones, J. (1975). Advanced placement—Taking a hard look. *NASSP Bulletin, 59*(393), 64–69.

Kirst, M., & Bracco, K. (2004). Bridging the great divide: How the K–12 and post-secondary split hurts students, and what can be done about it. In M. W. Kirst & A. Venezia (Eds.), *From high school to college: Improving opportunities for success in post-secondary education* (pp. 1–30). San Francisco: Jossey-Bass.

Klopfenstein, K. (2004). The advanced placement expansion of the 1990s: How did traditionally underserved students fare? *Education Policy Analysis Archives, 12*(68). http://epaa.asu.edu/epaa/v12n68/

Klopfenstein, K., & Thomas, K. (2005). *The Advanced Placement performance advantage: Fact or fiction?* American Economic Association. http://www.aeaweb.org/annual_mtg_papers/2005/0108_1015_0302.pdf

Lang, D. (1997). Accurate and fair RICs: One step closer with the RIC index. *ERS Spectrum, 15*(3), 26–29.

Lichten, W. (2000). Whither Advanced Placement? *Education Policy Analysis Archives, 8*(29). http://epaa.asu.edu/epaa/v8n29.html

Lockhart, E. (1990, Winter). Heavy grades. *Journal of College Admission, 126,* 9–16.

Marable, T. (1999). The role of student mentors in a precollege engineering program. *Peabody Journal of Education, 74*(2), 44–54.

Morgan, R., & Ramist, L. (1998). *Advanced Placement students in college: An investigation of course grades at 21 colleges* (ETS Report No. SR-98-13). Princeton, NJ: Educational Testing Service.

National Research Council [NRC]. (2002). *Learning and understanding: Improving advanced study of mathematics and science in US high schools*. Committee on Programs for Advanced Study of Mathematics and Science in American High Schools. J. P. Gollub, M. W. Bertenthal, J. B. Labov, & P. C. Curtis Jr. (Eds.). Center for Education. Division of Behavioral and Social Sciences and Education. Washington, DC: National Academies Press.

Niemi, R., & Smith, J. (2003). The accuracy of students' reports of course taking in the 1994 National Assessment of Educational Progress. *Educational Measurement: Issues and Practice, 22*(1), 15–21.

Noble, J., & Sawyer, R. (2004). Is high school GPA better than admission test scores for predicting academic success in college? *College and University, 79*(4), 17–22.

Pace, C., Barahona, D., & Kaplan, D. (1985). *The credibility of student self-reports*. Los Angeles: UCLA Center for the Study of Evaluation.

Rothschild, E. (1999). Four decades of the advanced placement program. *The History Teacher, 32*(2), 175–206.

Ruch, C. (1968). A study of the collegiate records of Advanced Placement and non–Advanced Placement students. *College and University, 44*, 207–210.

Rutledge, B. (1991, Fall). An alternative to ranking high school students. *Journal of College Admission, 133*, 5–6.

Sadler, P. M. (2007). Weighting for recognition: Accounting for Advanced Placement and honors courses when calculating high school grade point average. *National Association of Secondary School Principals Bulletin, 91*(1), 5–31.

Sadler, P. M., & Tai, R. H. (2007). Accounting for advanced high school coursework in college admission decisions. *College and University, 82*(4), 7–14.

Schneider, B. L., Kirst, M., & Hess, F. M. (2003). *Strategies for success: High school and beyond* (Brookings Paper on Education Policy No. 6). Washington, DC: Brookings Institution Press.

Seyfert, W. (1981). Rank-in-class—Another look at the guidelines. *Curriculum Report, 11*(1), 1–13.

Talley, N., & Mohr, J. (1993, Spring). The case for a national standard of grade weighting. *Journal of College Admission, 139*, 9–13.

Thompson, G. L., & Joshua-Shearer, M. (2002). In retrospect: What college undergraduates say about their high school education. *High School Journal, 85*(5), 1–15.

Venezia, A., & Kirst, M. (2005). Inequitable opportunities: How current education systems and policies undermine the chances for student persistence and success in college. *Educational Policy, 19*(2), 283–307.

Vickers, J. M. (2000). Justice and truth in grades and their averages. *Research in Higher Education, 41*(2), 141–164.

Wainer, H., & Steinberg, L. (1992). Sex differences in performance on the mathematics section of the Scholastic Aptitude Test: A bidirectional validity study. *Harvard Educational Review, 62*(3), 323–336.

Woodruff, D., & Ziomek, R. (2004). *High school grade inflation from 1991 to 2003* (ACT Research Report Series 2004-4). Iowa City, IA: ACT.

Ziomek, R., & Svec, J. (1997). High school grades and achievement: Evidence of grade inflation. *NASSP Bulletin, 81*(587), 105–113.

CHAPTER 14

Key Findings

Philip M. Sadler

One of the great pleasures of being a researcher is being able to spend time investigating those things that people believe to be true. Sometimes the evidence that people can muster to support a strongly held belief is utterly wrong.[1] But more often people possess only a bit of evidence that they have garnered from their own personal experience that they use to buttress their view. Nonresearchers have little opportunity to collect, analyze, or synthesize data; hence, the evidence that one tends to remember is selectively only that which confirms one's theories and beliefs. We all tend to ignore data that does not fit with our beliefs. As with the way the scientific community behaves when a new theory competes with an established one, evidence must be pretty overwhelming to change that which we strongly believe. We find this particularly true in the field of education, in which everyone has considerable personal experience. There is a common tendency to think that what worked well (or not) for us as individuals in our years of schooling will apply more generally to all students. Similarly, teachers of Advanced Placement may generalize about the success of their choice of materials, activities, or pedagogy based on the very few students with whom they have contact after they matriculate to college programs.[2] AP students may think that their own coursework is representative of that experienced by other AP students. By looking at Advanced Placement though a more scientific lens, the contributors to this book have had an opportunity to aggregate and analyze the experiences of very large number students and teachers, well beyond the life experience that any individual person could ever have.

263

In education there is far too little useful feedback for those who must make decisions about their own path through school or for those who are trying to best prepare students for success. Researchers tend to communicate more clearly with their academic colleagues though articles in professional journals than to the practitioners and policy makers who have more direct impact on schools, teachers, and students.

In this final chapter I attempt to summarize our research findings so they can be more generally applied by those who are making decisions concerning participation in and interaction with the AP Program. No doubt some may view our conclusions as overgeneralizations, lacking in the nuances of arguments for or against causality or in the conditions to which they apply. We admit that there are always exceptions to the rule in education. Yet to leave the reader with only the views of the individual contributors to this book and not to attempt to summarize across all the perspectives would be a missed opportunity to communicate the aggregate of our research findings. With such a wide range of researchers, hypotheses, foci, and methods, one may doubt whether any commonality can be found in the conclusions reached by our contributors. Yet there are two that bear examination. First, the impact of AP differs depending on the scale at which it is studied. Second, impact also varies depending on how one measures achievement of students who have taken AP courses.

Many advocates of the AP program make sweeping claims about its broad impact on students: that they graduate college earlier, that they switch college majors less often, and that they are better prepared for college. But at that gross scale, we find little evidence to support these claims and much evidence that contradicts it. Involvement in AP courses does not appear to bestow these global benefits on participating students beyond the habits and motivations that students already have on enrolling in advanced high school courses. AP also is not effective in universally countering the effects of poor preparation or lack of effort or in making a college education more affordable. Yet, on a finer scale, where one looks at particular subject areas (e.g., chemistry, calculus), there are definite advantages to participating in AP, although impact appears to vary by subject (and not all have been carefully studied). For example, on average AP chemistry students earn substantially higher grades in college chemistry. The benefits of AP can be substantial but appear to be restricted to effects within matched subject areas. Those looking for a panacea for what ails American education had best look elsewhere.

Second, AP experience is not uniform, even within a single subject. College Board audits notwithstanding, the quality of AP courses differ tremendously by high school and even by teacher. The key to understanding impact is the level of achievement attained by students in their AP course. Students may take an AP course and earn a grade from their teacher, or they may take other courses. They may take the AP exam and receive an AP exam score, or they may forgo the exam. Students who take AP courses and earn high grades benefit when applying to most college and universities, whereas AP exam scores do not usually play a role in college admission. AP-taking students often benefit from weighted GPAs, earning top honors for high school graduation. Some states offer automatic admission to public universities for these high achievers. Yet, simply taking an AP course appears to say little about future college performance. However, students who take an AP exam and earn a passing score enjoy significantly better performance in that subject in college. Students who take and pass the AP Calculus exam are much more likely to major in the physical sciences or engineering than those who do not. Although the College Board (2004) claims in its promotional materials that "AP isn't just for top students or those headed for college. AP offers something for everyone," there is little to recommend any benefit accruing to students who take and fail their AP exam. AP appears to offer an advantage only to students who perform well on the AP exam.

Researchers in the field of education study professionally a domain in which every citizen has a considerable personal history. This familiarity with good teachers and bad, with academic success and failure, with encouragement and discouragement makes schooling a most memorable experience. As adults, we often find ourselves advising students, whether our own children or others', to take advantage of educational opportunities and to avoid the pitfalls that we ourselves have experienced. The process of writing and assembling this collection of scholarly chapters by experts on the Advanced Placement program has garnered the attention of interested friends, colleagues, and even strangers who overhear conversations.

And so while the story we tell in this book is complex and nuanced, a few general recommendations can be made. For those who read the book in its entirety, these suggestions provide a concise summary. For those who skip to this last chapter needing to know "how the story comes out in the end" before venturing into the details of how the evidence was uncovered, we offer this advice to selected audiences:

- *Students.* Advanced Placement courses offer you an opportunity to study a subject in a very rigorous and demanding fashion. You will probably be in a class that has fewer students, those students will likely have stronger backgrounds, and there will be fewer student discipline issues than you have experienced in other courses. Your teacher will have a strong subject matter background and excellent teaching skills. Be prepared to work hard and put in more time than in other classes. Your best measure of your success at mastering college-level work is taking and passing the AP exam. The grade awarded to you by your teacher does not substitute for this, but your grade will be taken into account when you apply to college. You will have a better chance of getting into your first-choice college if you take the most demanding courses your high school has to offer and do well. Exploring other options, dual or concurrent enrollment with your local two- or four-year college is another great option for advanced study. Advanced coursework is a terrific way to explore a serious career interest while still in high school.
- *Parents.* Those students who enroll in AP courses should take the AP exam and pass it. AP coursework will not substitute for repairing a weak academic background. To avoid remedial courses in college, students should put extra effort into becoming proficient at writing, reading, and mathematics while still in high school. AP courses will require more time studying; your son or daughter must be willing to give these courses a high priority. While strong grades in AP courses will increase the chances of getting into a selective college, they rarely shorten the time to graduation or save money. To do this, students must have accumulated a semester or a year's worth of courses, and these must be accepted for college credit. Standards often vary by each college's or university's academic departments for awarding such credit. A passing grade on an AP exam does not guarantee credit at many colleges, especially selective ones.
- *Teachers.* AP students generally come with strong backgrounds, especially if they have taken and done well in a prerequisite course. You will find students willing to put in extra time on homework, writing assignments, and reading outside of class. Teaching an AP course is usually reserved for teachers with excellent academic backgrounds and many years of experience teaching a subject. While the grades you give to students will affect college admissions decisions, the best feedback you can receive about the quality of the AP course

that you teach is measured by having all students take the AP exam. Students who pass the exam are likely to perform better in college courses in the same subject area. Those who fail the exam have little to show for their year of study; there is little evidence that they are any better prepared for college success than when they first entered your classroom. Such students may be served better by taking a course that can strengthen their foundations, that is less rigorous, or one in a subject in which they are willing to put more time and effort.

- *School administrators.* Advanced Placement courses are best reserved for students who have done well in a prerequisite course. Students who are underprepared or who do not commit to putting in extra time and effort will fare poorly in AP classes. Your only accurate gauge of whether the AP courses in your school are successful is if students take and pass the AP exams. Failure indicates that the students are unprepared or not up to the challenge, or that the course does not have a proficient teacher or is lacking in resources. Professional development for teachers can help immensely, as can teachers taking a refresher course in the subject at a local college or university to relearn the content and experience the coverage that AP courses seek to emulate. AP courses in which few students take or pass the exam are not effective, and the resources, both material and personnel, should be considered for reallocation to improve lower-level courses. Some high schools choose to offer advanced courses in addition to or in place of AP courses, giving students the benefit of a particular teacher's expertise or building a student's capacity for independent research. Students can still take an AP exam after a non-AP course. Elite colleges generally want to see students take highly challenging courses; they need not be AP. Other opportunities for advanced coursework exist at local colleges that may better serve well-prepared students. Since advanced courses are more rigorous than others, grade point averages used for class rank and the award of graduation honors should be calculated with bonuses for honors and AP courses.

- *College admissions officers.* Students who have taken AP courses, and particularly those who pass the AP exam, will generally perform better than others in college courses in the same subject area. Those who passed AP exams will generally earn higher GPAs in college and will graduate on time. But simply taking an AP course does not foretell such benefits. High HSGPA, enrollment in rigorous high school courses, and high SAT/ACT scores all are predictors of college success. High school GPA is best recalculated to include bonuses for advanced courses and passing AP exam grades. AP courses are more common in private schools and wealthier school districts, so socioeconomic factors and school type should be considered when evaluating students' high school transcripts. The best available evidence suggests that dual and concurrent credit courses provide an opportunity that is equivalent to Advanced Placement coursework.

- *College professors.* Students who have taken an advanced course in high school typically show a stronger performance in that same college subject, particularly if they have taken and passed an AP exam. However, a passing exam score does not mean that students have mastered the content of your college's introductory course in that subject. Many colleges have increased the threshold for awarding college credit from 3 to a 4 or 5 AP exam score. While passing an AP exam raises the odds that a student will continue on to earn a degree in that field, some will use the course credit and choose not to go further in the subject. These students will not have an opportunity to learn about research from the perspective of scholars currently active in the field and possibly consider your field for a major or a career. While many students can skip introductory courses with strong AP scores, many find retaking an introductory course rewarding and interesting.

- *Policy makers.* Advanced placement is a large enterprise with strong and vocal advocates at many levels in the educational system. State and federal subsidies have aided in the dramatic expansion of the program, but they do not guarantee that this is money is always well spent. There is much evidence that students who do not take and pass the AP exam in a subject have not had a productive experience; hence, government support should require exams for all and monitor student success by classroom. In the absence of high AP exam passing rates, resources should be used to improve the AP course or be reallocated to better prepare students for later success when in college, avoiding the necessity of remedial college coursework and increasing opportunities for well-prepared students to take courses at local two- and four-year colleges.

- *The College Board.* With AP's strong brand recognition and large financial surpluses, the College Board has many options for improving American education. The intent on continual expansion of AP into more schools, with more students taking more tests each year, is reaching the point of diminishing returns. The College Board should embrace the efforts of all researchers and encourage a lively debate about its future efforts and direction. This can be done by listing all AP research appearing in peer-reviewed scholarly journals on its Web site, using surpluses to fund an independent foundation offering grants for the study of AP effectiveness to researchers unaffiliated with the College Board, and appointing scholars who conduct educational research to its board of trustees. The College Board should redouble its effort to develop and score AP exams to better ensure the equivalence of AP courses and introductory college courses. Having college students take AP exams is not sufficient to convince professors that standards have been maintained. Moreover, beneficial ways for spending the College Board's surpluses would include:

- increasing subsidies for professional development and mentoring of AP teachers;
- providing extensive feedback and support to AP teachers in underperforming schools;
- disseminating promotional information to students, parents, and educators concerning both successes and limitations of AP; and
- providing greater transparency and availability of AP data on a school and district basis so that independent researchers can determine how well the program works for students and identify directions for future improvement.

NOTES

1. Take, for example, the idea that people of Columbus's time thought the world was flat. The spherical shape of the Earth was known since antiquity, and its circumference had been measured by Eratosthenes in 240 BC to an accuracy better than 1 percent. The primary objection to funding his voyage was that Columbus had underestimated the size of the Earth and that he and his crew would die before their lightly provisioned ships made it the eleven thousand miles to Japan. Luckily, North America was in the way, only four thousand miles distant.
2. We have found that these are the usually the most gifted and motivated students and that they would succeed no matter their high school experiences.

REFERENCES

College Board. (2004). Get with the program. http://www.collegeboard.com/
    prod_downloads/prof/counselors/tests/ap/apminoritybroeng2.pdf

About the Editors

Kristin Klopfenstein earned her PhD in economics from the University of Colorado and is currently a senior researcher at the University of Texas at Dallas Texas Schools Project while on leave from a faculty position at Texas Christian University. She uses Texas' extensive student-level administrative database to study factors influencing the preparation of traditionally underrepresented students for postsecondary education and the workforce. Her most-cited research examines the access to and impact of the AP Program for low-income, rural, black, and Hispanic students in Texas. Klopfenstein's work has been funded by the Spencer Foundation, the Bill and Melinda Gates Foundation, the Communities Foundation of Texas, the National Science Foundation, and the U.S. Department of Education.

Philip M. Sadler earned a BS in physics from the Massachusetts Institute of Technology in 1973 and taught middle school science and mathematics for several years before earning a doctorate in education from Harvard University in 1992. As the F. W. Wright Senior Lecturer in Astronomy, Sadler teaches graduate courses in science education and undergraduate science at Harvard University. As head of the science education department at the Harvard-Smithsonian Center for Astrophysics, he carried out work that informs national policy debates on the teaching of science and professional development of teachers. Sadler has won awards for his research from the *Journal of Research in Science Teaching*, the Astronomical Society of the Pacific, and the American Institute of Physics. His research interests include assessment of students' scientific misconceptions and how they change as a result of instruction, the development of computer technologies that allow young people to engage in research, and models for enhancement of the skills of experienced teachers. He was the executive producer of *A Private Universe*, an award-winning video on student conceptions of science, and is the inventor of the Starlab Portable Planetarium and many other devices used for the teaching of astronomy worldwide. The materials and curricula that he has developed are used by an estimated fifteen million students every year.

Gerhard Sonnert is a research associate at the Harvard-Smithsonian Center for Astrophysics and associate of the department of physics at Harvard University. After receiving a doctorate in sociology from the University of Erlangen (Germany) and an MA in public administration from Harvard University, he entered the Harvard physics department in 1988 and conducted Project Access, a major empirical study of women's careers in the sciences. In 2006 he joined the Harvard-Smithsonian Center for Astrophysics, where he has investigated the effects of high school experiences on beginning college students' intentions for a career in the sciences and has also studied the factors influencing students' success in college calculus courses. Among his books are *Who Succeeds in Science? The Gender Dimension* (1995, with the assistance of Gerald Holton), *Gender Differences in Science Careers: The Project Access Study* (1995, with the assistance of Gerald Holton), *Einstein and Culture* (2005), and *What Happened to the Children Who Fled Nazi Persecution* (2006, with Gerald Holton).

Robert H. Tai is an associate professor of education at the Curry School of Education at the University of Virginia. He earned a BS in physics and a BA in mathematics from the University of Florida, an MS in physics from the University of Illinois, Urbana-Champaign, and an EdM and an EdD from the Harvard Graduate School of Education. His research agenda, which focuses on science education and scientific workforce issues, spans the range from grade six to postgraduate study and has been published in a variety of journals, including *Science*. He was a member of the 1995–1997 editorial board of the *Harvard Educational Review* and was the recipient of the 2008 Award of Leadership in Educational Research from the Council of Scientific Society Presidents. Prior to entering academia, Tai was a high school physics teacher for three years in Illinois and Texas.

About the Contributors

John T. Almarode is a former science and mathematics teacher who has taught all levels of physics, chemistry, and mathematics in the state of Virginia. His last three years in the classroom were at a specialized STEM high school. In addition to his secondary experience, he has worked with gifted and talented elementary school students in a STEM outreach program. Almarode is currently a doctoral student at the University of Virginia in science education. As a doctoral student, he is actively involved in several projects as well as helping to prepare elementary school teachers for science instruction. His research interests include factors that influence STEM success in college, the development and assessment of scientific reasoning, the impact of specialized high schools on STEM talent development, cognitive and neuroscience components of STEM education, and the trajectory of students through the STEM pipeline.

Henry Braun is the Boisi Professor of Education and Public Policy at Boston College. From 1979 to 2006 he was employed at Educational Testing Service (ETS) where he was the director of the Division of Statistical and Psychometric Research, vice president for Research Management, and a distinguished presidential appointee. He was elected a fellow of the American Statistical Association in 1991. Braun is a corecipient of the 1986 Palmer O. Johnson Award from the American Educational Research Association and a corecipient of the National Council for Measurement in Education's 1999 Award for Outstanding Technical Contribution to the Field of Educational Measurement. In recent years he has published on a variety of topics, including the black-white achievement gap, value-added modeling, comparative school effectiveness, applications of multilevel modeling, the role of literacy in economic and social welfare, test design, and standard setting. He currently chairs the Committee on Value-Added Methodology convened under the auspices of the National Research Council and the National Academy of Education.

Chrys Dougherty is a senior research scientist at ACT, Inc., and the National Center for Educational Achievement (NCEA), a subsidiary of ACT that specializes in research and training on effective schools and school improvement. He has written extensively on college readiness, the value of longitudinal student data, and the ten essential elements of statewide student information systems. He oversees procedures for selecting consistently higher performing schools as well as most of the NCEA's research projects using longitudinal student data. After teaching science in an elementary school in Oakland, California, Dougherty received his master's degree in public affairs from the LBJ School of Public Affairs at the University of Texas at Austin in 1985 and a PhD in economics from Harvard University in 1992. From 1992 to 1998 he taught statistics, economics, econometrics, and education policy courses at the LBJ School of Public Affairs and authored *Asking the Right Questions About Schools: A Parents' Guide* (2002). Dougherty joined Just for the Kids (later NCEA) in 1997 and became a primary designer of NCEA's innovative Just for the Kids School Reports.

William R. Duffy II is a senior vice president at Upper Iowa University located in Fayette, Iowa. While serving as an executive director at the University of Tennessee-Martin from 1995 to 2008, he established the dual credit program there, and it is currently the largest university dual credit program in Tennessee. He has received approximately $10 million in federal and state grants and funding to support dual credit offerings, educational access, and technology integration.

He served as a past president of the Tennessee Alliance for Continuing Higher Education, a statewide organization comprised of approximately sixty higher education institutions and three hundred members involved in continuing higher education. Duffy earned his master's degree in education and education specialist degree in higher education administration from Appalachian State University, and his EdD in higher and adult education from the University of Memphis. He is also a graduate of the United States Military Academy and a retired army infantry officer with more than twenty years of active duty service.

Maureen Ewing is an associate research scientist in research and development at the College Board. She received her doctorate in psychometrics in 2006 from Fordham University. She conducts research on the AP testing program and provides assessment design and psychometric support for AP exams. Her research interests include test construction, fairness, and validity.

Xitao Fan is the Curry Memorial Professor of Education in the Curry School of Education at the University of Virginia. He holds a PhD in educational psychology from Texas A&M University. He has been on the faculty of the University of Virginia since 2000. Prior to his current appointment, he was a member of the psychology department faculty at Utah State University. As a quantitative methodologist in education, he focuses on structural equation modeling, model fit assessment, and power estimation in modeling analysis, reliability, and validity issues in measurement, meta-analytic studies, etc. He has conducted numerous methodological and substantive studies involving large-scale longitudinal databases, studies about reliability and validity issues in measurement, studies on multivariate statistical techniques in general, and structural equation modeling and growth modeling in particular. He has been involved in numerous federally funded grants (e.g., NSF, IES, NIH) and currently serves as the editor of *Educational and Psychological Measurement*.

Kristen Huff is a senior research scientist in research and development at the College Board. She received both her masters degree (University of North Carolina at Greensboro) and doctorate (University of Massachusetts Amherst) in educational measurement. She has worked on Advanced Placement research, psychometrics, and assessment design since 2004. Before joining the College Board, Huff worked at Educational Testing Service on the development of TOEFL-iBT using evidence-centered assessment design. Her research areas of interest are assessment design, cognitive and item difficulty modeling, and diagnostic score reporting methodology. She is also active in several professional organizations and served as president of the Northeastern Educational Research Association in 2008–2009.

Pamela Kaliski is an assistant research scientist in research and development at the College Board. She received her doctorate in 2009 from James Madison University in assessment and measurement. She assists with Advanced Placement assessment design projects and conducts research using AP exam scores. Her research interests include test score validity, instrument development, hierarchical linear modeling, structural equation modeling, and mixture modeling.

Tim Lacy is a visiting assistant university historian for the Office of the Historian in the University of Illinois at Chicago. He researches, writes, lectures, and conducts oral histories on the history of the university. He completed his doctorate at Loyola University Chicago and is revising his dissertation, titled "Making a Democratic Culture: The Great Books Idea, Mortimer J. Adler, and Twentieth-Century America," into a book manuscript. Lacy's general subfields are intellectual and cultural history as well as the history of education, with specific topical interests in book culture, Catholicism, Chicago history, higher education, historiography, the history of philosophy, and print culture. He is published in the *Journal of the History of Ideas, American Catholic Studies, Journal of the Gilded Age and Progressive Era,* and specialized historical encyclopedias.

William Lichten is professor emeritus of physics and engineering and applied science at Yale University and a fellow of the Koerner Institute for Emeritus Faculty at Yale University. He has taught in the Yale physics department, the New Haven public schools, the Yale master of arts in teaching program, and undergraduate teacher preparation program. His recent research has been on the measurement of mental ability with standardized tests with application to education, diagnosis of mental retardation, and the nature of human intelligence.

Christine Qi Liu is a senior research analyst at the Association of American Medical Colleges. She earned a PhD in educational research from the University of Virginia, an MA in psychology from the University of Southern California, and an MS in biology from Purdue University. Her research interests are longitudinal structural equation modeling and multivariate analyses of large-scale data in science education. Liu has collaborated with other researchers on national surveys of science education in high school and graduate studies, faculty aging, promotion and retention issues in graduate medical education, as well as leadership organization and responsibilities in information resources in U.S. medical schools.

Lynn T. Mellor is a principal research manager responsible for the design and implementation of research at the National Center for Educational Achievement (NCEA). In addition to managing the research and evaluation of NCEA products and services, she oversees all research projects. Before joining NCEA, Mellor spent five years as director of research for a pharmaceutical research organization and eight years at the Texas

Education Agency, where she conducted research and evaluations on public school programs. Mellor earned her PhD in educational psychology from the University of Texas at Austin.

Pamela L. Paek is a senior associate with the National Center for the Improvement of Educational Assessment (NCIEA), working with states and other educational agencies to design and implement effective assessment and accountability systems. Prior to working with the Center, she served as a research associate at the Charles A. Dana Center at the University of Texas at Austin, leading the research and evaluation of secondary mathematics programs. She also worked as a psychometrician at ETS and PEM, and as a research scientist and manager at ETS studying teacher professional development and practices and the relationship of these with student achievement. Paek received a PhD in quantitative methods in education from the University of California at Berkeley.

Eva Ponte is an assistant professor of education at the University of Hawaii, Manoa. She received a PhD in education from the University of California, Berkeley. Her areas of research include teacher education, English as a second language (ESL), and assessment for learning. Her current project, "Expanding K–6 Teachers' Effective and Culturally Responsive ESL Pedagogy," provides embedded training to K–6 elementary in-service teachers in ESL and analyzes whether and how teachers translate newly acquired knowledge into classroom-based practices and dispositions that can enhance the learning process of ESL learners. Her work has appeared in the *International Journal of Interdisciplinary Social Sciences* and the *Journal of MultiDisciplinary Evaluation*.

Donald E. Powers received his doctorate in measurement and evaluation from the University of Pennsylvania. He joined Educational Testing Service in 1970 and is currently a principal research scientist in the research and development division. His interests are applied measurement and test validation, and his research has focused on sources of test variation that may hinder test interpretation and use. Powers has directed a wide variety of research projects and has been research coordinator for the Test of English as a Foreign Language program and for the Graduate Record Examinations program.

M. Kathleen Thomas is an associate professor of economics at Mississippi State University. She also serves as a research affiliate with the Texas Schools Project at the University of Texas at Dallas, and as codirector of the Mississippi State University Center for Economic Education and Financial Literacy. Thomas earned her PhD in economics from Georgia State University. She specializes in state and local public finance with particular interest in education policy and minority access to higher education. Her recent research involves score gaps on the SAT II between white and minority students, where Texas students sent their SAT scores after the Fifth District Court eliminated affirmative action programs, trends in college entrance exam choice, and the AP Program and its influence on college outcomes.

Catherine Trapani is a senior program administrator in the Automated Scoring & Natural Language Processing Group at the Educational Testing Service (ETS). She earned a BA in physics from Rutgers University and an MS in statistics from Montclair State University. She is currently studying for her doctorate in psychometrics at Fordham University. Trapani has worked on a variety of projects within ETS's research and development division and is currently responsible for the operational integrity of the automated scoring engines. Her other research includes work for SAT I, Advanced Placement, Graduate Record Exam, National Assessment of Educational Progress, National Board for Professional Teaching Standards and Test of English as a Foreign Language. Her main interests lie in modeling univariate and multivariate data, using exploratory data analysis and graphical methods to present data in simpler displays, and applying decision theory to judgments.

Index

AP advancement into inner-city
schools (*continued*)
correlation between low SAT
schools and high AP failure
rates, 234–235, 236, 237f
lack of critical evaluation of the
surge program, 239–240
push to put AP classes into all
schools, 233–234
questions about the outcomes of
the AP surge, 236–237
questions over the subjectivity of
testing promotion, 237–238
questions regarding the
qualification scale, 238
AP Biology Teacher's Guide, 78
AP biology teachers study
classroom context, 73
content coverage, 74–75
goal of the study, 64–65
implications of results, 81–82
instructional and assessment
practices, 73–74
limitations, 81
methods, 65, 69–71
potential advantages of the AP
program for students, 63
practices related to student
performance (*see* teacher
practices linked to student
performance)
preferred teaching strategies, 74
sample population, 66
school context, 72–73
survey construction, 65–66
survey variables, 67–69
teacher characteristics, 71–72
teachers' importance to the success
of the course, 63
teaching and contextual variables
related to student outcomes,
69–71
test-specific instructional activities
and practices, 75

AP course enrollment and long-
range educational outcomes
concerns about the STEM
workforce, 109–110
definition of AP participation
used, 111
implications for improving the
STEM workforce, 116
introduction to study, 109–111
methodology, 111–112
odds of earning a degree in science
related to AP participation,
114
results and discussion, 112–115
AP participation's effect on time to
college degree
analysis and results
assumptions in the study, 204–
206, 205t
dual credit courses and time to
degree, 207–208
evidence of little gain towards
early graduation, 207
impact of selected variables,
204–206
implications of evidence that
program results are student-
specific, 208
methods, 190
predicted hazard functions,
206–207
survival analysis use, 202–204
cost-benefit analysis
descriptive statistics, 211t
expected return for AP subsidies,
208–210
expected return for dual credit
programs, 210–212
cost-benefit analysis conceptual
framework
AP experience's effect on time to
degree, 192–193
cost impact of extended time to
degree, 192

expected return for AP subsidies
based on early graduation,
208–210
fail rates of subsidy recipients,
181–182
goal of making AP courses
available to disadvantaged
students, 220
ineffectiveness of AP incentive
programs in increasing passing
rates, 223–224
lack of return from AP program
subsidies, 213–214
minority student participation
in dual credit programs,
143–144
original ideal of increasing access
to high-level coursework for
motivated students, 41
participation's impact on closing
the achievement gap, 182
public policy moves to extend
program coverage (*see* AP
advancement into inner-city
schools)
public return from accelerated
learning subsidies, 195–196
recommendations to include SES
in admissions decisions, 255
success based on a strong
educational pipeline, 184
themes of causality and social
equity when discussing
effectiveness, 7, 8
Southwest Regional Educational
Laboratory, 179
Sputnik, 32
Stand and Deliver, 37
Standards for Educational and
Psychological Testing, 88
STEM (science, technology,
engineering, and mathematics),
8, 109–110, 116
Stewart, Donald M., 39

students and the AP program
backgrounds for the FICSS study,
54–56
eighth grade coursework and (*see*
preparing students for advanced
placement)
financial benefit of taking AP
courses (*see* costs and benefits
of AP participation)
high school coursework and (*see*
high school AP and success in
college science courses; high
school coursework and college
admissions)
low-income and minority (*see*
socioeconomic status (SES) and
the AP program)
recommendations based on
studies' results, 266
subsidies and the AP program
expected return based on early
graduation, 208–210
fail rates of subsidy recipients,
181–182
ineffectiveness of AP incentive
programs in increasing passing
rates, 223–224
return from, 195–196, 213–214
"Synthesis of Research on Advanced
High School Coursework in
Science and Mathematics,"
6–7

Taylor, Wendell H., 27
teacher practices linked to student
performance
most significant variables, 77
regression analysis results, 77
teachers' use of the Internet and, 79
time spent in test prep one month
before the test, 80
time students' spent studying and,
79